THE LITTLE TREASURY OF GOLF

THE
LITTLE
TREASURY OF
GOLF

EDITED BY J. P. RESNICK

BLACK DOG & LEVENTHAL PUBLISHERS
NEW YORK

Published by

Black Dog & Levnthal Publishers, Inc.
151 West 19th Street
New York, NY 10011

Distributed by

Workman Publishing Company
708 Broadway
New York, NY 10003

Designed by Martin Lubin

Typesetting by Brad Walrod/High Text Graphics

Manufactured in the United States of America

ISBN: 1-884822-50-9

h g f e d c b a

Library of Congress Cataloging-in-Publication data
The little treasury of golf / edited by J. P. Resnick
     p.   cm.
   Includes index.
   ISBN 1-884822-50-9
   1. Golf—anecdotes. 2. Golf—Miscellanea. I. Resnick,
Jane Parker.
GV967.L46   1996
796.352—dc20   96-12653
                               CIP

Foreword

In 1771, Tobias Smollett wrote, "Hard by, in the fields called the Links, the citizens of Edinburgh divert themselves at a game called Golf, in which they use a curious kind of bats tipped with horn, and small elastic balls of leather, stuffed with feathers."

Two centuries later, only the equipment has changed. The passion of golfers for their game has never waned. Indeed, their addictive enthusiasm has built golf courses in nearly every country in the world. Courses exist on terrain with bone dry desert climates, tropical jungles, and precipitous mountains, albeit with unique obstacles. Golfers are ubiquitous.

And they have never been people of a few words. One cannot say enough about golf; there is never a definitive statement. The game is compelling, frustrating, fascinating, aggravating, tantalizing, thrilling, and maddening, almost all at the same time. Golf has been, and continues to be written about in all forms of literature: essay, fiction, humor, biography, autobiography, and, volumes and volumes of instruction. It is a noble body of work and gems from every genre have been included in this book. There are recollections of St.

Andrews at the turn of the century; eloquent odes to the game's attractions; analyses of its mental demands; descriptions of the euphoria of a well-played round; explorations, without conclusion, about golf-as-obsession; details of the perfect swing, the right putt, and the wrong move; and serious and humorous explanations of what makes golfers the superior group they so clearly are.

Golfers belong to an exclusive universal club—not single 18-hole courses with clubhouses. Their membership began in the 18th century and is swelling into the 21st. Their connnection is not bound by time or geography. It is in the spirit and joy of the game. That is what the book is about.

Contents

THE LITTLE TREASURY OF GOLF

of anxiety, and swing anyhow. In such circumstances a really natural and proper swing is rarely accomplished, and, before the golfer is aware of the great injustice he has done himself, his future prospects will probably have been damaged. But if he has no ball before him he will learn to swing his club in exactly the way in which it ought to be swung. His whole mind will be concentrated upon getting every detail of the action properly regulated and fixed according to the advice of the tutor, and by the time he has had two lessons in this way he will have got so thoroughly into the natural swing that when he comes to have a ball teed up in front of him he will unconsciously swing at it in the same manner as he did when it was absent, or nearly so. The natural swing, or some of its best features, will probably be there, although very likely they will be considerably distorted.

At the same time the young golfer must not imagine, because he has mastered the proper swing when there is no ball before him, that he has overcome any considerable portion of the difficulties of golf, for even some of the very best players find that they swing very much better without a ball than with one. However, he may now taste the sweet pleasure of driving a ball from the tee, or of doing his best with that in view. His initial attempts may not be brilliant; it is more than likely that they will be sadly disappointing. He may take comfort from the fact that in ninety-nine cases out of a hundred they are so. But by and by a certain confidence will come; he will cease, under the advice of his tutor, to be so desperately anxious to hit the ball anyhow so long as he hits it, and then in due course the correctness of swing which he was taught in his first two days will assert itself, and the good clean-hit drives will come. There will be duffings and toppings and slicings, but one day there will be long straight drive right away down the course, and the tyro will be told that the professional himself could not have done it better. This is an extremely pleasurable moment.

The Complete Golfer

Mind-Bending Game

WALTER SIMPSON

Golf has some drawbacks. It is possible, by too much of it, to destroy the mind . . . For the golfer, Nature loses her significance. Larks, the casts of worms, the buzzing of bees, and even children are hateful to him. I have seen a golfer very angry at getting into a bunker by killing a bird, and rewards of as much as ten shillings have been offered for boys maimed on the links. Rain comes to be regarded solely in its relation to the putting greens; the daisy is detested, botanical specimens are but "hazards," twigs "break clubs." Winds cease to be east, south, west, or north. They are ahead, behind, or sideways, and the sky is bright or dark, according to the state of the game.

The Art of Golf

A Worm's Paradise

B. RADFORD

"We believe that to take charge as most clubs do three or four guineas entrance and a like subscription is ridiculous and unreasonable, and that there are scores of would-be golfers who are prevented from playing on the grounds of expense alone."

These are the remarks made by the chairman at a meeting called for the purpose of forming a golf club, and the meeting decided that, as 46 ladies and gentlemen had promised to become members, they would for a club, and before the meeting broke up they agreed that the entrance fee and subscription should be one guinea. They had already selected the ground on which to lay out a nine-hole course, and a committee was formed to enter into negotiations with the farmer.

Now, without wishing to damp the enthusiasm of these good people, I am of opinion that they are asking for trouble. They evidently know very little of the expenses connected with the making of a golf course, even on a modest scale. I know the ground that they propose to rent, and at the outset they are up against a stiff proposition in the person of the farmer. This same son of the soil had formerly let a portion of his land to a club, but as he persisted in turning his cattle in, to the detriment of the greens, they had no choice but to shift their quarters. The professional who was attached to this club has related to me the story of how on one occasion he turned the cattle off the links. This coming to the ears of the farmer brought him to the scene with a loaded gun. The timely warning of a caddie probably saved the pro's life, for when he arrived at the clubhouse the pro was nowhere to be found.

However small the club is, a nine-hole course cannot be brought into play under an expenditure of £250. The cost of labour, horse hire, machines, etc., would soon swallow up this amount, and there is always something required even when the committee think everything is in order. There are few, if any, courses that are as they were originally laid out, for it is not until they are played over that faults appear, and then begins the real work on a course. This bunker is in the wrong place, and that tee is dangerous, or it may be that more bunkers are necessary.

For a club with a membership of 200, possessing an eighteen-hole course, the subscription should be at least three guineas, for it is not possible to keep everything as it should be with a less sum, and when a club is formed the members should realize this, and not fix the entrance fee at a guinea as an inducement for others to join, for sooner or later they will awake to the fact that good golf cannot be obtained at this price, and if they do manage to rub along and keep the right side of the balance-sheet, the result will be seen in the condition of the course.

It is a curious fact that the largest and most exclusive clubs, such as Westward Ho!, Hoylake, or St. Andrews, do not spend as much per year on the upkeep of the course as do some of the small Metropolitan clubs on the upkeep of the 90 acres usually known as a worm's paradise. It is on this type of links that greenkeeping is an art, and the seaside course calls for little skill on the part of the custodian.

To all enthusiasts I would suggest that before the club is formed they should see that from a financial point of view there is nothing to fear, and to get rid of the idea that good golf can be obtained for a subscription of one guinea.

Golfing

Golf has probably kept more people sane than psychiatrists have.
HARVEY PENICK

Golfluenza

L. LATCHFORD

Golf is not a mere disease, infectious and contagious, which once acquired cannot be shaken off. Once a golfer always a golfer—there's no help for it!

The game exercises a spell, a thrall over the man who has once swung a club. You begin promiscuously and experimentally. A golfing friend casually hands you a driving iron and asks you to have a "whang" at a golf ball. Well! you "whang" and your fate is sealed. You are a golfer from that moment. Most likely you missed the ball and, like the man who ordered another pound of beetle powder, vowing that "he'd kill that confounded cockroach before he'd done," you mutter between your teeth that you'll go on whanging till you knock that ball into the next field. Or you, by the veriest chance (as you discover later), give the ball a fine swinging smack and to your delight see the lively bit of white gutta-percha soaring in the air to alight a full hundred yards off.

Then with a mild chuckle you hand back your friend his iron and exultantly observe that you think this game would "suit you" thoroughly. Whatever your luck—whether you hit or whether you miss—you are a golf-infected person. The incipient stages of the disease are rapid. You buy a set of clubs, clandestinely and ill-advisedly, seeking no advice, and probably acquiring tools which indeed prove "ill adapted for putting the little balls into the little holes." Then you sally forth covertly to practice and to fret away your soul in vain endeavours to "drive." You practice "putting"—which looks so easy, but is so tricky—on your lawn, and you fume and perspire at your own ineptitude.

Thenceforward you are known to talk of nothing but mashie strokes, bunkers, long putts, stymies and cuppy lies. A course of golf reading almost inevitably follows, the quality of the golf-links decides for you your summer holiday resort, you betake yourself to see the professional tournaments, you talk familiarly of Harry Vardon, Braid, Sandy Herd, and Jack White, and you breathe the name of "auld Tom Morris" with caressing veneration. Then you are fully ensnared—the royal and ancient game is your fowler.

The Young Man

Measure for Measure

HARRY FULFORD

K. Richard—
We are amaz'd; and thus long have we stood
To watch the fearful bending of thy knee.
Because we thought ourselves that it were right;
And if we be, how dare thy joints forget
To do their rightful duty in our presence?
If we be not, show us again the swing
Lest we dismiss the from thy post;
For well we know, as you have shown us oft
We grip the handle of our driver right.

Romeo—
Boy, give me my mashie, or the lofting iron.
And now take heed that thou movest not,
See thou betrayest not thy life if I charge thee
Whate'er thou hear'st repeat it not.
And do not speak to me upon the course.

Why I consent to play upon these links
Is, partly to confound Capulet,
Who hath a record, complished.
I am not jealous, but by Heaven
It rankles in mine bosom. Though
If I may trust the feeling that's within me,
This day will see an end to my revenge.

Hamlet—
To tee, or not to tee, that is the question:
I have oft heard it said that he
Who scorneth sand, wherewith his ball
May be brought closer to his reach,
Is tempting providence. Inasmuch
He causeth it to ascend unduly.
Therefore it behooves us, Horatio,
To take heed of this precept.
It is mine honour.
And being, as I trust, most honourable, It will
    enhance mine honour
To keep my passion within bounds,
Lest in the losing of it, I lose my match.

(He strikes)—
"Tis sad. Despite my most careful attention
It has flown, to the country from whose bourne
No ball returns.

Golfing

There are no absolutes in golf. . . . No two people swing alike.
KATHY WHITWORTH

Golf Dreams

JOHN UPDIKE

They steal upon the sleeping mind while winter steals upon the landscape, sealing the inviting cups beneath sheets of ice, cloaking the contours of the fairway show.

I am standing on a well-grassed tee with my customary summer foursome, whose visages yet have something shifting and elusive about them. I am getting set to drive; the fairway before me is a slight dog-leg right, very tightly lined with trees, mostly conifers. As I waggle and lift my head to survey once more the intended line of flight, further complications have been imposed: the air above the fairway has been interwoven with the vines and wooden crosspieces of an arbor, presumably grape, and the land seems to drop away no longer with a natural slope but nicely hedged terraces. Nevertheless, I accept the multiplying difficulties calmly, and try to allow for them in my swing, which is intently contemplated but never achieved, for I awake with the club at its apogee, waiting for my left side to pull it through and to send the ball toward that bluish speck of openness beyond the vines, between the all but merged forests.

It is a feature of dream golf that the shot never decreases in difficulty but instead from instant to instant melts, as it were, into deeper hardship. A ball, for instance, lying at what the dreaming golfer gauges to be a 7-iron distance from the green, has become, while he glanced away, cyndrical in shape—a roll of coins in a paper wrapper, or a plastic bottle of pills. Nevertheless, he swings, and as he swings he realizes that the club in his hand bears a rubber tip, a little red-rubber tab the color of a crutch tip, but limp. The rubber flips negligi-

○ **9** ○

bly across the cylindrical "ball," which meanwhile appears to be sinking into a small trough having to do, no doubt, with the sprinkler system. Yet, most oddly, the dreamer surrenders not a particle of hope of making the shot. In this instance, indeed, I seem to recall making, on my second or third swing, crisp contact, and striding in the direction of the presumed flight with a springy, expectant sensation.

After all, are these nightmares any worse than the "real" drive that skips off the toe of the club, strikes the prism-shaped tee marker, and is swallowed by weeds some twenty yards *behind* the horrified driver? Or the magical impotence of an utter whiff? Or the bizarre physical comedy of a soaring slice that strikes the one telephone wire strung across three hundred acres? The golfer is so habituated to humiliation that his dreaming mind never offers any protest to implausibility. Whereas dream life, we are told, is a therapeutic caricature, seamy side out, of real life, dream golf is simply golf played on another course. We chip from glass tables onto moving stairways, we swing in a straitjacket, through masses of cobweb, and awake not with any sense of unjust hazard but only with regret that the round can never be completed, and that one of our phantasmal companions has kept the scorecard in his pocket.

Even the fair companion sleeping beside us has had a golf dream, with a feminist slant. An ardent beginner, she says, "I was playing with these men, I don't know who they were, and they kept using woods when we were on the green, so of course the balls would fly miles away, and then they had to hit all the way back. I thought to myself, *They aren't using the right club,* and I took my putter out and, of course, I kept *beating* them!"

"Didn't they see what you were doing, and adjust their strokes accordingly?"

"No, they didn't seem to *get* it, and I wasn't going to tell them. I kept *win*ning, and it was *won*derful," she insists.

We gaze at each other across the white pillows, in the morning light filtered through icicles, and realize we were only dreaming. Our common green hunger begins to gnaw afresh, insatiable.

Hugging the Shore

Instructions in Etiquette

DOUGLAS ERSKINE

Etiquette is described in the dictionary as "the conventional rules or ceremonial observed in polite society; good breeding."

I have a friend who wanted to teach me golf and whose first lesson consisted of a dissertation on the value of golf as a teacher of etiquette.

"The game gives you the best idea of etiquette," he said. "Every golf player continually bears in mind the fact that he is playing a game which depends for its success and advantages on the amenities and on the strict observance of rules of etiquette that are based on the highest ideal of human fellowship."

He took me to a golf course, walked me around a couple of miles of up-hill-and-down-dale real estate, reduced me to a physical wreck and a mental derelict and it was all due to that etiquette of which he had boasted.

"Before you take the club in your hand," said this Chesterfield of the links, "I want you to come with me and watch a match between two good players. You will observe the courtesy with which they will act towards each other, the good fellowship that will prevail throughout the match, the cordiality with which the loser will congratulate the winner, and the heartiness with which the spectators will offer their felicitations to the winner and their condolences to the man who loses. And above all, you will notice with what superior consideration for the feelings of the players the gallery will act from start to finish."

I made up my mind to act in such manner that none of the professors of etiquette in that gallery would have occasion to point the finger of scorn at me, but as Bobby Burns once sagely remarked: "The best-laid schemes of mice and men gang aft agley."

Mine went agley before the match started.

One of the players took a bit of sand, placed it on the grass and gingerly planted his ball on the top of it. The gallery bent its gaze on the player with a collection of benevolent looks that would have done the young man a lot of good had he not been busily engaged in wiggling his stick and taking alternate looks at the ball and a point in the middle distance about 250 yards from where we were standing.

"Well, he's on his mark. Why don't the starter give the signal?" I asked.

My friend grabbed me by the wrist and a chorus consisting of the entire gathering whistled "Sh-Sh-Sh."

Right away I knew I was in wrong and, with great presence of mind, I looked about as if to discover the culprit. But it was no use. From each eye there shot a dagger right at me and the young man with the club stepped ostentatiously back from the ball and regarded me with a baleful gleam in his eye.

I could see that my remark showed ignorance of the rules and that the young man was extremely peeved about it. Evidently he had been used to playing before a deaf-and-dumb academy, so I said no more until he had sent the ball close to that point 250 yards away which had so attracted his attention.

I was relieved to notice, when the other player stepped up to take his turn at bat, that he was an old friend, with whom I used to play baseball when the belt he was wearing would have gone around him twice. I knew nothing would disturb him in his hitting. Hadn't I seen him knock home runs when thousands were shouting at him and calling him names, of which Fathead and Bonehead were the most flattering?

He wiggled his bat just like he used to do when he was trying to rattle the pitcher and I knew that the time for encouragement had arrived.

"That-a-boy, Bill," I yelled. "Slam it right over second."

One look at Bill's face showed me that etiquette had done its deadly work on him. That wild-running, reckless-sliding ball-player, who had ripped many a stocking with his spikes and opened wounds in umpires' feelings that never could be healed, glowered at me without a look of recognition.

"If the party with the raucous voice and the vacant mind will kindly remember that this is a gentleman's game, I shall feel greatly obliged to him," said Bill, and that gallery of etiquetters actually applauded.

Raucous voice, indeed! And that same Bill used to

say I was the best coacher on the team because they could hear me all over the diamond.

Vacant mind! Why, I taught that big stiff all the inside baseball he ever knew.

"Now, will you be good?" said my companion. "You see what you get for failing to observe the rules of etiquette, which demand that deep silence prevail when the players are making their shots."

Etiquette and I got along fine together until they had the balls on the green. Then I got in bad again by laughing when Bill missed the hole when he only had to roll the ball a foot. Anybody would have laughed. It was so easy a man with two wooden legs could have kicked it in.

"Vacant mind, indeed! I don't see any jostling or over crowding in his upper story," I remarked, loud enough for the etiquetters to hear. But I could see that they did not appreciate my resentment at Bill's remark to me.

"Hard luck," they murmured.

"Sure," I said. "The same kind of hard luck that makes a fellow fall for the hidden ball trick."

My instructor in etiquette had a busy time for the next few holes. I had to promise solemnly that I wouldn't say a word loud enough for anybody to hear, especially the players, and it was maybe just as well that I kept my promise. If they had heard what I was saying to myself I would have been eligible for every blackball in every etiquette club in the world.

By the time we got to the seventh tee, as my friend called it, Bill was "down." That's what they told me, and he looked to me as if he was down, and out as well. I could see that what he need was support of some kind. So I determined that he should have it. Was my old sidekicker to lose because no one would show their faith in him? Not if I could help it.

"Come on, Bill," I shouted. "The lucky seventh. Here's where we knock one out of the lot."

Etiquette could stand no more. Bill showed that the new cult had him in its grasp.

"You will be doing me a great favor," he said, icily, I thought, "if you will get away as far as you can from this game and stay there. You have about as much idea of the usages of polite society on the links as a rabbit has of the internal economy of a greyhound's kennel. If you hurry you will be able to get to the ball park before the game starts and there you can get rid of that abundance of oratory which seems to be beyond your control. Mounted on a soap-box at a street corner, you might be all right, but on a golf links you are an anachronism."

Bill had the house with him and all I could do was to go. But before I went I wanted to show him that I forgave him.

"Well, I wish you luck," I said. "But you'll never make the big league playing this game. You step back from the plate as if you expect to get beaned by the ball you're hitting and you'll raise dissension in the team with that mean disposition of yours. If I was the manager of this club, I'd release you and sign a busher."

Crushed by the coldness and indignant at the sneers of the gallery, I went off, aided by my friend, who stopped me from going back and telling them another hard thing I had just thought of.

Fortunately etiquette does not prohibit a member from buying his quest a drink, and I was *en rapport* for the first time that day when we got to the smoking room club.

I see by the papers that Bill won his match, but I'll bet he doesn't appreciate how much he owes me for my efforts on his behalf. He probably thinks he won on his etiquette.

Pacific Golf and Motor

My Own Swing

SAM SNEAD

[In the golf swing, the] *feel* is more important than mechanical action. If I'd become tangled up in the mechanics of the swing when I first hit shots, chances are I'd have been only an average player.

My secret is that I learned by feeling my way along— and "feel" still is the biggest word in the world to me. If my grip or stance on the tee didn't feel right when I began playing, I asked myself, "Why not?" Then I studied on it until it did feel comfortable and right and the results were good.

As that system worked out, I don't remember ever having shot a 90 on a golf course, and mighty few 80s.

Golfers depend too much upon outside help and worrying over details and not enough upon their own senses. For example, having chopped plenty of wood as a boy, I knew you didn't jerk the ax back. And you didn't give deep thought to swinging it down. You only brought back the ax with as little effort as possible, took a half second or so to aim, and laid the blade on the block of wood where you wanted it. Hands, arms, and feet all worked by feel. I felt confident that I'd split the block from the time I spit on my hands because of the long practice and no agonizing over how I'd do it. If I happened to miss, I took a breath, slowed up a little on the swing, and corrected the mistake—just by sensing what needed to be done.

Golf wasn't that simple, but by making mistakes, experimenting, and correcting by myself, rather than having others tell me what to do, I put together a game almost entirely by feel. I don't say most beginners shouldn't have pro lessons. But after they have the basic information, and trouble appears, they should practice, practice, practice, until their own brain and nerves have solved the problem. They'll be ten times as strong as the average player for it....

The practice swing of most ordinary players almost always carries most of the main ingredients. The fundamentals are there. But when they are in a match, the difference is terrific. The feet are no longer easily set. There is a cramped body turn. Hands and wrists are rigid. When this happened to me, I began thinking in terms of *performance*, not *results*. By this I mean I had no thought beyond the ball—of traps, ponds, rough, or out of bounds. All I did was to go back to my practice swing, on which I could count, and then to think *with* my swing—not *ahead* of the swing. This takes will power, but it isn't so hard to let your mind relax and say to yourself, "Here goes my practice swing—and I don't care where the ball lights or lands. If I can't play like a good golfer in actual play, at least I can go back to my practice swing and let nature take its course."

Call on your will power to "let the rest of the world go by," and dust that thing with the form you have when nobody is watching—and watch your score go down.

Climb inside your old, regular personality, not the one that wants to take over when the pressure is on.

Education of a Golfer

The Necessary Evil

The caddie is one of the necessities of Golf—as indispensable as the ball itself—too often he is the "necessary evil" which figures in all human enjoyments; but I wonder whether the influence of the caddie has ever been duly balanced by a thoughtful golfer.

This is not referring to the caddie's capabilities in the matter of advice or instruction, but I allude to his personal attributes and characteristics, what one might call his moral being.

A clean, cheerful caddie, who maintains an even demeanour, neither elating his master with undue praise, nor depressing him with an ill-concealed scorn, is a rarity, and one to be cultivated and encouraged; but it must be admitted that the generality of the tribe have tricks and failings calculated to rasp the susceptibilities of the highly-strung golfer; and most golfers are highly strung when keen on the game, and materially influence his play.

There is the officious caddie, who offers gratuitous advice and criticism, too often from a slender stock of knowledge. He produces the club he thinks most suitable for a stroke, and looks supercilious if you select another which you fancy for yourself. He is conventional, and while patting up a tee imparts voluntary and undesired information.

This caddie may be endured on a day when your play

seems all that you have longed for it to become, but on a bad day he is more aggravating than you play itself, and his conduct is conducive to manslaughter.

Then we have all met the languid and indifferent caddie, who fails to appreciate your most brilliant performances. He can never render a straight answer, being of an undecided temperament, and is a poor hand at "spotting" your balls.

The indifferent caddie is only a shade more bearable than his sympathetic brother. This individual condoles with one in a way that is maddening.

"Seen you drive over that bunker very often, sir," he will remark when you have sent your ball into the cruel thickset furze. Later on he will tell you that Mr. Smith, whom you consider the worst player in the club, is not so much ahead of you after all. It is possible to ignore your butler, and even to despise your valet, but a caddie forces himself upon you, and you cannot overlook his presence.

Golf

Hope on Ford

Bob Hope

If I were ever backed into a corner and forced to name the people whom I've most enjoyed playing golf with it would, of course, be a difficult task. I've had so much fun on the golf course with so many persons. But very high on my list would be Gerald R. Ford, thirty-eighth President of the United States, genuine good guy and the most dangerous 14-handicapper in the land—in more ways than one.

Jerry Ford's fame as an erratic hitter, capable of

beaning anyone within a range of 260 yards, is richly deserved. He's rattled a number of shots off heads and backsides of the fearless followers in his gallery. The President doesn't really have to keep score. He can just look back and count the walking wounded.

I play maybe fifteen or twenty rounds a year with the President, mostly at pro–ams on the PGA Tour including, naturally, the Bob Hope Desert Classic. We also get together at his invitational tournament, which has pros and amateurs, each year at Vail, Colorado. And sometimes we'll just go out and play a social round in Palm Springs, with no gallery except his Secret Service personnel. It's a little different playing with those guys around. I once saw him hit a shot off line and a cactus threw it back onto the fairway.

In the last half dozen years or so President Ford and I have become very close friends. I love the guy. He's so human, so natural. He gets happy when he hits a good shot or sinks a long putt, and I can tell you that he's pretty good at both. But he's also got a temper, and I've seen him fume after missing a shot.

Ford plays golf with the same fierce determination he showed on the football field for University of Michigan back in 1932, '33, and '34. He battles you all the way for a $1.00 nassau. He reminds me a lot of Ike in that way. Ford has never shaken one habit of his football days when he played center—he still putts occasionally between his legs.

I've gotten a lot of mileage out of my Jerry Ford jokes. The public enjoys them, because they know that the President does hit a bunch of wild shots, that he loves to play golf as few men do and that he contributes so much to the game. The PGA Tour, in fact, made him an honorary member.

So it's fun to introduce him at dinners with lines like "You all know Jerry Ford—the most dangerous driver since Ben Hur." Ford is easy to spot on the course. He drives the cart with the red cross painted on top.

Whenever I play with him, I usually try to make it a foursome—the President, myself, a paramedic and a faith healer. One of my most prized possessions is the Purple Heart I received for all the golf I've played with him.

Confessions of a Hooker: My Lifelong Love Affair With Golf

My Golf

CHARLES BATTELL LOOMIS

I am naturally very nervous. All my friends say that I lack repose, that I am too strenuous. "Take up golf, old man," said one. "It is what you need. It will keep you out in the open, it will teach you the value of deliberation, and it will cure your nervousness, and give you a repose of manner that you can get in no other way."

I am spending the summer in the country, and although there is no course near us, the country-side is full of natural advantages for the pursuit of the game, and I determined to take it up.

I did not care to go to the expense of a whole outfit, as I might not like the game after I had learned it, but the next time I went down to New York I bought a driver, thinking to practice repose with it.

I bought a particularly stout one that cost me five

dollars, as I figure that if I put a little more into the purchase price I'd gain in the end. But now I'm sorry that I did not buy a very cheap one, because then, when I had tripped up the old gentleman in the Fourth Avenue car on my way to the Grand Central it would have broken the club, and that would have ended my golf. But the stick was stout, and the old gentleman fell and broke his leg instead, and also dropped a bottle of wine that he was taking home, having just received it from a returning sea-captain.

He told me that he did not mind the break in his leg, because he had broken it before in the same place, and he knew just how long it would take to mend it, and he needed a rest from business cares, anyway, which he never would have taken if he had not been forced to it in some such way; but he was all broken up over the spilt wine, as it was a very rare vintage, and he never expected to receive any more.

I apologized all I could and offered to put him up at any hospital he might select, but he wouldn't hear of it, and as the wine was priceless, there was nothing left for me to do except to feel miserable and show it plainly, which I did.

He was an old golfer himself, and after I had helped him out of the car (and lost my train by so doing) he showed me the proper way to hold my stick so that I shouldn't trip up anybody else. The pleasantest part of my golf experience was while we were waiting for an ambulance—for I had telephoned for one at my own expense. We sat on the curbstone, and he wouldn't hear of my accompanying him; said he believed in the rigor of the game, like Sarah Battle, and he ought to have seen that I was a beginner and kept out of the way of my club.

He was so entertaining that I was really sorry when the ambulance came and he rolled off toward his home.

As for me, I had missed the last train for the day, so there was nothing to do but to put up overnight at a hotel, and that with dinner and breakfast cost me four dollars more. So far, the game had come to nine dollars, and I had yet to make my first inning.

I will hastily pass over the broken car window on the way up in the train next morning. I might have pushed an umbrella or a cane through it, and I contend that it was not because it was a golf-stick, but because I lacked repose, that I did break the glass. Of course I had to settle with the conductor, but I think that three dollars was too much to charge me for the glass. The car was ventilated after I had opened the window in this artificial way, and thousands rose up and called me blessed in different parts of the car, for, needless to say, the car was warm and the other windows were too tightly wedged to open, even with superhuman efforts. I should like to recommend to the Consolidated Company a judicious use of golf-sticks on their windows; then there would not be so much smothered profanity on the part of the men, and overstrained muscles on the part of women who foolishly attempt the impossible.

I hold that the London way is preferable to ours. There you know that the bus windows cannot be opened, that they were manufactured shut; but in this country you know that a car window may be opened in a perfectly normal way under proper conditions. The fact that the conditions never are proper, coupled with the knowledge that the windows were meant to open, is what makes travel in summer in America so absolutely unendurable.

But I digress.

I was unable to do any golfing after I had reached my abiding-place in the country, as I found in the mail an order for a Christmas story, and as it was July the affair cried haste and kept me busy all day. But next morning I awoke early, aware that the golf fever had seized me, and I was up before any one else in the house, as every one else knew, for my lack of repose caused me to express my exuberance of spirits in merry roundelays—that is, they were merry to me, but disastrous to the dozers.

My youngest son soon joined me, and was delighted at my request that he act as my caddie. He prepared my tee—I had coffee in bed: I never take exercise with stomach empty.

I adjusted the ball, gazed earnestly at the object I desired to approximate, swung my club in the air, made several false starts in the most approved fashion, and then I let drive.

My next-door neighbor, a wealthy gentleman from New York, was awakened by the crash of glass, and came running down-stairs in his pajamas. I tried to cultivate repose as I reflected that I had disturbed his, and while cultivating it I went over to see just what damage I had inflicted. I had put quite a curve on the ball, for it was fifty feet to the left of its intended destination.

I walked over and gazed at the ten-dollar opening I had made in his plate-glass window. MY son was overjoyed both at the crash and at the jagged opening. That is youth. I felt no joy.

My neighbor was not gazing at the opening I had effected, but a little faience vase which had tried in its ineffectual way to stop the rapid progress of the ball.

Even as the old gentleman of two days before had

overlooked the broken glass, but the vase was an heirloom and virtually priceless.

Here let me stop long enough to ask why it is that people will load up their summer houses with priceless treasures. I never yet bought anything that was priceless; in fact, I always insist on having the price plainly marked. And when people give me priceless things I do not put them in my summer house. I go even further than that. The place where I spent my winters I regard simply as a house of detention until I can return to my summer place, so I never load it up with priceless treasures; therefore at no season of the year could such an accident have befallen me as I had caused to fall upon my neighbor.

He would not hear of my buying him another vase,—he is a little deaf,—and I was glad he would not, nor did I raise my voice. My golfing had cost me enough already, and when I buy faience I want it for my self.

But he was somewhat sarcastic at my expense, and that I did not like. I like sarcasm to be repaid, although I like to do the shipping myself. He said that I was not cut out for an athlete, and that at my time of life if I did want to take up games of skill I'd better go out to the Bad Lands, that couldn't be damaged, or to the Desert of Sahara. Altogether he made me feel very sorry that I had not bought a putter instead of a driver. Putting is wholly innocuous and innocent. Those who made a name for themselves in the late sixties at croquet, as I did, should be able to putt with ease, while driving of all kinds is and always has been dangerous and difficult.

Still, there is too much of the sportsman in my make-up to allow me to submit tamely to setbacks. It was now break-fast time, and I had a little ten-dollar practice,—

for of course I insisted on paying for the pane I had caused to be broken,—and, like Dewey at Manila, I felt that breakfast was necessary; but afterward I would go on with the fight and master driving.

The morning mail brought me an order for a hundred-dollar story that an editor wanted while he waited in his office; that is to say, he wanted it within twenty-four hours.

I generally pay immediate heed to such orders, because I think that editors who take the trouble to order things in this world, where so much is forced upon the unwilling, ought to be encouraged; but the golfing fever was on me, and after breakfast, instead of going into my workroom, I secured my son once more and sallied forth to try a little more driving.

This time I went farther from the haunts of men, and took up my station in a very wild field full of shrubs and weeds, and, as I supposed, containing nothing valuable—certainly no vases or rare wines.

I have heard people say that they found it hard to hit the ball squarely; that they generally dug up earth, or chipped slices of gutta-percha from the cross-hatched sphere, or fanned the circumambient air. But my troubles were of a different nature. I hit the ball every time I strove to, and the first time I hit it in that field I seemed to conceal it in a lusty whortleberry-bush some fifty feet distant.

My son and I consumed nearly the whole of a pleasant morning looking for that ball. We visited every bush and shrub that was big enough to harbor a ball, but we could not find it, and at last, after several hours' search, I reluctantly gave up and sent my boy home after another one. While he was gone I threw myself down upon the grass to rest, and I found the ball, or, to speak more accurately, my hip found it. And it wasn't ten feet from the place where I had stood when driving. I can account for this only one way. When people lose their way in the great woods they circle round and round, and at last bring up where they started from. I dare say that lost balls do the same, and that this one was on its way back when I found it.

While yet my son was gone, I placed the new-found ball on a little tee of my own making, and with a strength born long waiting I whirled my club through the soft July air and smote the ball.

Will somebody tell me why farmers in New England should raise Angora goats, and if so, why they select wild and shrubby pastures to raise them? I am told that it is a profitable industry, and that in a few years, instead of the cattle upon a thousand hills, it will be the thousand Angoras on a single hill, so prolific and so useful are they. But they are inimical to golf, and hard as their heads are, they are not so hard as a ball driven by a strong man with a five-dollar club.

There were little kids in that field not worth more than twenty-five dollars apiece, and they were scot-free after my horrible drive. They bleated and leaped and cropped the rank herbage, all unaware of the fact that the father of the herd, imported from Turkey, had been laid low by a golf-ball. My son saw him drop, and my son found the ball on the ground in front of him.

I did not know that he was highly valuable, but small boys have a way of picking up information, and my son told me that Mr. Hermance, a gentleman farmer and a neighbor of mine, who had just gone into the industry, had paid one thousand dollars for this miserable animal that was now worth no more than its wool and its hide and its carcass would bring. It did not interest me to recall, as I did immediately, that I had read in a afternoon paper that Angora leather made the best golf-bags in the market. I did not care to buy a golf-bag just then.

I decide quickly. I took the next train for New York and proceeded to get insured for one thousand dollars in favor of Mr. Hermance. Then I registered an oath to play no outdoor games more dangerous than puss-in-the-corner.

Then I returned to my summer home to write the story that the editor was waiting for so patiently, and nothing better coming into my head, I wrote up my experiences at golf under the foregoing title. While they were not written by an expert golfer, they should hold much of interest to the average beginner, and if the reading of them shall save the world a few pieces of faience, a few rare vintages, a few legs, and a few Angora rams and other cattle, I shall not have written in vain.

The First Lesson

E. J. HOLLINGWORTH

The links were swept by a strong north-easter; the sea, dashing against England's whitish cliffs, was also visibly affected. I myself was past caring about the weather, and the Great Man apparently did not notice it. He took fourteen balls from an adoring acolyte and led the way in silence to the first hole.

The wind howled. It flapped the graceful profusion of his nether garments. The Great Man walked with the gait peculiar to his profession, a delicate blending of the retired sea captain and the gorilla. 'Why do they all bend their knees so much?' I asked myself. I was soon to find out the reason.

At a deserted and uninviting spot near a little flag we halted. He took a club, bent his head devotionally, wriggled rapidly like a kitten about to spring, then suddenly turned parts of himself back to front. This he did three times before my fascinated gaze.

'That's all I'm going to teach you this afternoon,' he said. 'All you want to practice is the swing. It's a little tricky at first, but you'll soon get into it. How many grips do you know?'

I confessed complete ignorance of them all.

'Have you ever seen this?' he inquired very gently, twining his fingers in and out among one another and the stick.

'It is a little like something I was once shown, only that was done with a string,' I replied, making honest efforts to follow his directions.

The Great Man took three more vicious swings. Then he said, 'Now grasp the club, fix the eyes on this weed, bend the head slightly—no, keep the body upright and the back stiff. Now raise the head of the club slowly with the left hand, guiding it with the right. Stand firm with the right foot and rise upon the ball of the left toe, bring the left shoulder round under the chin, always keeping the head bent and the eyes fixed. Arch the right wrist. Now slightly bend the left knee; no, keep the right knee stiff. You are now in a position to begin the downward stroke. Let the club-head travel smoothly down, passing through the point upon which the eyes are fixed and allow it to carry through to its natural position over the left shoulder, taking care to swing only from the shoulders, keeping the wrist stationary, at the same time elevating the right heel and transferring the weight of the body from the right foot slightly inward and bend the right knee. Now arch the left wrist, keep the eye fixed on the one spot and stiffen the back. You are now at the correct finish. But always remember that the only way to acquire the swing is to let yourself do it naturally. Self-consciousness is the ruin of good style.'

'I'm afraid I'm not doing it quite right,' I said after ten minutes of earnest effort.

The Great Man was most patient. Seventeen times I essayed the swing, but, alas, whenever the right knee was becomingly bent the left wrist was sure to be unarched. If the left shoulder came fittingly into contact with the chin the right heel was shirking its responsibility. Should all the knees and wrists be functioning satisfactorily the head would be found to be unbent and the eyes would be caught surveying, perhaps pardonably, the harmonious whole. Should the eyes, recalled to duty, rest immovably on the fixed spot, the effort would always entail an unstiffened spine or drooping shoulders.

'You'll soon get the knack,' said the Great Man doubtfully. 'Now we'll try with balls.'

He placed one on a small eminence.

'Hit in the direction of the sea,' he said.

I took courage. This was much better than being told to try and hit one little patch of grass.

I hit. The ball rose well.

'Good,' he said, putting down a second. I hit again, into a hedge twenty yards to the right. At the third shot I scored a green-mower. The fourth went into a little hole some way off to the south-west. The fifth, sixth, seventh and eighth were rather oblique shots. The ninth bagged a groundsman in the middle distance, but the tenth, eleventh, twelfth and thirteenth were somewhat disappointing. As I was addressing the fourteenth I saw the Great Man glance at his watch. This put me on my mettle.

Resolutely keeping the head bent, the eyes fixed, then raising the club with the left hand, arching the right wrist, rising on the ball of the left toe, placing the left shoulder beneath the chin, I paused for one exalted second, then down came the club-head, round came the right shoulder, down sank the left heel, up rose the right. The left knee stiffened, the right knee bent, the ball of the right toe transferred the weight to the left foot. After its splendid natural swing and follow-through the club came to rest above the left shoulder, and through it all the back had remained stiffened, the head bent, and the eyes even now were fixed—on the ball.

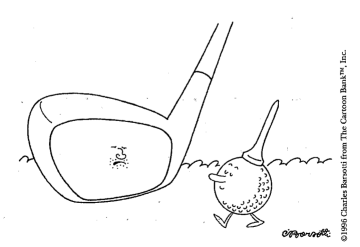

"You've got style, kid."

Patience

HORACE G. HUTCHINSON

If you happen to be a really long driver the fact will be generally admitted without your emphasizing it, to the annoyance and even peril of your neighbors, by always firing off your tee shot the moment the parties in front of you have struck their seconds. To bear and to forbear is a necessity of golfing existence.

Hints on Golf

Golf

H. J. WHIGHAM

It is natural that a game which has formed the chief recreation of the Scottish people for several centuries should have by this time a large literature of its own, so much so that two of the best volumes in the whole domain of sporting history are devoted to this subject. It will be unnecessary and superfluous therefore to enter upon a full description of the game's development in the remote past, for are not its annals written in the pages of the Badminton book upon golf and did not Sir Simpson go back farther yet and invent a pretty legend to explain the origin of the pastime?

All this has been done for us already. It is needless to recount how the popularity of the game began in the seventeenth century seriously to menace the profession of the soldier and the pursuit of religion; how great Montrose preferred a friendly contest at Musselburgh to raiding the base Lowlander, or how Charles I forfeited his crown and his life because he allowed the Irish Rebellion to break out while he was sacrificing his royal duties to indulge in this ancient sport. More recent passages in history tell the same tale. The one fact of importance which has been related of the predecessor of Queen Victoria on the throne of England is that he was elected captain of the St. Andrews Golf Club, and it is certain today that Mr. A. J. Balfour would refuse the premiership of the British Government if he could by so doing become the amateur golf champion of Scotland and England.

In order, then, to avoid returning over ground that has been so often trodden before, it will be well to confine ourselves to the more recent incidents in the growth of the game, more especially those which have to do with its spread in this country. Fore even Mr. Horace Hutchinson's excellent work in the Badminton series was contributed before England became thoroughly converted. Nine years ago, at the English universities, not only was the game played by a very small body of undergraduates over the half-inundated cricket fields during the winter months, but the ignorance displayed by all who did not belong to this devoted band was simply appalling to one who had been born and educated north of Tweed. The point of view taken by most Englishmen was well expressed when it was proposed about a year later that the members of the team selected to represent Oxford in the inter-university golf match should be allowed the privilege of wearing a "half-blue"—the full "blue" being the reward for services in the Rowing Eight, Cricket Eleven, or football teams. The president of the "blues" committee was at the time one of the best all-round athletes in Oxford, and he very strongly objected to extending any university recognition to the exponents of the game which—as he put it—did not include perspiration. In other words, he confirmed the general opinion of outsiders that golf is not an athletic pursuit at all, but merely a mild recreation for old men.

Now, although it is perfectly true that children of ten and octogenarians can trudge round the links and enjoy the fresh air and the mild exercise involved in trapping the ball, it is entirely wrong to suppose that the game when properly played does not require the same muscular strength, skill, and endurance which are requisite for the pre-eminence in all the higher branches of sport. Golf was never intended to be a game for team matches, and for that reason it is probably right to leave it out of the reckoning in university athletics. On the other hand we need only look for a moment at the career of the best amateur players in the world to see the truth of the assertion upon which I should like to lay some stress that strength, skill, and training are absolutely necessary for success in the royal and ancient game; for if it were really a pastime for old men, women, and children, as so many seem to imagine, or if it were simply a society fad, as it would appear to a large section of the American public, who have been unaccustomed in the past to any form of athletics which can be indulged in by a man after he has left college, then the best players would be drawn indifferently from the ranks of the strong and the weak, the young and the aged.

This, however, is not the case. Every prominent golfer whose name comes readily to mind has achieved success in other branches of sport. Mr. F. G. Tait, the amateur champion of Great Britain for 1896, was a fair cricketer at school and a first-rate football player. He did not go through a university career, and so his prowess on the football field was not widely known; but he was one of the strongest players at Sandhurst, the training school for the army, where strong men are rife. His predecessor, Mr. Leslie Balfour-Melville, whose record as a golfer is a long and glorious one, was for years the best all-round athlete in Scotland. He was one of the few cricketers from the North who could ever rank with the English exponents of the game; at school he was one of the most brilliant football players in the country; his skill at lawn-tennis was far above the average, and it may be remarked in passing that he is a billiard-player of no mean ability, for curiously enough, accuracy in billiards and golf seem to go together in a great many cases.

Then, again, we are not surprised to find that Mr. J. E. Laidlay, who is without doubt the most brilliant match play of all the first class amateurs, was one of the most remarkable school cricketers when he was a boy at Loretto; and so instances might be multiplied. Mr. Horace Hutchinson was a good cricketer in his college days, Mr. Mure Fergusson, the Blackwells, and Mr. John Ball, are all men of great physical strength and muscular activity. The last named player had the distinction of being the first amateur to win the open championship, and although there are others who in the last two or three years have met him on even terms, he was for a short time quite unique in the power and accuracy of his play, and it is certain that he could never have reached such perfection if it had not been for the country life which allowed him constant practice and plenty of hard physical exercise.

It may be taken for granted then, that although a man can play the game as long as he can walk or even ride round the links on a pony, the real science of golf can only be acquired by men of athletic capacity. To saunter round the eighteen holes on a summer afternoon, with intervals for tobacco and conversation, is one thing. It is another and a very different undertaking to go through a championship tournament, playing thirty-six holes a day, when every drive must be hit hard and clean, every approach must be accurate, every put must be true to a hair's breadth. A football match is a matter of less than two hours; from the instant the ball is in play, the nervous strain is removed and the constant action requires a sound wind and fleetness of foot, but not the absolute freedom and yet control of the muscles which is requisite for steady driving, nor anything like the strain on the nerves which is kept up from the start to the finish of a close encounter at golf.

It was probably an awakening to the fact that golf was, after all, a real branch of athletics that brought about its sudden and extraordinary popularity in England eight or nine years ago. The conversion of the South began when many of the prominent cricketers discarded the bat to take up the golf club. Having for many years dismissed the Scotch game with various disparaging terms, such as "parlor skittles" or "Scotch croquet," they at length discovered that it only required a single trial to enamour them of this much despised pastime. Moreover, it became apparent that for those who had left college and settled down to a regular profession cricket was a vain and elusive pursuit, making far too strenuous demands upon the time and purse to come within the reach of any but the rich and idle.

Golf, on the other hand, could be freely enjoyed by all who were able to spare an afternoon a week. No sooner, therefore, were the floodgates opened than the new waters threatened to inundate the whole field of English sport. The staunchest cricketers were found among the proselytes, lawn-tennis became a thing of the past, the crack shots from the midland counties would tarry on the links of St. Andrews late in the year when the partridges and pheasants were waiting to be killed at home; even the rabid fox-hunter found himself wasting whole days when the frost was out of the ground, chasing the gutta-percha instead of the brush. Heretofore in Scotland inland links were exceedingly rare; but now they sprang up in every county of Great Britain. Old lawns, on whose immemorial turf it had been reckoned a sin even to walk, were ruthlessly hacked to pieces by the iron of the golfing tyro; the cattle were robbed of their pasturelands in order that the putting-greens should not be disturbed; and last but not least the Sabbath was freely violated by the men and women who had never before missed a morning service in church.

Needless to say, this sudden enthusiasm was regarded with supreme distrust by the conservative Scotchman. New elements were introduced into the game which he could least endure. Formerly the only prizes in the year had been the autumn and spring medals at the leading clubs, and these were coveted for glory and not for their intrinsic value, which amounted to less than that of the expense in clubs and balls which it cost to win them. The real game of golf was to be found only in match play, and the counting of scores was regarded with the utmost abhorrence except on those rare occasions, twice in the year, when it was absolutely necessary.

The Englishman, however, looked upon the matter in a very different light. Long practice in lawn-tennis tournaments had inured him to the vicious habit of pot-hunting, so that golf for him was a new and unending source of joy. Tournaments and sweepstakes were matters of weekly occurrence, a system of handicapping was instituted, and the young golfer was chiefly engaged not so much in improving his game as in defeating the vigilance of the green-committee; nor was it at all rare to find a veritable duffer in possession of many valuable trophies, any one of which would have bought up all the medals in the keeping of the best first-class player in Scotland.

It can hardly be wondered then that the term "English golfer" became one of reproach upon the Northern courses. The pilgrims from the South were in fact a terrible nuisance. They had no respect for the sacred traditions of the game; they appeared on the classic heath of St. Andrews adorned in flaring "blazers," which filled the mind of the orthodox Scot with loathing, they never played a match, but toiled round the links with pencil and card, intent on deceiving themselves into the belief that they were daily lowering their record. A famous old caddie at North Berwick expressed the general feeling of his outspoken class when he pointed to one of these misguided individuals busily engaged with his card on one of the putting-greens, utterly oblivious to the fact that he was delaying the field while he worked in the higher branches of arithmetic, and remarked in a loud tone the contempt to one of his party, "D'ye see yon man? D'ye ken the best club in his set—it's his pencil."

This was only one aspect of the movement, however, and now that the pencilling disease has more or less abated, it is only fair to admit that the new impetus given to the game by its sudden popularity outside of Scotland has been in the long run most beneficial. The competition has of course become far greater, and as young athletes have taken up the sport more and more, the standard of excellence has proportionally increased. I am quite willing to believe that "Young Tom" Morris was one of the greatest golfers that ever lived, but I am equally convinced that there were no amateur in his time who could compare with the players of to-day. The conditions are certainly in our favor. Not only have the greens become easier, and straight driving less essential, but the implements of war are far more efficacious.

The quality of the balls has greatly improved, and the introduction of the "bulger" has revolutionized the art of driving. With the old-fashioned long-headed club it was practically impossible to hit hard with accuracy, the slightest deviation in aim involving a terrific slice or pull. Nowadays the curve on the face of the club, and the more compact volume of weight, makes the matter of direction so much easier that a far greater force can be given to the stroke. Twenty years ago a man who was a long driver was at once stamped as an erratic player, not to be relied upon. Now, unless a certain average of distance is maintained no one can rank as a first-class player.

But it was not merely the old-fashioned weapons which handicapped the amateurs of the past generation. We have only to consider who they were to see that, other things being equal, they could not possibly have competed with the best players of today. In the first place, they were far behind the professionals, which is not the case at present. Secondly, they were for the most part middle-aged men; so much so that it was considered an impertinence for any youngster to play against them. They kept up the pleasing fiction for a long time that golf, as at whist, the ripeness of long experience was necessary for success, and it required many expositions of the game to persuade them that the cracks of the younger generation, men like Mr. J. E. Laidlay and the Blackwells, were introducing a new and superior kind of play. When, for instance, Mr. Ted Blackwell used to drive across the corner of the railway at St. Andrews—a carry of about one hundred and seventy yards—his feat was regarded as a sort of circus trick, wonderful to look at, but quite outside the true sphere of golf. After awhile, however, it became apparent that not only could the trick be repeated, but what was more important, Mr. Blackwell almost invariably beat his opponent, and gradually the old order began to change, making way for the new, which was hastened in its coming by the fresh impulse from athletes in England.

In other words, the kind of golf which could be played by an elderly Scotch judge on Monday afternoon at Musselburgh in a stiff collar and a high silk hat ceased to be regarded as the best standard of excellence which could be reached by the amateur. It was recognized now that to play the game to its full advantage a man must be in good health and training, with muscle and eye in perfect accord; and we must thank the English cricketer for helping to impress this fact upon the hardy but conservative Northerner.

It is now time to turn to the growth of the game in this country, which is the main theme of the present article. We have seen that the sudden spread of golf in England was almost contemporaneous with a new development in the evolution of the sport. It remains to inquire how far that development has been appreciated in America. The particular genius of the American has a tendency to reduce sports of all kinds to a scientific basis, and therefore it is expected that sooner or later the lovers of the game in this country will be able to throw some new light not only upon the methods of play, but upon the interpretation of the rules, which has always been a difficulty since golf passed out of the hands of the few into the possession of the many who cannot be controlled by tradition alone, but need the assistance of hard and fast laws. It seems to me that so far the players in this country have been more exercised over the proper reading of the regulations than they have over the development of the game itself. And since it is extremely important that no radical changes should be made in the rules, which long experience has proved to be best adapted to the government of the game before, at least, it is definitely understood what the game is, it may be well to point out a few of the main shortcomings of the golf that is played on this side of the Atlantic.

You cannot play golf without links, any more than you can make bricks without straw, so that the first consideration is that your links should be as good as possible. It is five or six years since the game was introduced into the United States, and yet the fact remains that there is hardly a course in the country that in any way approximates a first-class links in the proper sense of the term. Of course allowances must be made for the many drawbacks which have to be overcome in the way of climate and soil, but there are so many errors in the best courses in the country which might easily be remedied, that it seems necessary to indicate exactly what are the features of the best courses in England and Scotland, and what is the standard at which we have to aim.

To put it as shortly as possible: Great Britain is encircled for the most part by a belt of sandy soil from a half a mile to a mile in breadth, which has been formed by the receding of the ocean. This belt of land is of an undulating character, with occasional abrupt sand-hills, and the whole surface is covered with a short velvety turf which stands a great deal of wear and tear, but is always smooth and soft; even in the rainiest summer the grass seldom grows long enough on the regular course to conceal a golf-ball from sight, while the climate of the British Isles is such that a drought seldom comes to parch the young blades, or scorch the putting greens.

Such a thing as a stone or a tree is practically unknown on the best courses; good play will always secure good lies on perfect turf, while the putting greens are simply part of the regular course, not laid out with the natural roll of the land, which greatly increases the necessity of skill and accuracy in negotiating the finer part of the game. The only hazards admissible are sand-bunkers, which occur naturally at irregular intervals, the long grass which on the seashore is called "bent," and which generally bounds the edge of the course to prevent wild driving, the gorse which is an incident of most Scotch links, and, if nature happens to supply it, a water hazard in the shape of a pond or stream. There are cases of stone-walls on Prestwick and North Berwick, two of the finest courses in Scotland, but they are there of necessity and not by choice, and to imagine that they are proper adjuncts, would be equivalent to considering that every racket-court must have a cracked wall, because there happens to be a slight fissure in the best court at Lords.

Now the courses which are laid out on this sand-belt of Great Britain are not held to be best because they are recommended by custom, but because it only requires a single day upon any of them to find that the game takes on new features of interest which it never possessed before. A man who has once ridden upon a modern safety with pneumatic tires would never go back to the old-fashioned high bicycle with thin cushions; so one who has played golf at Prestwick or St. Andrews knows at once what are the possibilities of the game. Imagine, therefore, the astonishment of a Scotch golfer upon reading the accounts of some of the prominent courses in this country.

Here are a few examples: "It is an inland course of stone-wall hazards, rocky pastures bordered by ploughed fields and woods, and is prolific in those little hollows known as cuppy lies;" or this: "The hazards are mainly artificial; there are some stretches of sand, railroad embankment, and deep roads that are tests of skill and temper;" or this: "There are nine holes in the course which furnishes great variety in its hazards of hills, stone-walls, railroad embankments lined with blast furnace slag, apple-trees, and a combination of terrors in front of what is known as the Devil's Hole, consisting of brook, boulders, and road, which has spoiled many a score;" or, best of all: "A player who has done a round at the Country Club will have passed over various points of avenue, steeple-chase course, race-track, polo-fields, and pigeon-shooting grounds; he will have come triumphantly through a purgatorial stone-wall jump, a sand-bunker and bastion, a water jump and finally a vast gravel pit or crater... Stone-walls, trees, ploughed fields, fences, and chasms present excellent sporting requirements on a course."

Many more instances might be quoted, but these are quite sufficient to explain exactly what a golf-links ought *not* to be. A golfer is not a quarryman that he should go down into a gravel-pit to extricate his ball from the midst of boulders; nor is he one of the hewers of wood or drawers of water that he should slash the trees with his niblick like a modern Don Quixote, or cover himself with a mire from a muddy ditch. It is understood, of course, that Nature cannot entirely be overcome. The coast of Maine, where there is enough moisture in the air to keep the greens in good condition, is too rocky, while the summer climate of Long Island prevents the courses there from being kept in first-class condition, although the quality of soil is equal to anything in Scotland or England. Still, even if the ideal links can never be quite attainable, it is possible, by aiming in the right direction, to get a course which shall be for all practical purposes a perfect test of golf.

To arrive at such a consummation, it is necessary always to keep the ideal in view; and the first object, therefore, should be to procure the best possible turf all through the course and the putting greens. Next it should be remembered that, if possible, all the hazards, with the exception of a stream or a pond, should be sand-bunkers. Long grass is admissible, but should be avoided in the direct line of play, because it leads to so much waste of time in hunting for lost balls. Every single tree on the links should be ruthlessly cut down. If a picturesque landscape is insisted upon it is easy enough to leave the woods which may happen to lie on the confines, but they should be regarded as out of bounds and never played through. Every boulder and stone should be removed with assiduous care, for they are merely responsible for broken clubs and loss of temper, and have nothing in the world to do with the game.

Finally the putting greens should be left as Nature made them, except in so far as they are kept in perfect condition by rolling and mowing. They ought not be laid out on a dead level so as to preclude any nicety in the judgment of curves, but should be gently undulating and always guarded in some way by a hazard. In this country it is generally necessary to water them, that they may not become parched and inordinately keen; on the other hand it must be remembered that the smoother and keener they are up to a certain point, the greater will be the skill called into play both in putting and approaching.

A man who has been accustomed to pitch the ball boldly on to slow level-putting green with fair accuracy, will find himself hopelessly at sea when he has to contend with a keen slope where a hair's breadth deviation from the true direction will lead to instant perdition. To take cases in point, the putting greens at Shinnecock, where the championship meeting was held last year, were far too small and keen, although they were beautifully true. Those at Meadowbrook, on the contrary, are perfect condition, but they are for the most part so level and slow, that approach play is rendered comparatively easy.

So much for the nature of the ground. A word or two remains to be said upon the laying out of the eighteen holes. I say eighteen advisedly, because a course of half the distance can never be placed in the first class. The expenses incurred in laying out of golf-links in this country are generally so great, that it has been deemed best in most cases to get nine good holes rather than eighteen of an inferior nature. But this should always be regarded as a temporary measure. It is not merely a matter of convenience in tournaments which can only be held with any satisfaction on a full course; but in every-day play a nine-hole round becomes very monotonous and does not allow sufficient scope for versatility in the game.

As far as I am able to judge there are many nine-hole courses in the East which are admirably constructed—Meadowbrook, for instance, being very well laid out—but there is not one of the eighteen-hole rounds that approaches perfection. Take Shinnecock, for instance, which, from the nature of its soil, ought to be an almost ideal field for play, there is hardly a single hole of a good length; that is to say, the distances are so arranged that not only is the prowess of the good golfer seldom brought into evidence, but the chances of good and bad are in a fair way of being equalized. The chief thing to aim at in distributing the holes is to arrange them in such a way that each can be reached from the tee by one or two or three *full* shots, as the case may be. That is practically the whole gist of the matter. For it is obvious that, under such conditions, a player cannot miss a single shot, cannot even play an indifferent stroke without being penalized.

If, on the other hand, the length of a hole is such that it cannot be covered in one shot, and yet if the drive off the tee goes only a hundred yards or so, it can still be covered in two, by the aid of a good second; then it is evident that one drive is, for all practical purposes, as good as another. When there are many holes of such a description, a player may make a bad drive off every tee and yet defeat an opponent who never misses a single shot in the round. A careful study of the best courses in Great Britain will show that the number of holes measuring from two hundred and forty to three hundred yards is exceedingly rare; in other words, the rule referred to above is the essential toward excellence.

As for the hazards, they should be sand bunkers, as far as possible. Sand should be procured, even at considerable cost, because there is no other kind of hazard which answers the purpose so well. They should be of such a nature that a good player can always extricate himself from the difficulty in one stroke, and they should, above all things, be varied in their construction.

The everlasting line of cops seen on so many of our inland courses are both an offense to the eye and the intelligence. The difficulties thrown in the path of a discriminating golfer should be of a far more subtle nature. In driving off the tee it is generally well to have something in front to catch a missed ball, and the hazard ought to be large and well defined; a little ditch, at one hundred and twenty yards distance, is not nearly sufficient because it punishes only a few out of the many bad shots. If possible, the hazard should extend in many cases over the whole distance between the tee and the carry of a moderate drive.

Then, as regards the hazards near the putting green, particular care should be taken to have them placed in various shapes and positions. A single bastion in front of every hole is more often an aid to the success than a ground for misfortune; it is an easy guide to the eye, and induces a player to be bold in his approach, a quality in which he is often deficient. Hazards should be placed on every side of the hole, more especially beyond it, so that every approach may call for careful calculation. Finally let me repeat that trees and stones must, at all cost, be removed; and the requirements of a good golf course will have been fairly stated.

When we have arrived at such a measure of excellence as this, the difficulties of the rules and regulations of the game will begin to solve themselves. The United States Golf Association, for instance, passed a rule permitting a player in a match to lift his ball out of any difficulty at the penalty of two strokes. Now this was in direct opposition to the original idea of the game that the ball should always be played under any circumstances, or else the hole should be given up. The excuse for the change made by the Executive Committee was that there were many courses in the country where conditions were different, and where it would often be impossible to hit the ball at all. The answer to such an argument is apparent. Such a course is not fit for the proper exercise of the game and ought not be admitted to membership in the Association. Although it is impossible always to reproduce the perfect turf and bracing sea-air of the Scotch links, it is quite feasible to lay out a course in such a way that it may be as good a test as possible of proficiency in the game.

Take, for instance, the Chicago Golf Club links at Wheaton. The course has been in existence only two years, and yet, when a few additional bunkers are finished, which are at present under construction, it will present as fair a field for the settling of rival claims as any links outside of the first half dozen or so in Great Britain. Of course the quality of soil is different from that of St. Andrews or Prestwick, but the turf is excellent; a good drive is hardly ever punished by a bad lie; the hazards are of the proper sort, chiefly consisting of sand bunkers, with an occasional water-jump, and above all there are no trees, stones, or buildings on the course.

The holes are laid out in such a way as to eliminate, as far as possible, the element of chance; and taking it all in all it is probably the only eighteen-hole course in the country which can compare with the best links abroad. I state this, not as a matter of prejudice, but because it is an incontrovertible fact, and one which should be taken into consideration by all green-committees; for it is a simple proof that nearly all the Eastern courses could be improved to a similar extent by keeping the true ideal constantly in view.

The rules of golf have always presented a difficulty to those who are entrusted with the care of framing them, and since there are many points under discussion at the present moment of writing it will be well to take only a general view of the case. It is quite certain that many of the existing regulations as they stand are faulty, chiefly because while they have the right aim in view, they leave so much ground for argument and discussion; and it is equally certain that before long the American golfers, who are not bound hand and foot by tradition, will introduce one or two remedial measures which will incense the conservative Briton but will probably aid the true development of the game. Already an excellent innovation, for which the United States Association is responsible, is the method of deciding the Amateur Championship.

It was considered a great step in the right direction when the competition by holes was first introduced into Great Britain, not by a Scotch club but by the green committee of Hoylake in England. Since the hole game is the only true golf, it seemed a pity that the Amateur Championship should not be decided by any other way. A difficulty, however, has since arisen on account of the unwieldy size of the field which threatens to make the tournament a very protracted affair.

It remained for American golfers to solve the problem by inventing the dual method of play; first weeding out the poorer players by two rounds of medal play, and then selecting the champion by several rounds of hole play—a plan which sounds very obvious and satisfactory as soon as it is suggest; for it cuts down the list of entries very quickly, and also necessitates excellence in both branches of the game; and after all the patience and accuracy brought out in medal play ought to count for something.

Now, however, there is a proposal to go still farther into the weeding out process by fixing a definite scratch score for every links based upon the distances of the holes, and accepting no entry from anyone whose handicap at his home club is about a certain limit. Whether this suggestion should be carried out or not is entirely a matter of expediency. If it is found that so many entries are made as to seriously militate against the success of the tournament, it will be necessary to adopt some such scheme for keeping out all those who have really no chance of winning, but merely enter for practice or amusement. The national tournaments not a nursery for embryo golfers, not is it fair that a good player should be handicapped by having to go through the preliminary rounds with a duffer who has not the ghost of a chance of winning.

One of the arguments against the acceptance of a definite scratch based on distance, is that it can be so easily obviated by a slight alteration of tees so as to make the score as high as possible and include a number of players who would not otherwise have qualified. Still it must be remembered that it is always easy to defeat the ends of any government for the time being, and a certain reliance must be placed upon greens committees to do their best, not only for the interests of their respective clubs, but for the future of the game itself.

In this matter of qualification experience alone will show whether a new regulation is necessary or not; but as a general principle it ought to be remembered that golf is still a very new game in the country, and the would be iconoclasts should be discouraged from taking any premature action which would alienate us from golfers on the other side of the Atlantic in the meantime, and in the long run prove to be quite unnecessary.

Those who look for instruction in the science of golf must turn to the pages of the Badminton book which is still the highest authority on the subject; but it may not be out of place to throw out a few suggestions as to the spirit in which the book should be read. It must be remembered in the first place, that nearly all the men who have taken up the game in America of recent years, have reached an age when it is impossible to acquire the easy suppleness of youth. They ought accordingly to modify the instructions which come to them, not only from the literature upon the subject, but from many of the professional teachers who always seem to forget that their pupils have not had the same advantages in early youth themselves.

It is nearly always wrong for a grown man to attempt a full swing to start with. I have so constantly heard the most promising beginners reproached for what the conventional book learned player calls a lack of form, that it seems very necessary to point out that a short clean sweep at the ball is not only far more effective, but far better form than the angular contortions which go to make up what many beginners are pleased to call a full swing. In driving the ball the main object is to keep the head of the club traveling as long as possible in the direct line of flight, and this must be achieved, at first, by letting the club go back only so far as is possible without making an angular bend in the swing. If this steady sweep is constantly kept in view, the beginner will find that gradually he is able to swing farther and farther back as the muscles become more accustomed to the motion, until finally he attains the proud distinction of possessing a real St. Andrew's swing. In all other things, moreover, he should exercise his common sense and make up his mind that it is his duty to hit the ball clean every time, even if in so doing he sacrifices a good many yards in distance.

Above all let him watch the best players and get into their style by unconscious imitation. If our beginners would only walk round with their professional teachers, and feel, as it were, the easy method of sweeping away the ball, they would learn far more than they do in a hundred verbal lessons; and when they play they should always play matches and not trudge round the links with a pencil and score card—trying to lower a record or their own which is absolutely meaningless. The young player who can take odds from his elders and betters and compete with them more or less successfully, is far nearer the road to grace, although his total score should mount up ever so much higher than the record of the solitary and introspective knight of the pencil.

Life would be far more worth living on a golf links if there were a rule in every club forbidding a member to mention his score or talk at length about the lowering of a record which nobody but himself cares about, and even he himself only half believes in. The game was originally intended to be a friendly contest of skill; the middle-aged beginner has made it a fruitful source of lying and self-deception, and very scourge to his friends.

One word should be said about the courtesies of the game. There is no pursuit in life which exhibits the best and the worst of a man so freely as the game of golf. That a control of the temper is absolutely essential for success goes without saying, and there are many little points which suggest a loss of control if certain rules of etiquette are not strictly observed. The most important of these is the way in which the rules are interpreted, and there seems to be only one way of dealing with the matter.

First of all, if a penalty is incurred for any reason, the player should at once admit it without waiting for his opponent to call his attention to it, and no matter how trifling the breach of rule, or how unimportant the game, the full penalty should be conceded whether the opponent desires it or not. On the other hand, if the opponent should move his ball, for instance, in addressing it, it is his business to count the stroke, for stroke it is just as much as the longest drive that was ever struck from the tee; and except when playing for a medal he should be left entirely to himself in the matter.

To put it shortly, the word "claim" has no place in the golfer's vocabulary. It may be argued, of course, that your opponent may then take advantage of you. If he does, your remedy is simple—never to play with him again. In the meantime, if every golfer were intent upon acting up to the very letter of the law, there could never be any possibility of dispute. After all it is a game for gentlemen, and unless that is kept in mind, unpleasantness becomes endless. Perhaps it is this very fact which has made it so popular in this country, where the other great games are in danger of getting entirely into the hands of professionals.

That being the case, it is most important that the tendency to multiply tournaments and lavish handsome trophies on indifferent players should be checked at the outset of our golfing history. Ten years ago the best players in the world were content with the custody of one or two small medals which they could not even keep, and I confess that in the best interests of the game, I wish the same state of things existed now. Possibly we shall have a revulsion of feeling in a short time, and golf will take on again its garb of Caledonian simplicity.

The Right Whack!

HARRY VARDON

The way to drive far is to comply with the utmost care with every injunction that I have set forth, and then to hit hard by the proper use of the swing. To some golfers this may be a dangerous truth, but it must be told: it is accuracy and strength which make the long ball. But I seem to hear the young player exclaim, "When I hit hard you say 'Don't press!'" A golfer is not pressing when he swings through as fast as he can with his club, gaining speed steadily, although he is often told that he is. But it most frequently happens that when he tries to get this extra pace all at once, and not as the result of gradual improvement and perfection of style, it comes not smoothly but in a great jerk just before the ball is reached. This is certainly the way that it comes when the golfer is off his game, and he tries, often unconsciously, to make up in force what he has temporarily lost in skill. This really is pressing, and it is this against which I must warn every golfer in the same serious manner that he has often been warned before. But to the player who, by skill and diligence of practice, increases the smooth and even pace of his swing, keeping his legs, body, arms, and head in their proper places all the time, I have nothing to give but encouragement, though long before this he himself will have discovered that he has found out the secret of the long ball.

The Complete Golfer

A Review of the Future

We have no wish to be unnecessarily harsh in our estimate of this book by J.A.C.K.—Golf in the Year 2,000, or What We Are Coming To—for those whose excursions into literary pastures, as he tells us in the preface, himself shall hardly account, still, candour compels the admission that J.A.C.K., if the unpleasant pleasantry be allowed to pass, is not exactly a "ripper" in the arts and graces of authorship.

Like Rip Van Winkle, the narrator falls into a trance, and sleeps for a hundred and eight years, at the end of which time he awakens to find, not unnaturally, that he and his surroundings have "suffered a sea of change."

Several wonderful things happen; shaving has been improved out of existence, in lieu thereof a magical depilatory removes the beard by touch; when dinner time arrives the table is found to be "made of three concentric circular pieces, and the middle one sank down through the floor, leaving intact the outer one, which formed the edge of the complete table"; "the dumb waiter portion reappeared, bearing two plates of soup on it."

The Chief Inspector when the time arrives for serious business, gives his guests the choice of a green on which to have a match; "They are all equally convenient, from Thurso to Penzance; if you cared, we could even play a round on both of the greens I've mentioned." So by means of an electric tubular railway, they find themselves at St. Andrews almost before they have time to wink. Arrived there, it is necessary to procure a set of clubs, and a golfing coat, this latter a garment which subsequently develops unexpected, not to say alarming qualities. The staring is managed by phonograph, in conjunction with a board outside the window, on which board every man's name appears when his turn arrives. It is satisfactory to find that due sense of order and decorum prevails; in fact, no one is at the tee but the opponent.

The schoolboy, if under age of fifteen, has no place in this economy, nor are there any caddies—none in the flesh, that is to say. As substitutes there are perpendicular rods about four feet high, weighted at the foot and hung upon wheels, the magnetic qualities of the employer's golfing jacket serving to keep them in tow, at a respectful distance of twelve feet. The clubs have advanced with the age, and are fitted with a dial apparatus for automatically registering every shot played, for there is a competition everyday, and "we have got handicapping as near perfection as possible, for we have a record of every round a man plays, and by taking his average from day to day and from week to week, we soon arrive at this right figure."

Another automatic apparatus registers the length of every carry; the thickness of the grip can be altered at will in a moment, and the shape of the clubs, all made of steel in one piece, is such that they can be used either right or left-handed. The niblick is a work of genius; when swung over the shoulder its queerly-shaped double head begins to revolve on its own account with exceeding velocity, like a paddle-wheel, only faster, and ejects out of the bunker clouds of sand sufficient to keep "Old Tom's" greens going for a twelvemonth. Moreover, the golfing jacket shouts "Fore" every time a drive is made, to the detriment, until one becomes habituated to it, both of the stroke and the temper.

Not without a touch of humor does the author allow his imagination free play in dealing with the future of the game, when match play shall have been almost improved out of existence, and the self-acting putter does everything short of telling you the line of your putt. The pity of it is that the ideas are clothed in such slip-shod English, grating on one at every turn, itself sufficient to mar the effect of the whole, however rich the imagination, or amusingly extravagant the general conception.

Golf

Disposing of Tommy

R. Browning

According to the definition, when two persons playing one ball between them contend against a third person playing his own ball, the match is called a "threesome." I explained all this to Milly on the way to the first tee. For on the principle that a beginner's enthusiasm is more likely to be encouraged by a real game than by any amount of practice, we had agreed that Milly's first lesson should take the form of a match between us two on the one side and her youngest brother on the other.

Milly was rather huffy at the start because I picked out the oldest and dirtiest ball I had got to tee up for her.

But I know what ladies' golf is. You would think that they don't swing the club with any strength at all, and yet I have seen a girl, playing for the first time, cleave a brand-new Haskell to the mid-riff in a manner that Ivanhoe himself might have envied.

However, her first shot—I mean the first one she hit, for, of course, we were not counting misses—was such a rattling good one that it made her quite pleased again. We were on the green in two to Tommy's three. "Do you know," said Milly, as she held out her hand for the putter, "I think women, though, of course, they can't hit as far as men, should be able to do the wee shots on the green better." I admitted that a delicate touch was everything in putting; and pointing to a spot about half way between the ball and the hole, "You try and play it to there," I said.

Milly laughed—she had a particularly nice kind of laugh—and asked me if I thought she knew no more about golf than that. "Well, if you're going to play for the hole," said I, "be sure not to hit too hard. The ball flies off far faster than you are apt to think." "Oh, I know," said Milly, and played the ball straight for the hole. It was a longish putt, but I believe if she had hit the ball with just about one-quarter of the strength it would certainly have gone in. As it was, I was able to play the ball back on to the putting-green again with my next, but Milly's second putt was so timid that we had never any chance.

After that, we wrestled along pretty comfortably until the sixth hole, though Milly never came near repeating the success of her first shot. But at this point I had to help Tommy to hunt for his ball which he had lost in a patch of whin, and when I got back to Milly I found that she had played her ball and had not the slightest notion where it had gone. All that she could say was that she thought it was a pretty far shot, although she had "hit the earth a little too." However, we hunted for it in vain.

At last I suggested that we might have better chance of guessing whereabouts it had gone if she would take us back to where she played it from. Ye gods! she certainly had "hit the earth a little too." I would never have dreamed that so much strength lay in these slight wrists. For there lay a fine tough divot of about four inches by six, not taken clean out certainly, but folded over, for all the world like the lid of a milk-can.

"I don't think the ball would go very far, when you took the earth as heavily as that," I said, and stooped to replace the divot. Never was wisdom more quickly justified—for the ball lay underneath. All the same Milly need not have been so angry just because I laughed.

However, by the time we had played two holes more, and Milly was playing with so little heart that Tommy won both with ease, I saw that her enthusiasm for golf had pretty well evaporated. Yet if I suggested stopping I knew what a nuisance Tommy would make himself. It was time for desperate measures. The way the tenth hole is bordered by a fence on the right-hand side, with a stretch of heather beyond. I teed a brand new two shillings' worth before Tommy's gleaming eyes, and adopting the stance which Vardon recommends for the player who wishes to slice, I sent the ball curving gracefully into the heather.

"Ugh!" said I, "There's small use in searching for it there!"

"You don't mean to say you're going to leave it?"— Tommy's youthful thrift was instantly in arms against such heedlessness. I explained that I thought it a bit too tiresome for Milly to wait while he and I hunted for a ball that we might never find. "But if you like to have a search," I added, as indifferently as I knew how, "you can hang on to it if you find it."

"Right-oh!" said he, "I've got my eye on just about the very place." And with that he was over the fence like a shot.

The Stymie by "Han-Kan"

To Play and Play and Play

TONY LEMA

Playing the tour presents two very compelling challenges that so many of us find impossible to resist, challenges that have nothing to do with money. First of all, for pro and amateur alike, there is the challenge of the game itself. Golf requires a technique that none of us ever quite master, but which we all think we could master with just a little more playing and a little more practice. In our effort to reach this unreachable perfection we become very much like hounds at the dog track. We are chasing a rabbit that we are never going to catch, but this is what makes the game so fascinating, so hypnotic. We all know that we are never going to catch the rabbit, but we are getting a terrific bang out of trying. Everything takes second place to the chase. A job that keeps you at a desk from 9 o'clock in the morning to 5 o'clock at night—Lord, what a bind! Happiness is a fine day and a fine golf course. A non-golfing girl I know once said that she thought the greatest torture God could devise for a golfer would be to one day empower him to hit every drive, every iron and very putt perfectly. Imagine his anguish when, returned to his mortal golfing self, he ties to play again. Well, every golfer has actually had these moments. The hacker who suddenly fired a burst of seven straight pars that seemed as effortless as breathing. The really good amateur who breaks the course record one day and decides he could really play this game well if he could play it more often. The desire to play and play and play and play becomes overwhelming. For some there is no solution to this problem. For others there is the pro tour.

Golfer's Gold

The True Line

JOHN L. LOW

There is hardly such a thing as an unfair bunker. Even the hazard right in the middle of the course at the end of a long tee shot, like the ninth hole bunker at St. Andrews, is really quite a fair risk. That it is only a good shot which goes into it is often the complaint we hear. True, true, gentle grumbler, but not good enough. If the player is going to drive to one side or the other, there is plenty of room on either flank. . . . Golf need not be played in bee-lines. It is a mistake to suppose that because you hit a ball straight down the middle of the course and find it bunkered you are to fill up the offending hazard. Next time you will play on the true line, not on the bee-line and all will be well. . . . For the little pot so near the bee-line, I would submit that it, too, is a good hazard. . . . By going very near the difficulty we gain just a little distance and a slightly better position. The greedy golfer will go too near and be sucked into his destruction. The straight player will go just as near as he deems safe, just as close as he dare. Just as close as he dare: that's gold and that's a hazard of immortal importance: for golf at its best should be a contest of risks.

Concerning Golf

The Doubter's Fate

HENRY LEACH

The is a very simple job,
And when I have holed the ball,
I shall be certain of my half-crown,
Still, I must be careful.
It is very easy to miss these short putts;
And I have missed many thousands, costing me
Many pounds—scores of pounds.
And now that I am up against it,
And looking at this putt,
It does not seem quite so easy as it did at first.
It will require most careful management—
a most delicate tap,
And very accurate gauging of strength.
One needs to be very cool and
deliberate over these things.
One's nerves, and stomach,
and liver must be in prime condition.
I wish I had not been out to dinner last night.
Was it Willie Park or Ben Sayers
Who said that a man who could putt
could beat anybody?
I believe him—Willie or Ben.
This is really a most awkward putt.

The green looks slower than the others.
It is very rough.
Why don't the committee sack the greenkeeper,
Who ought to be a market gardener?
It is like a bunker between
My ball and the hole. Such very rough stuff.
One, two, three—six—nine—why?
There are eleven big blades of grass
Sticking up like the rushes at Westward Ho!
The grass becomes so very stiff and wiry
in this very hot weather.
(Yes, it is too hot to putt properly).
My ball will never break through this grass.
It is one of the hardest putts I have ever seen.
I wish I had more loft on my putter.
I was an ass not to bring that other one
out from my locker,
here it is eating its head off (so to speak).
I think, also, that a little cut
would do this putt a lot of good.
But how? The green slopes from the left;
Yet it seemed to slope from the right.
Also, it goes downwards to the hole.
This is a perfect devil of a putt!
I know my stance for putting is not good,
But Harry Vardon says that every man
has his own stance,
So perhaps it is all right.
But I had better move my left foot; it seems in the way.
I see that two—six—seven of the pimples on his ball
Are quite flat.
Nobody can putt with a ball like that.
A man ought to be allowed to change his ball

Even on the green at all times like this,
I must allow for those pimples.
Confound that fellow Brown!
He seems to be waiting.
And he is smoking his dirty shag so much
That I can hardly see the hole for smoke.
If I lose this hole I shall lose the match.
I am quite with Johnny Low in his new idea
for handicapping.
When he says some of us should be allowed to play
Our bad shots over again.
In that case I would have one good smack at this ball
To get the strength and the hang of
Everything. And I am certain—
yes, I am quite absolutely certain—
That I would hole the ball next time.
However, what does it matter?
Better men then I have missed such putts,
And I am not a chicken—life a hard life—lot of work—
Office tonight—awful day tomorrow.
And as the wife was saying—
Let me see. Oh! hang this putt!
He can have his half-crown if he wants it,
But I am going to have one good smack
At this ball. Now—
No, that was wrong. Now, yes, yes—

. . . .

My godfathers!
And my godmothers!
I have missed that putt again!

The Spirit of the Links

Post-Round Practice

TOM WATSON

The most valuable time to practice is right after your round, when your mistakes are fresh in your mind. Replaying the strengths and weaknesses of a round on the practice tee immediately after finishing play is a good discipline and excellent learning tool. I like to correct a pattern of poor shots as soon as I can. If I had trouble with short left-to-right putts and a particular bunker shot, I might putt a hundred left-to-right putts until I find the problem and then go to the practice bunker and try to solve that problem as well.

I usually spend more time practicing after a round than I do before. Before the round, I'm just warming up the engine. It's a good way to wind down. Many times I can work out a problem I was having, which gives me a boost of confidence for the next round. And I sleep better that night.

Getting Up and Down

Winter Dreams

F. SCOTT FITZGERALD

SOME OF THE CADDIES were poor as sin and lived in one-room houses with a neurasthenic cow in the front yard, but Dexter Green's father owned the second best grocery-store in Black Bear—the best one was "The Hub," patronized by the wealthy people from Sherry Island—and Dexter caddied only for pocket-money.

In the fall when days became crisp and gray, and the

long Minnesota winter shut down like the white lid of a box, Dexter's skis moved over the snow that hit the fairways of the golf course. At these times the country gave him a feeling of profound melancholy—it offended him that the links should lie in enforced fallowness, haunted by ragged sparrows for the long season. It was dreary, too, that on the tees where the gay colors fluttered in summer there were now only the desolate sand-boxes knee-deep in crusted ice. When he crossed the hills the wind blew cold as misery, and if the sun was out he tramped with his eyes squinted up against the hard dimensionless glare.

In April the winter ceased abruptly. The snow ran down into Black Bear Lake scarcely tarrying for the early golfers to brave the season with red and black balls. Without elation, without an interval of moist glory, the cold was gone.

Dexter knew that there was something dismal about this Northern spring, just as he knew there was something gorgeous about the fall. Fall made him clinch his hands and tremble and repeat idiotic sentences to himself, and make brisk abrupt gestures of command to imaginary audiences and armies. October filled him with hope which November raised to a sort of ecstatic triumph, and in this mood the fleeting brilliant impressions of the summer at Sherry Island were ready grist to his mill. He became a golf champion and defeated Mr. T. A. Hendrick in a marvelous match played a hundred times over the fairways of his imagination, a match each detail of which he changed about untiringly—sometimes he won with almost laughable ease, sometimes he came up magnificently from behind. Again, stepping from a Pierce-Arrow automobile, like Mr. Mortimer Jones, he strolled frigidly into the lounge of the Sherry Island Golf

Club—or perhaps, surrounded by an admiring crowd, he gave an exhibition of fancy diving from the springboard of the club raft. . . . Among those who watched him in open-mouthed wonder was Mr. Mortimer Jones.

And one day it came to pass that Mr. Jones—himself and not his ghost—came up to Dexter with tears in his eyes and said that Dexter was the—best caddy in the club, and wouldn't he decide not to quit if Mr. Jones made it worth his while, because every other—caddy in the club lost one ball a hole for him—regularly—

"No, sir," said Dexter decisively, "I don't want to caddy any more." Then, after a pause: "I'm too old."

"You're not more than fourteen. Why the devil did you decide just this morning that you wanted to quit? You promised that the next week you'd go over to the State tournament with me."

"I decided I was too old."

Dexter handed his "A Class" badge, collected what money was due him from the caddy master, and walked home to Black Bear Village.

"The best—caddy I ever saw," shouted Mr. Mortimer Jones over a drink that afternoon. "Never lost a ball! Willing! Intelligent! Quiet! Honest! Grateful!!"

The little girl who had done this was eleven—beautifully ugly as little girls are apt to be who are destined after a few years to be inexpressibly lovely and bring no end of misery to a great number of men. The spark, however, was perceptible. There was a general ungodliness in the way her lips twisted down at the corners when she smiled, and in the—Heaven help us!—in the almost passionate quality of her eyes. Vitality is born early in such women. It was utterly in evidence now, shining through her thin frame in a sort of glow.

She had come eagerly out on to the course at nine o'clock with a white linen nurse and five small new golf-clubs in a white canvas bag which the nurse was carrying. When Dexter first saw her she was standing by the caddy house, rather ill at ease and trying to conceal the fact by engaging her nurse in an obviously unnatural conversation graced by startling and irrelevant grimaces from herself.

"Well, it's certainly a nice day, Hilda," Dexter heard her say. She drew down the corners of her mouth, smiled, and glanced furtively around, her eyes in transit falling for an instant on Dexter.

Then to the nurse: "Well, I guess there aren't very many people out here this morning, are there?"

The smile again—radiant, blatantly artificial—convincing.

"I don't know what we're supposed to do now," said the nurse, looking nowhere in particular.

"Oh, that's all right. I'll fix it up."

Dexter stood perfectly still, his mouth slightly ajar. He knew that if he moved forward a step his stare would be in her line of vision—if he moved backward he would lose his full view of her face. For a moment he had not realized how young she was. Now he remembered having seen her several times the year before—in bloomers.

Suddenly, involuntarily, he laughed, a short abrupt laugh—then, startled by himself, he turned and began to walk quickly away.

"Boy!"

Dexter stopped.

"Boy—"

Beyond question he was addressed. Not only that, but he was treated to that absurd smile, that preposterous smile—the memory of which at least a dozen men were to carry into middle age.

"Boy, do you know where the golf teacher is?"

"He's giving a lesson."

"Well, do you know where the caddy-master is?"

"He isn't here yet this morning."

"Oh." For a moment this baffled her. She stood alternately on her right and left foot.

"We'd like to get a caddy," said the nurse. "Mrs. Mortimer Jones sent us out to play golf, and we don't know how without we get a caddy."

Here she was stopped by an ominous glance from Miss Jones, followed immediately by the smile.

"There aren't any caddies here except me," said Dexter to the nurse, "and I got to stay here in charge until the caddy-master gets here."

"Oh."

Miss Jones and her retinue now withdrew, and at a proper distance from Dexter became involved in a heated conversation, which was concluded by Miss Jones taking one of the clubs and hitting it on the ground with violence. For further emphasis she raised it again and was about to bring it down smartly upon the nurse's bosom, when the nurse seized the club and twisted it from her hands.

"You damn little mean old *thing!*" cried Miss Jones wildly.

Another argument ensued. Realizing that the elements of the comedy were implied in the scene, Dexter several times began to laugh, but each time restrained the laugh before it reached audibility. He could not resist the monstrous conviction that the little girl was justified in beating the nurse.

The situation was resolved by the fortuitous appearance of the caddy-master, who was appealed to immediately by the nurse.

"Miss Jones is to have a little caddy, and this one says he can't go."

"Mr. McKenna said to wait here till you came," said Dexter quickly.

"Well, he's here now." Miss Jones smiled cheerfully at the caddy-master. Then she dropped her bag and set off at a haughty mince toward the first tee.

"Well?" The caddy-master turned to Dexter. "What you standing there like a dummy for? Go pick up the young lady's clubs."

"I don't think I'll go out to-day," said Dexter.

"You don't—"

"I think I'll quit."

The enormity of his decision frightened him. He was a favorite caddy, and the thirty dollars a month he earned through the summer were not to be made elsewhere around the lake. But he had received a strong emotional shock, and his perturbation required a violent and immediate outlet.

It is not so simple as that, either. As so frequently would be the case in the future, Dexter was unconsciously dictated to by his winter dreams.

II

NOW, OF COURSE, the quality and the seasonablility of these winter dreams varied, but the stuff of them remained. They persuaded Dexter several years later to pass up a business course at the State university—his father, prospering now, would have paid his way—for the precarious advantage of attending an older and more famous university in the East, where he was bothered by his scanty funds. But do not get the wrong impression, because his winter dreams happened to be concerned at first with musings on the rich, that there was anything merely snobbish in the boy. He wanted not association with glittering things and glittering people—he wanted the glittering things themselves. Often he reached out for the best without knowing why he wanted it—and sometimes he ran up against the mysterious denials and prohibitions in which life indulges. It is with one of those denials and not with his career as a whole that this story deals.

He made money. It was rather amazing. After college he went to the city from which Black Bear Lake draws its wealthy patrons. When he was only twenty-three and had been there not quite two years, there were already people who liked to say: "Now *there's* a boy—" All about him rich men's sons were peddling bonds precariously, or investing patrimonies precariously, or plodding through the two dozen volumes of the "George Washington Commercial Course," but Dexter borrowed a thousand dollars on his college degree and his confident mouth, and bought a partnership in a laundry.

It was a small laundry when he went into it but Dexter made a specialty of learning how the English washed fine woolen golf-stockings without shrinking them, and within a year he was catering to the trade that wore knickerbockers. Men were insisting that their Shetland hose and sweaters go to his laundry just as they had insisted on a caddy who could find golf balls. A little later he was doing their wives' lingerie as well—and running five branches in different parts of the city. Before he was twenty-seven he owned the largest string of laundries in his section of the country. It was then that he sold out and went to New York. But the part of his story that concerns us goes back to the days when he was making his first big success.

When he was twenty-three Mr. Hart—one of the gray-haired men who like to say "Now there's a boy"— gave him a guest card to the Sherry Island Golf Club for a week-end. So he signed his name one day at the register, and that afternoon played golf in a foursome with Mr. Hart and Mr. Sandwood and Mr. T. A. Hendrick. He did not consider it necessary to remark that he had once carried Mr. Hart's bag over this same links, and that he knew every trap and gully with his eyes shut—but he found himself glancing at the four caddies who trailed them, trying to catch a gleam or gesture that would remind him of himself, that would lessen the gap which lay between his present and his past.

It was a curious day, splashed abruptly with fleeting, familiar impressions. One minute he had the sense of being a trespasser—in the next he was impressed by the tremendous superiority he felt toward Mr. T. A. Hendrick, who was a bore and not even a good golfer any more.

Then, because of a ball Mr. Hart lost near the fifteenth green, an enormous thing happened. While they were searching the stiff grasses of the rough there was a clear call of "Fore!" from behind a hill in their rear. And as they all turned abruptly from their search a bright new ball sliced abruptly over the hill and caught Mr. T. A. Hendrick, in the abdomen.

"By Gad!" cried Mr. T. A. Hendrick, "they ought to put some of these crazy women off the course. It's getting to be outrageous."

A head and a voice came up together over the hill:

"Do you mind if we go through?"

"You hit me in the stomach!" declared Mr. Hendrick wildly.

"Did I?" The girl approached the group of men. "I'm sorry. I yelled 'Fore!'"

Her glance fell casually on each of the men—then scanned the fairway for her ball.

"Did I bounce into the rough?"

It was impossible to determine whether this question was ingenuous or malicious. In a moment, however, she left no doubt, for as her partner came up over the hill she called cheerfully:

"Here I am! I'd have gone on the green except that I hit something."

As she took her stance for a short mashie shot, Dexter looked at her closely. She wore a blue gingham dress, rimmed at throat and shoulders with a white edging that accentuated her tan. The quality of exaggeration, of thinness, which had made her passionate eyes and down-turning mouth absurd at eleven, was gone now. She was arrestingly beautiful. The color in her cheeks was centered like the color in a picture—it was a not "high" color, but a sort of fluctuating and feverish warmth, so shaded that it seemed at any moment it would recede and disappear. This color and the mobility of her mouth gave a continual impression of flux, of intense life, of passionate vitality—balanced only partially by the sad luxury of her eyes.

She swung her mashie impatiently and without interest, pitching the ball into a sand-pit on the other side of the green. With a quick, insincere smile and a careless "Thank you!" she went on after it.

"That Judy Jones!" remarked Mr. Hendrick on the next tee, as they waited—and some moments—for her to play ahead. "All she needs is to be turned up and spanked for six months and then to be married off to an old-fashioned cavalry captain."

"My God, she's good-looking!" said Mr. Sandwood, who was just over thirty.

"Good-looking!" cried Mr. Hendrick contemptuously, "she always looks as if she wanted to be kissed! Turning those big cow-eyes on every calf in town!"

It was doubtful if Mr. Hendrick intended a reference to the maternal instinct.

"She'd play pretty good golf if she'd try," said Mr. Sandwood.

"She has no form," said Mr. Hendrick solemnly.

"She has a nice figure," said Mr. Sandwood.

"Better thank the Lord she doesn't drive a swifter ball," said Mr. Hart, winking at Dexter.

Later in the afternoon the sun went down with a riotous swirl of gold and varying blues and scarlets, and left the dry, rustling night of Western summer. Dexter watched from the veranda of the Golf Club, watched the even overlap of the waters in the little wind, silver molasses under the harvest-moon. Then the moon held a finger to her lips and the lake became a clear pool, pale and quiet. Dexter put on his bathing-suit and swam out to the furthest raft, where he stretched dripping on the wet canvas of the springboard.

There was a fish jumping and a star shining and the lights around the lake were gleaming. Over on a dark peninsula a piano was playing the songs of last summer and of summers before that—songs from "Cin-Chin" and "The Count of Luxemburg" and "The Chocolate Soldier"

—and because the sound of a piano over a stretch of water had always seemed beautiful to Dexter he lay perfectly quiet and listened.

The tune the piano was playing at that moment had been gay and new five years before when Dexter was a sophomore at college. They had played it at a prom once when he could not afford the luxury of proms, and he had stood outside the gymnasium and listened. The sound of the tune precipitated in him a sort of ecstasy and it was with that ecstasy he viewed what happened to him now. It was a mood of intense appreciation, a sense that, for once, he was magnificently attune to life and that everything about him was radiating a brightness and a glamour he might never know again.

A low, pale oblong detached itself suddenly from the darkness of the Island, spitting forth the reverberate sound of a racing motor-boat. Two white streamers of cleft water rolled themselves out behind it and almost immediately the boat was beside him, drowning out the hot tinkle of the piano in the drone of its spray. Dexter raising himself on his arms was aware of a figure standing at the wheel, of two dark eyes regarding him over the lengthening space of water—then the boat had gone by and was sweeping in an immense and purposeless circle of spray round and round in the middle of the lake. With equal eccentricity one of the circles flattened out and headed back over the raft.

"Who's that?" she called, shutting off her motor. She was so near now that Dexter could see her bathing-suit, which consisted apparently of pink rompers.

The nose of the boat bumped the raft, and as the latter tilted rakishly he was precipitated toward her. With different degrees of interest they recognized each other.

"Aren't you one of those men we played through this afternoon?" she demanded.

He was.

"Well, do you know how to drive a motor-boat? Because if you do I wish you'd drive this one so I can ride on the surf-board behind. My name is Judy Jones"— she favored him with an absurd smirk—rather, what tried to be a smirk, for, twist her mouth as she might, it was not grotesque, it was merely beautiful—"and I live in a house over there on the Island, and in that house there is a man waiting for me. When he drove up at the door I drove out of the dock because he says I'm his ideal."

There was a fish jumping and a star shining and the lights around the lake were gleaming. Dexter sat beside Judy Jones and she explained how her boat was driven. Then she was in the water, swimming to the floating surf-board with a sinuous crawl. Watching her was without effort to the eye, watching a branch waving or a sea-gull flying. Her arms, burned to butternut, moved sinuously among the dull platinum ripples, elbow appearing first, casting the forearm back with a cadence of falling water, then reaching out and down, stabbing a path ahead.

They moved out into the lake; turning, Dexter saw that she was kneeling on the low rear of the now uptilted surf-board.

"Go faster," she called, "fast as it'll go."

Obediently he jammed the lever forward and the white spray mounted at the bow. When he looked around again the girl was standing up on the rushing board, her arms spread wide, her eyes lifted toward the moon.

"It's awful cold," she shouted. "What's your name?"

He told her.

"Well, why don't you come to dinner to-morrow night?"

His heart turned over like the fly-wheel of the boat, and, for the second time, her casual whim gave a new direction to his life.

The Short Stories of F. Scott Fitzgerald

A Superior Set of Men

J. KERR

It is your caddie's business to find out how far you drive with each club, and since a life-long experience will have taught him the exact relative position to the hole of each blade of grass on the links, he ought to be always able to put into your hand the right club, almost without your asking for it. He will also know the idiosyncrasies of your play, to what extent he may allow you to "greatly dare," out of what lie you may be permitted to play with a brassy, and all such little niceties.

Almost since he was born (in the year 1847) "Fiery" has been connected with Golf, and it is a proof of his excellence as a caddie that young Willie Park has had him for helper in all his famous tournaments. He is one of these caddies who rank as high as the best professional, but who are purely carriers and coaches. "Fiery" probably plays Golf, but not better than a second-class amateur. There is a batch of such men at Musselburgh. They are mostly very illiterate, but in their own way very respectable and deserving of respect.

My usual caddie, Flinn, is one of the same lot. He carries well, knows his employer's game and almost never needs to be asked for a club—he has always the right one ready. His employer's clubs he keeps in good order. He is always sober during the day—at least, nearly always.

These men have no wish to do anything more than earn a living. Neither Flinn nor "Fiery" attempt to sell balls, nor offer to remake them. They simply carry. They will have nothing to do with caddies who have ever been in gaol for theft, etc. Neither Flinn nor "Fiery" would beg. They often starve. "Fiery" is a very reticent man. No one knows more than he is a bachelor, and lives in a lodging. No man ever saw him with his cap off, nor knows why he refuses to let his head be seen. He and his lot are quite heathens. They look on churches as for their betters, just as much as clubs. (This statement of Sir Walter's requires some qualification. Some of them, we happen to know, are good churchmen.) They would as soon expect to be invited to lunch in the one as to worship in the other.

I believe that in their own way "Fiery" and his set are most reliable men ... Whether "Fiery" is better educated or merely more intelligent, than most of his set I don't know; but he is a man of suave and polished manners. Yet he and two other caddies to whom we once gave a glass of champagne at St. Andrews because we happened to have no whisky unpacked, all said they have never tasted wine before. "Fiery" alone seemed to appreciate it. He disagreed with the others who did not wish to taste it again, and said he "could see that men might come to like that, but for his part he did not think it had 'eneuch o' grip.'"

Prints of William Gunn (Caddie Willie), a curious character of the golf links, are familiar in Scottish clubhouses. One of the strangest peculiarities of this eccentric ancient caddie was the way in which he wore his clothes, and the extraordinary profile he presents in the prints of him is accountable to the fact that he continually carried his wardrobe on his back. All the clothes he got he put on his back, one suit above another. To admit of his wearing three or four coats at once, he had to cut out the sleeves to let them on. True to the uniform which invariably distinguished golfers in those days, an old red coat was always worn outside of them all. He also wore three or four vests, an old worn fur one being outermost. It was the same with his trousers—three or four pairs on, and the worst outermost; and three bonnets, sewed one within the other. He head his quarters at Bruntsfield, renting a garret.

Willie was very honest, paying his rent regularly, and for his bread and milk as he got it. He lived entirely on baps and milk, never having a warm diet or a fire in his garret, even in the coldest winter. "Caddie Willie" was a Highlander, and could only speak English imperfectly. He was in the habit of tramping from Edinburgh to his Highland home every autumn when the golfing season closed. In 1820 he left. From that journey poor Willie never returned, and all the inquiry golfers made never elicited his fate.

Golf

Golf is a wonderful game. . . . It is the one game in which a stationery player hits a stationary ball. The fact that a player must generate his own power is one of the fundamental reasons that golf is perhaps the most difficult of all the major games to play consistently well.

HERBERT WARREN WIND

Obsession of Robinson Brown

W. G. SUTPHEN

You may say that you can't live by golf alone. But please, don't try to budge Mr. Robinson.

When the Marion County Golf Club was first organized, upon the list of charter members appeared the name of Robinson Brown, of the old-established firm of McTavish & Brown, ship-chandlers and general dealers in marine stores at No. 6014 Burling Slip. But it must not be rashly inferred from this circumstance that Mr. Brown was a golfer, or that he took any particular interest in the naturalization of the royal and ancient game. On the contrary, being an American of the Americans, and well into his fifth decade, Mr. Brown had long ceased to care for athletic amusements, either in an active or in a vicarious capacity, and he even held some old-fashioned notions upon Saturday half-holidays and the propriety of using public money for the establishment of municipal playgrounds. He rejoiced when croquet became obsolete; he viewed with disapproval the introduction and overwhelming popularity of tennis; he found himself in entire sympathy with the attitude of his favorite evening newspaper towards college football, and he prided himself upon his inability to distinguish between a base hit and an error. For exercise he depended upon walking (by the doctor's orders), and the Swedish movement cure (also by the doctor's orders), and he found amusement and abundant mental relaxation in occasional attendance at trotting matches and his regular after-dinner rubber at seven-point whist. Simple in his tastes and habits, he desired nothing more of To-day than that it should follow in the comfortable groove of Yesterday, and, with the disappearance of his waist, he had insensibly lost the capacity of any emotion unconnected with cutlets and the state of the money market. Such, then, was Mr. Robinson Brown in the year of grace eighteen hundred and ninety-five.

It may seem at first sight that in joining a golf club Mr. Brown was acting decidedly at variance with his well-considered and often-expressed opinions, but he had been prompted to the step by several ulterior considerations. In the first place, he had seen the game played while on a visit to a country-house at Southampton, and he was thoroughly convinced that it had only to be tried once to be found forever wanting. In point of hopeless inanity it could not be improved upon, and Mr. Brown reasoned very acutely that its colossal imbecility could not be better established than by public exploitation of its claims to recognition. The statue had only to be set upon its pedestal for the clay feet to crumble, and Mr. Brown confidently hoped that in falling it might hit some other things, perhaps the manager of a college football team, or even a young woman on a bicycle.

Secondly, Mr. Brown was heavily interested in the development of the particular suburban section which would be advantageously opened up to public inspection by the establishment of a well-appointed country club, and if he could clear some thousands of dollars by the sale of lots before the boom in golf collapsed, the investment of a hundred or so in stock and dues would manifestly be a good business stroke. And, finally, it would make a pleasant break in the monotonous round of his daily constitutional drive along the Monkton Road to stop for a few moments at the clubhouse and enjoy the mild refreshment of a "Sam Ward" upon its shady piazzas. He had always thought that the town club should maintain a country annex during the summer months, and the golfing madness, while it lasted, would at least insure a respectable article of Scotch whiskey. And so the Marion County Golf Club took to itself a local habitation and a name, and the signature of Robinson Brown stood first upon the roll of incorporators.

It was evident from the start that the new organization was to be a great success, and, strange as it may appear, it was the golf that made the club so popular. Mr. Brown was forced to acknowledge that the interest in the new game was as profound as it was inexplicable, and it was an extraordinary fact that the middle-aged members were even more enthusiastic than the young people. Mr. Brown, from his corner seat on the wide, cool piazza, watched the development of the craze with ever-increasing astonishment. Respectable citizens, hard-headed business men, against whose commercial standing there had never been a breath of suspicion, one after another fell victims to the fascination of the "green," and the surrender once made was invariably absolute. The conversation in the smoking-room was all of phenomenal "long puts." The state of the market was of distinctly minor importance to these lunatics so long as the great questions of "stance" and "grip" remained unsettled, and Mr. Brown found his disgust that the popular bond issue and the attitude of the government towards Venezuela were as nothing compared to the establishment of a new record on the course. He raged inwardly at the senile folly of his former friends, and openly made sarcastic comments upon the appearance of their legs, but all to no avail. The most he could hope for was that the craze might be as short-lived as it was furious. But the days slipped away into weeks, and the end was not yet.

Now it happened upon a certain pleasant afternoon that Mr. Brown appeared at the club somewhat earlier than was his wont. He was indulging in the rather unusual luxury of a holiday from business, and, truth to tell, he did not know what to do with it. He was tired of being driven up and down the Monkton Road, so he ordered the coachman to turn in at the club. There were only half a dozen of the members about, and Mr. Brown saw to his disgust that they were all confirmed worshippers of the goddess of Golf. He stalked gloomily down to the teeing-ground to watch the players drive off, the strong men bobbed and scuffled and writhed and scraped in their futile endeavors to render meet obeisance to this new Baal.

The last three players had been waiting to play a "foursome," but the fourth man had failed to put in an appearance and they had decided to play a three-ball match. They were Hardinge, the secretary of the club; Mason, who was an acknowledged power in the wholesale-grocery world; and Woodhouse, better known as *The Fiend*, from the fact that he took all his meals at the club-house, and was popularly supposed to sleep upon the course while engaged in practice for the monthly medal. Now Hardinge and Mason had been erstwhile bosom friends with Robinson Brown, and it irritated him to see them so completely given over to this senseless infatuation. He jeered at Hardinge when he "topped" his drive, and sarcastically suggested "the side of the house" to Mason after that gentleman had "missed the globe" five times running and had broken his favorite play-club. The players bore Mr. Brown's badinage with ill-concealed impatience, but Woodhouse was winking expressively, and they remained silent.

"Perhaps you'd like to take a hand, Brown," said *The Fiend*, carelessly, as he teed his ball and struck off. "Not a 'foursome,' you know, but just a four-ball game around the short course." And thereupon, with an ingratiating smile, he actually forced a club into Mr. Brown's astonished hands just as a drag full of people rumbled along the drive and pulled up directly in front of the teeing-ground.

It was a very embarrassing position for Mr. Brown, this public discovery of Saul also among the prophets, and his first impulse was to employ the club upon Mr. Woodhouse's impertinent person. But another and sweeter form of revenge instantly presented itself—to surpass by one brilliant and overpowering stroke *The Fiend's* own drive (which was really rather ordinary), and then to scornfully retire from the contest upon the ground that it was too easy to be interesting. Not the shadow of a doubt as to his ability to perform the feat clouded Mr. Brown's mind, and it is therefore not surprising that he even exceeded his own expectations. The ball went off the club with the most perfect accuracy, and actually fell dead at the hole 170 yards away. Mr. Brown's revenge was ready to his hand, but he did not take it; he could have crushed *The Fiend* with a single word, but he did not say it. Silently, and yet with the air of a man who knows when he has done a good thing, Mr. Brown proceeded to the putting-green and waited majestically for the other players to come up. It is hardly worth while dwelling upon this remarkable inconsistency on Mr. Brown's part. No explanation would be satisfactory to the non-golfing mind, and to that of the golfer none is needed.

As Mr. Brown's ball rested on the very lip of the cup it was impossible for him to foozle the putt, and the hole was his in two—"a record, by Jove!" as Hardinge exultantly proclaimed. Mr. Brown felt impelled to tell exactly how he did it, and he was pleased with the respectful attention accorded to his remarks. "And now whose honor is it?" concluded Mr. Brown, cheerfully. "You play straight over that flag, I believe. Hey there, you boy! Fore!"

Mason managed to draw *The Fiend* to one side. "What on earth!" he began—

"Sh!" interrupted *The Fiend*, warningly. "It simply means that I haven't forgotten what that man Brown once said about my legs."

Mr. Brown finished the round in very fair figures for a beginner, and, although it was growing late, persuaded Woodhouse into taking a turn around the full eighteen holes. It was long past the Brown dinner-hour when they had finished, but the new convert did not appear to attach any importance to that fact. He insisted upon driving *The Fiend* home, and before they separated an agreement had bee reached for a meeting at the club the next afternoon.

"And be sure you hunt me up that address—where I can get a red coat, you know," bawled Mr. Brown, standing up on the back seat of the rapidly receding carriage. *The Fiend* laughed as he entered the house, and the sound was not a pleasant one.

It is a remarkable fact that Mr. Brown bought no less than thirty-seven drivers before finding one whose length and "lie" exactly suited him, and as he broke that one on the very first round he began to have a realizing sense of the exacting nature of the fascination to which he had yielded himself. Of course the first ambition of every true golfer is to possess an absolutely perfect set of clubs, and Mr. Brown felt very much annoyed at his misfortune. However, his collection of irons was perhaps unequaled in the country. His driving-cleek was a noble instrument, purchased at about its weight in gold from a celebrated professional player whose identity may be thinly disguised, under his familiar sobriquet of "Willie." It was really a good cleek, and Mr. Brown expected to do wonders with it at the next monthly handicap. For practice work he bought several others exactly like it in appearance, and unfortunately got the lot all mixed up through the stupidity of a caddie. This was even more disheartening than the loss of his driver, and, although the professional was called in and commissioned to pick out the masterpiece, Mr. Brown never felt quite sure that the lost treasure had been recovered. Assuredly the cleek did not play the same as when "Willie" had used it in establishing a new record for the course, and Mr. Brown felt vaguely that he had been swindled. There could be no doubt, though, about his wooden putter, a monstrosity that bore the name of "Philp," and which was guaranteed to have once belonged to Allan Robertson himself. It was a glorious weapon, and as Mr. Brown invariably used an iron putter he never lost his confidence in the playing qualities of his treasured antique.

All this, of course, cost more or less money, and the size of the club-maker's bill rather startled Mr. Brown when it was presented at the end of the month. "Though, after all," he thought to himself, "I should probably have spent as much in 'Sam Wards' and been none the better for them." Of course the unhappy man had entirely ignored the fact that his consumption of "Scotch and soda" was increasing in inverse ratio to his abstinence from other forms of liquid refreshment; but the delusion is not an uncommon one among the fraternity of golfers, and nothing is misleading as statistics, with the possible exception of "Scotch and soda" itself.

One afternoon, about ten days after Mr. Brown's conversion, Mrs. Brown was surprised to receive an early morning call from Mr. McTavish, the senior partner in the firm. On descending to the drawing-room she found that a gentleman in a state of unusual excitement, and it was with some difficulty that she finally gathered that he had come to inquire as to the whereabouts of Mr. Brown. On her informing him that Mr. Brown had taken the day off, and was spending it upon the golf course, Mr. McTavish drew a long breath of relief, but it was evident that he was both surprised and annoyed. It appeared that Mr. Brown had given no intimation of his intended absence, and as he held the combination of the safe it had been impossible to transact any business at the office. In this emergency Mr. McTavish had taken the first train out to Lauriston to find out what was the matter. "And I was prepared, madam, for the worst," he concluded, gravely.

"Apoplexy, perhaps," hazarded Mrs. Brown, smilingly.

"Or Canada," retorted Mr. McTavish.

Well, of course, it was unjustifiable, this insinuation on the part of the senior partner, but it must be remembered that Mr. McTavish was a very dignified old gentleman, with a tendency to suppressed gout, and Mr. Brown's dereliction had put him to a great deal of bodily inconvenience and mental discomfort. It was annoying to find that all this pother had been caused by a ridiculous game of golf, and Mr. McTavish considered that he did well to be angry. Nevertheless, Mrs. Brown resented the imputation, and some warm words passed.

"I shouldn't have cared," said Mr. McTavish, bitterly, "if Brown had broken his leg or had been killed on the railroad—that would have been *some* excuse."

"Oh, indeed!" put Mrs. Brown.

"But to find him playing golf with the market liable to go to pieces at any moment— I don't know what I can say to *that*, I really don't." And Mr. McTavish stopped short, in the consciousness that the English language was entirely unequaled to the due expression of his feelings.

"Perhaps you've said quite enough already," remarked Mrs. Brown, icily; "but I don't know what you are to do about it unless you go in for golf yourself."

"I go in for golf!" gasped Mr. McTavish.

"Why not? It would help you to understand Mr. Brown's position and be an excellent thing for your health. Mr. Brown was never better than since he took to golf. It keeps him in the open air, he has a splendid appetite, an excellent temper, and he hardly ever drinks a 'Sam Ward' nowadays, a point which some other people might do well to bear in mind at this hour in the morning."

And then Mrs. Brown gathered up her skirts and sailed majestically out of the room, leaving Mr. McTavish to don the conversational cap at his leisure. Whereupon the senior partner hurried back to town and immediately sent for his lawyer and a safe expert.

When Brown came home that night, fresh from a glorious victory over *The Fiend*, Mrs. Brown told him of her visitor and his extraordinary behavior. Mr. Brown only smiled at the prejudices and narrow-mindedness of the non-golfing class, and went out on the lawn to practice up his "approaching."

It must be confessed, however, that as time went on Mrs. Brown was not wholly satisfied with Mr. Brown's attitude towards all things outside of golf. She smiled indulgently at his fancy of taking a cleek to church in lieu of a walking-stick, but she frowned when she discovered that he had laid out a course of short holes among the flower-beds, and she was annoyed to see that the front lawn looked as though a "Sir Roger de Coverley" had been performed upon it by a select company of patent harrows and steam-ditchers. It was also very provoking, upon the occasion of a grand dinner-party, that Mr. Brown should have brought up from the city a dozen golf balls instead of French artichokes that he had been instructed to procure. The cook had done his best, but even a marvelous sauce could not make them go down with the guests, and the chef had given warning the very next day. It was too bad, for he had been a veritable treasure, a real pearl among cooks.

Mrs. Brown finally felt impelled to have a serious conversation with her husband. She pointed out to him the fact that he had not been near the office for a month, and although Mr. McTavish had offered no remonstrance either verbally or otherwise, his very silence was portentous. As Mr. Brown's income was derived solely from his interest in the business, he could not afford to entirely ignore his responsibilities, and, after all, golf was simply an amusement and not the real business of life. Mr. Brown listened attentively to what Mr. Brown had to say, and acknowledged frankly that he had been doing wrong. He would go to town, effect a reconciliation with

Mr. McTavish, and take up his duties with new zeal and fresh determination. Yes, he certainly would do that—it was the only proper course.

"But when will you go?" urged Mrs. Brown.

"Just as soon as the monthly handicap is over," answered Mr. Brown, firmly.

Mrs. Brown said no more, but she turned away with a sigh, and with an uncomfortable foreboding of what the future might bring forth.

Two or three days after this conversation it happened to be wet, and Mrs. Brown had occasion to go to town. On returning home at evening she was surprised to see the house brilliantly lighted from top to bottom, and on entering she was still further amazed at the sight that presented itself. All the furniture from the hall and the rooms opening into it had been removed from its proper place and piled up here and there in fantastic heaps. There were dents and scratches on the polished mahogany, and Mrs. Brown's face grew rigid as she saw two or three "stars" in the big mirror over the library mantelpiece. There was a heap of wet sand on the costly Bokhara rug at the far end of the hall, and, even as she gazed, unable to believe her own eyes, Mr. Brown appeared from the butler's pantry, attired in full golfing costume and attended by Robinson Brown, jr., with his bag of clubs. Mr. Brown carefully teed his ball, and, with a loud shout of "fore," drove it the whole length of the hall and drawing-room, to the utter destruction of a unique Sevres vase that was as the apple of Mrs. Brown's eye. Little Robinson clapped his hands, and Robinson, sr., proudly announced that his score was only thirty-six from the first tee in the third-story bath-room, not at all bad considering that he had been bunkered in the china-closet.

"The china-closet!" repeated Mrs. Brown, mechanically.

"Now then, Robinson," said Mr. Brown, gleefully, "get me another cutglass tumbler, so I can hole out. No, never mind, this inkstand will do."

Mrs. Brown, unable to speak or move, sank helplessly upon a fauteuil which had not been needed for bunker-building, and watched Mr. Brown with fascinated eyes as he proceeded to execute an approach shot over a Louis Seize mirror laid face upward on the floor in lieu of a water hazard. Unfortunately the ball fell short and rolled directly on the mirror, forcing Mr. Brown to call for his "president." Mrs. Brown groaned as the niblick crashed into the glass, but Mr. Brown exulted vociferously, for the ball plumped squarely into the inkstand, sending a shower of stygian drops over the lace curtains.

"Forty for the nine holes," announced Mr. Brown as he restored the club to the bag and turned to find himself what could only be described as the "PRESENCE" of Mrs. Robinson Brown.

Now just what happened during the subsequent interview does not concern us, but the fact remains that early the next morning Mr. Brown started for his office in the city. On the train he took up a daily paper, and was unpleasantly surprised to see among the business announcements a notice of the forthcoming dissolution of the partnership now existing under the firm name of McTavish & Brown, ship-chandlers and general dealers in marine stores at No. 6014 Burling Slip. Mr. Brown felt in his heart of hearts that Mr. McTavish was amply justified in his action, but he went on in the faint hope of inducing him to reconsider it. But the interview was in vain. The senior partner treated Mr. Brown with dignity and had no reproaches to make. But his resolution was inflexible—the business must be wound up.

Mr. Brown returned home and talked over the situation with Mrs. Brown. It would, of course, take some weeks to adjust all the interests of the firm, and in the meantime they would have little or no income for current expenses. Mrs. Brown suggested sending for her Uncle Henry, who could advise and perhaps assist them in their embarrassing emergency. A wire was accordingly despatched to Mrs. Brown's Uncle Henry, and that gentleman was good enough to respond to the appeal by taking the first train out to Lauriston. As he stepped out of the carriage at the Brown mansion a small, white, round, and excessively hard object struck him squarely on the leg, causing him several moments of exquisite anguish. Mr. Brown, who had been experimenting behind the icehouse with a new driver, was profuse in his apologies, but Mrs. Brown's Uncle Henry refused to enter the house and took the first train back to town.

It was some three days before Mrs. Brown could bring herself to speak calmly to Mr. Brown, but she could not forget that she had once loved him and was still his wife. She forgave him fully and freely, but it was hard to feel that Mr. Brown's inconsiderate act had not only deprived them of the hope of immediate assistance, but would in all probability have a serious effect upon the ultimate disposition of the old gentleman's property.

"It all will go to the Asylum for Aged Gold-beaters," said Mrs. Brown, sadly, and Robinson Brown ground his teeth in silence.

Still, Mrs. Brown did not wholly despair of the future, for Mr. Brown had now signed a solemn pledge of total abstinence from golf. There was yet time for him to retrieve his past errors, and Mrs. Brown helped him like the true woman that she was. She gave up nearly all of her time to playing parlor croquet and Halma with Mr. Brown, and although these simple amusements were but melancholy substitutes for the royal game, yet they afforded some temporary relief from the awful craving that at times nearly overpowered him. And as the days went by Mrs. Brown felt almost hopeful again. It was now three weeks since Mr. Brown had touched a golf-club, and the legal formalities of winding up the business were fast drawing to completion. In another fortnight Mr. Brown would have his money at his disposal and be ready for a fresh start in life. They would move to some Western city where there was no club and where public golf was not allowed. Surely there must be some such haven of refuge, and once more removed from the possibility of temptation, all would be well again. Mrs. Brown's face grew hopeful and tender as the vision rose before her. Ah! how happy they would be!

It was drawing on to luncheon-time, and Mrs. Brown, dismissing her daydream with a half-smile at her girlish romanticism, stepped out into the hall on her way to the dining-room. As she passed the closet where Mr. Brow's clubs and golfing paraphernalia were stored she saw with a sickening sense of fear that the lock had been forced and that the closet was empty. Hardly breathing, she flew out upon the lawn. Gracious heavens! Her worst fears were indeed realized, for there stood Mr. Brown, wearing his awful golf face and surrounded by his entire collection of eight-seven clubs and a dozen carefully teed balls. And as she stood with aching heart and tear-dimmed eyes, she saw by his side Robinson, jr., the eldest boy and the pride and joy of the Brown family. She heard

Mr. Brown speaking to him in a coaxing tone, as in a dream she saw the besotted, cunning smile with which he sought to force a club into the innocent child's hand. The wretched man placed a ball in front of the boy and showed him how to grip the club. "And now remember," said Mr. Brown, "slow back! Don't press! Keep your eye on the ba'l!"

Mrs. Brown never clearly remembered just how she managed to do it, but in the next instant she had dashed in between father and son, snatched the accursed thing from the child's hand and hurled it far out upon the lawn, farther indeed than Mr. Brown had ever been able to drive a ball.

Husband and wife faced each other.

"Mr. Brown," said Mrs. Brown, "for myself I have nothing to say. But there is no law, human or divine, which can compel me to stand by and see my innocent child deliberately started upon the dreadful road that can only end in 'Walkingshaw's Grave.' There shall be no open scandal, but I shall take Robinson, jr., and the other children and go to my Uncle Henry's by the four train."

Robinson Brown was sober enough now. He turned perfectly white, but his voice was clear and firm.

"You are quite sure, Mary, that you are justified in taking this step?"

"Yes quite sure."

"And there is nothing, absolutely nothing, that I can do or say to alter your determination?"

He spoke quietly, but there was a note of stress in his voice that betrayed the strong man's agony.

"Absolutely nothing."

"Very well," said Robinson Brown. "While you are packing, I think I'll go and work up my putting a bit."

For the sequel to this remarkable story I am indebted to *The Fiend*, who told it the other night to a select company of the "Old Guard" in the smoking-room of the club.

"As you all know," he began, "it was useless to try and straighten out the tangle, for after Mrs. Brown's departure poor Brown, relieved of all restraint, entered upon a perfect orgy of golf, and for three weeks the niblick was hardly ever out of his hand. Then he seemed to brace up for a time, but the tone of his system had been so lowered by his long-continued dissipation that the reformation was only temporary, and he soon fell back into his old courses—or, shall I say, links. It was pitiable, and no one realized his condition more acutely than he did himself; but what was there to be done? Poor Brown was absolutely unable to pass a golf club without dropping in for a round or so, and at last he lost all sense of decency and openly frequented public golf courses. The Green Committee felt very sorry for him, and as he had no regular home he was tacitly allowed to take up his quarters in the Great Sahara bunker, just this side of the eleventh hole. He had been accustomed to spend most of his time there anyhow, and I suppose that it seemed familiar and homelike to him. Hoe he managed to live I don't know.

"Well one day Brown was in the bunker, as usual, working away with his niblick. He had just missed the ball for the seventeenth consecutive time and was about to say as much, when the words suddenly died away on his tongue; a new and peculiar sensation pervaded his entire being; he stood stockstill, astonished and almost terrified. Little by little the dark clouds were rolling back from before his tortured eyes, the crushing weight was being lifted from before his aching brain, a heavenly calm was stealing gently over his agonizing soul, his tired muscles were relaxing into peaceful rest, and with a great gulp of unspeakable relief Robinson Brown realized that he was a free man, saved as by fire and at the eleventh hole.

"He bent down and picked off the burrs from his stockings, his heart almost bursting with its mingled emotions of thankfulness and praise. Then, straightening up, he looked with new eyes upon his surroundings. That awful Great Sahara bunker! What a horrid place this was! How could he have possibly endured its dismal presence throughout all these weary weeks and months? And that wretched ball! What a loathsome-looking object! all hacked and scarred and paintless. Well, if he never got it out, why should he care? *He didn't care!* Ah, the intoxicating ecstasy of that bare thought—HE DIDN'T CARE! With a sudden movement of his heavy heel he ground the ball deep into the soft sand, and turned his back forever upon the Great Sahara bunker.

"Clothed and in his right mind, Robinson Brown quickly made up his mind as to what he should do. It was a hard step to take, but he had sinned and he must take the consequences like a man. Reparation, atonement! at least he could make acknowledgment of his error. Forgiveness! but forgiveness is divine.

"Mrs. Brown's Uncle Henry lived at Rhinebeck, and he could just make the connection with the Saratoga Express. As fast as stem could carry him he was whirled up the river and, arrived at his destination, took a hack out to Uncle Henry's place. He hardly dared to think even for a moment of what was coming, of what might come. Mrs. Brown, Mrs. Brown's Uncle Henry, Horace

McTavish—and he who had been a golfer! For the moment his heart stood still, he was about to order the driver to pull up; but he stayed his hand and the hack rolled on.

"On reaching the gate, Brown dismissed the vehicle, intending to steal quietly up to the house by making a shortcut across the south lawn. The grounds were surrounded by a high evergreen hedge, and as he approached it he heard voices. His heart leaped as he recognized Mrs. Brown's well remembered tones, and Robinson jr.'s boyish treble. Surley, too, that was Uncle Henry's deep bass, and most remarkable of all, he could distinguish the unmistakable Doric accents of his old partner, Horace McTavish. There was a moment's silence, and then followed an extraordinary and confused medley of shrieks, laughter, and muttered abjurations. What *could* it mean? Almost suffocating under stress of so many and complex emotions, Robinson Brown noiselessly stepped up to the hedge and looked over.

"*Mrs. Robinson Brown, Uncle Henry, Mr. Horace McTavish, and Robinson Brown, Jr., were playing a 'foursome' at golf, and Mrs. Brown's Uncle Henry had just laid Mr. McTavish a stymie.*

"Well, they heard the sound of the fall, Brown being a heavy man, and after some trouble they managed to get him into the house and sent for the resident professional. The latter looked grave at first, but after a short, careful examination of all the symptoms he was enabled to assure Mrs. Brown that the case was by no means hopeless. Hard work and business distractions would be the best remedial agencies, and of course golf in every form must be strictly tabooed. Uncle Henry and McTavish were all kindness and sympathy, and the latter immediately had new partnership papers drawn up and executed. Uncle Henry made his will in Robinson Brown's own presence, and the satisfactory nature of its provisions went far towards restoring the invalid to his wonted spirits. As soon as the Browns could get moved back into their old home, Mr. Brown resumed his daily trips to his office in the city, and from that on his improvement was rapid. Of course Mrs. Brown's care and devotion were unceasing. Nothing that could remind Mr. Brown in any way of golf was allowed about the house, and Mrs. Brow even went so far as to have a red coat, belonging to Robinson, jr., packed away in a tin box and carefully buried at the end of the vegetable garden, where Mr. Brown never went by any possibility. With all that it was a long, hard struggler, and at times Mrs. Brown felt almost discouraged. For months Mr. Brown was obliged to drive to the railway station by a round-about and inconvenient route in order to avoid passing by the golf-grounds, and he fainted dead away on the train one day when a friend, carrying a newly purchased cleek, happened to enter the car and thoughtlessly took a seat beside him. But the day of deliverance was at hand.

"For a week Mr. Brown had secluded himself every evening in his library, and Mrs. Brown was beginning to feel a trifle anxious. All her efforts to penetrate the mystery were in vain. Mr. Brown was preoccupied, uncommunicative, and certainly up to something. Yet he seemed to be cheerful, even hopeful, and there was a new note of tenderness in his voice when he did speak; it was all very perplexing to Mrs. Brown.

"It was Friday evening and Mrs. Brown's birthday.

Mr., Brown rose from the dinner-table, but instead of proceeding alone to the library, in accordance with his usual custom, he silently intimated to his wife that she should bear him company. Pale and trembling, Mrs. Brown obeyed. Robinson Brown carefully locked the door, and then taking an odd-looking object from a secret closet, he presented it to Mrs. Brown. She started back affrighted; what was this monstrous implement, with its glittering, hammer-like head and strange, double handed grip?

"'The Robinson Brown patent pendulum and self-compensating putting-cleek,' said Mr. Brown, proudly, 'and I invented it myself.'"

Finally, the *Man-in-the-Corner* broke the silence:

"Well, and what then?"

"I do not think," answered *The Fiend*, gravely, "that any words of mine could fitly describe the scene that followed. There are some things, sir, that should be sacred even to a golfer."

The *Man-in-the-Corner* fell back abashed; *The Fiend* took a sip of "S. and S.," and then went on: "Ah! but it is a beautiful sight to see Robinson Brown on the links, surrounded by his re-united family, and restored comfort, happiness, golf, and his own self-respect. He has never succeeded in getting round under 120, even with the aid of the patent putter, but the sum of earthly felicity is not necessarily made up of the material figures of a score-card."

"But I don't see yet—" began the *Man-in-the-Corner*.

"Simple enough," interrupted *The Fiend*. "Robinson Brown had temporarily over golfed himself."

Golficide and Other Tales

Golf in the Old Country

C. W. WHITNEY

To the occasional or casual observer there appears in the Englishman's demeanor on the links no departure from his usual placidity. He stalks upon the grounds with habitual solemnity, and takes up the game in the same seriousness that has been associated with him at play. If the on-looker follows the player around the course, he seeks in vain for any visible sign of that joyous spirit which he, likely as not, has imagined fitting accompaniment to athletic contest.

But in golf the Briton is a contradiction. He gives no outward evidence of perturbation, though, to borrow topical opera slang, he boils within. It is only to his familiars in the club-house and around his own board that the Englishman reveals himself, and there, by the softening influences of good cheer, may you discover how hopeless a victim he is to the ancient and royal game.

Before he has finished his Scotch and soda he will play over again every stroke of that last round in which he has beaten a single hole, and then take up in elaborate detail certainly every bunker and almost every brae on the course, until he has at length decided to his complete satisfaction on the identical stroke and spot that caused his downfall. I should be willing to give long odds in a wager on every golfing enthusiast in great Britain being able to find, blindfolded, any given hazard on his home links, and the great majority of hazards on every course in England or Scotland. To hear them discuss strokes to evade, I was near saying, almost every bit of whin, and locate every sand dune is to gain some idea of the range and strength of golf mania.

I was prepared to find the country gone golf-crazy, but I found instead a condition bordering on what I have called golf-insomnia, though I should add that my observations were made from esoteric vantage-ground. At first I was disappointed, and ascribed the stories I had heard of the golf-furor to the newspaper license; I had looked for some familiar token by which I might recognize the craze—signs such as in America indicate unmistakably that a boom is on. But my first visit to links so depressed me that I nearly reached determination to pass by golf altogether in my pilgrimage—in the eventual failure of which resolution my readers have my heart-felt sympathy.

It was a disillusioning experience, that first sight of the much-heralded and antique game. Speaking retrospectively, I am not sure I have a very distinct recollection of just what I reckoned on viewing; I do not believe I expected to see players astride their clubs prancing about the teeing-ground in ill-concealed eagerness for the affray, nor a dense and cheering throng of spectators surrounding the putting-green of the home hole, nor triumphantly shouldered victors borne from the field amid hosannas and tumultuous applause by the populace.

Even as I write now I can feel again the dejection that came over me in successive and widening waves as I looked for the first time on the game that is reported to have converted in the last two or three years more disciples than any other in the country. At first I thought I had gone on the links during a lull in the play. Then I persuaded myself that I had arrived on a day set apart for the convalescents of some near-by sanitarium, but as I discovered my error in the ruddy imprint of health on their cheeks, my wonder grew that so many vigorous, young, and middle-aged men could find amusement in what appeared to me to a melancholy and systematized "constitutional."

Once recovered from the initial shock, I found amusement in the awful solemnity that enveloped the onlookers about the putting-green, every mother's son of whom watched the holing out with bated breath. One, standing next to me in the crowd, and whose pleasing face gave encouragement, while the frequency with which he had trod on my toes seemed to me to have established a sufficient *entente cordiale* between us, bestowed upon me, when I asked why no one called the number of strokes each player had taken, so we would all know how they stood, such a look of righteous horror as I am sure would have caused any but an irrepressible American to wish the earth might open and swallow him. But being an American it simply increased my thirst for knowledge, and at the next sally I upset him completely by asking why a player, who was executing the "waggle" with all the deliberate nicety of one thoroughly appreciative of that important prelude to the flight of the ball, did not hit it instead of wasting so much time and energy flourishing his "stick" above it.

To have alluded with levity to one of the rudimentary functions of the game was appalling enough in all conscience, but to have called a club a stick was too much for my neighbor, and he of the aggressive feet moved away from the tee with a pained expression clouding the open countenance that had tempted my golfing innocence.

Subsequent and solitary wanderings about the links brought but little solace to my joyless sporting soul, for it seemed that every turning I was challenged by loud and emphatic cries of "fore," the significance of which I did not understand, while the air appeared to be filled with flying balls that whizzed past at uncomfortable proximity, or alighted just behind me, after a flight of a hundred and fifty yards or so, with a thud far from reassuring. It does not seem probable such a situation could under any circumstances have a humorous side; but it may, and I have laughed until my head ached over the comical consternation of some luckless and obstinate duffer, who, instead of permitting, as courtesy and tradition teach, more skillful following players to pass him, continued on his laborious and turf-bruising way, driven into by those immediately back of him, and damned by every golfer on the links. Given an irascible and stubborn and indifferent (a combination that has been known to exist) leading player, with following balls dropping around him, and I fancy even an Englishman, if he is not playing, will acknowledge the picture mirth-provoking.

What broke the gloom of that first day of my experience, and turned indifference to a desire for knowledge, were the individual maneuvers on the putting-green, which, sometimes grotesque, frequently picturesque, and invariably fraught with the weightiest meditation, convinced me that any game requiring such earnest play must improve on acquaintance. The putting-green presents a scene for the student of human nature, with its exhibitions of temperaments and varied styles of play: one will make a minute and lengthy survey over the few yards of turf that separate his ball from the hole, and attain the climax of his joy or woe by a short sharp tap with the club; another devotes his critical attention to the lie of the ball, followed by a painfully deliberate aim that seems never to quite reach the explosive point; some appear to acquire confidence by the narrowing of the human circle around the hole; others wave all back save their caddie, who, like a father confessor, remains at their side administering unction of more or less extremity to the last.

The duties of the caddie are manifold, including the responsibilities of preceptor, doctor, and lawyer. He will be called upon to device means of escape from soul-trying bunkers, administer to the wounded pride of the unsuccessful, and turn legislator at a crowded teeing-ground: he must even at times serve as a foil to the wrath of the disconsolate player who has "foozled" a drive that was confidently expected to carry him safely beyond a formidable hazard. There are caddies and caddies, to be sure, but when of the right sort, no servants, I fancy, receive such marked evidence of their master's regard. Most of them Scotch, some of them the most picturesque figures on the golfing-green.

To obtain a full appreciation of the charms and difficulties of golf you should have acquired a settled conviction of its inferiority as a game requiring either skill or experience; you must have looked upon it with supreme contempt, and catalogued it as a sport for invalids and old men. When you have reached this frame of mind go out on the links and try it. I never believed a club could be held in so many different ways but the right one until I essayed golf, nor dreamed it so difficult to drive a ball in a given direction. The devotion of the golfer to his game is only equaled by the contempt of him who looks upon it for the first time. You wonder a great many things when you first see it played, but your wonderment is greatest that a game which appears so simple should have created such a furor.

The secret of its fascination rests largely in the fact

that it beats the player, and he, in his perversity, strives the harder to secure the unattainable.

The game is by no means easy; in fact, one of England's foremost players asserts that it takes six months of steady play to acquire consistent form. You must hit the ball properly to send it in the desired direction, and you must deal with it as you find it; you cannot arrange the ball to suit your better advantage, nor await a more satisfactory one, as in baseball and cricket. The club must be held correctly and swung accurately in order to properly address the ball, from which the player should never take his eye, while at the same time he must move absolutely freely, and yet maintain an exact balance. Besides which, it demands judgment and good temper, and if you fail in the latter your play will be weakened on the many trying occasions that arise.

It is a selfish game, where each man fights for himself, seizing every technicality for his own advantage, and there is no doubt that to this fact its popularity may in a large measure be attributed. Unlike cricket, baseball, or football, one is not dependent on others for play. You can usually find some one to make up a match, or you may go over the course alone, getting the best practice and fairly good sport, or at least there is always a caddie to be had for the asking, and the usual small fee.

The exercise may be gentle, but whosoever fancies golf does not test the nerves should play a round on popular links. I cannot say if the native views it in the same light, but I concluded before I had half finished my tour that the attraction of golf was as much due to the atmosphere of tradition on the links and good-fellowship in the clubs as to the qualities of the game itself. I doubt if we in America will ever be able to extract so much pleasure from it. Our dispositions, our temperaments, are not golf-like; we hurry through life at too rapid a gait; we have not the time to give golf in order to gain that responsive charm the game holds for the leisurely suitor.

What I have endeavored to show here is the breadth and depth of the spirit which has made the golfing widow an accepted national institution, seized the serene Briton by the ears, and set him putting into tumblers and whisking off the heads of daisies overnight, that in the morrow's play his aim may be the truer and his swing the deadlier.

Harpers Monthly Magazine

Links to Conquer

JOHN L. LOW

Nothing contributes more to the popularity of golf than its almost endless variety. No two courses are the same, even though they be similar in character; no two shots are alike, even though the same distance has to be accomplished. This variety is a very distinct feature of the game. Football or cricket grounds, if good, do not vary much from one another. Certain soils, no doubt, lend themselves better to turf-growing than others, and the sticky patches favour the bowlers, but the conformation of the cricket and football field remains the same. In golf it is quite otherwise; each course has its own features, and each demands a fresh variety of strokes. The play at St. Andrews or Hoylake is quite different from the play at Sandwich—so different that the clubs suitable for the hard turf of the North Country greens would require modification if used on the softer turf on the South Kent course. The golfer who has grown weary of one set of strokes has only to leave his home green and pay a visit to some other course, and he will find new difficulties to be encountered and have to devise fresh methods of overcoming them. No golfer has ever been forced to say to himself with tears, 'There are no more links to conquer.'

Concerning Golf

Silent Greens

HORACE G. HUTCHINSON

Do not get into the habit of pointing out the peculiarly salient blade of grass which you imagine to have been the cause of your failing to hole your putt. You may sometimes find your adversary, who has successfully holed his, irritatingly shortsighted on these occasions. Moreover, the opinion of a man who has just missed his putt, about the state of that particular putting green, is usually accepted with some reserve.

Hints on Golf

The Heart of a Goof

P. G. WODEHOUSE

It was a morning when all nature shouted "Fore!" The breeze, as it blew gently up from the valley, seemed to bring a message of hope and cheer, whispering of chip-shots holed and brassies landing squarely on the meat. The fairway, as yet unscarred by the irons of a hundred dubs, smiled greenly up at the azure sky; and the sun, peeping above the trees, looked like a giant golfball perfectly lofted by the mashie of some unseen god and about to drop dead by the pin of the eighteenth. It was the day of the opening of the course after the long winter, and a crowd of considerable dimensions had collected at the first tee. Plus fours gleamed in the sunshine, and the air was charged with happy anticipation.

In all that gay throng there was but one sad face. It belonged to the man who was waggling his driver over the new ball perched on its little hill of sand. This man seemed careworn, hopeless. He gazed down the fairway, shifted his feet, waggled, gazed down the fairway again, shifted the dogs once more, and waggled afresh. He waggled as Hamlet might have waggled, moodily, irresolutely. Then, at last, he swung, and taking from his caddie the niblick which the intelligent lad had been holding in readiness from the moment when he had walked to the tee, trudged wearily off to play his second.

The Oldest Member, who had bee observing the scene with a benevolent eye from his favourite chair on the terrace, sighed.

"Poor Jenkins," he said, "does not improve." "No," agreed his companion, a young man with open features and a handicap of six. "And yet I happen to know that he has been taking lessons all the winter at one of those indoor places."

"Futile, quite futile," said the Sage with a shake of his snowy head. "There is no wizard living who could make that man go round in an average of sevens. I keep advising him to give up the game."

"You!" cried the young man, raising a shocked and startled face from the driver with which he was toying. "*You* told him to give up golf! Why I thought—"

You must bear in mind that Jenkinson's is not an ordinary case. You know and I know scores of men who have never broken a hundred and twenty in their lives, and yet contrive to be happy, useful members of society. However badly they may play, they are able to forget. But with Jenkinson it is different. He is not one of those who can take it or leave it alone. His only chance of happiness lies in complete abstinence. "Jenkinson is a goof."

"A what?"

"A goof," repeated the Sage. "One of those unfortunate beings who have allowed this noblest of sports to get too great a grip upon them, who have permitted it to eat into their souls, like some malignant growth. The goof, you must understand, is not like you and me. He broods. He becomes morbid. His goofery unfits him for the battles of life. Jenkinson, for example, was once a man with a glowing future in the hay, corn, and feed business, but a constant stream of hooks, tops, and slices gradually made him so diffident and mistrustful of himself, that he let opportunity after opportunity slip, with the result that other sterner, hay, corn, and feed merchants passed him in the race. Every time he had the chance to carry through some big deal in hay, or to execute some flashing *coup* in corn and feed, the fatal diffidence generated by a hundred rotten rounds would undo him. I understand his bankruptcy may be expected at any moment."

"My golly!" said the young man, deeply impressed. "I hope I never become a goof. Do you mean to say there is really no cure except giving up the game?"

The Oldest Member was silent for a while.

"It is curious that you should have asked that question," he said at last, "for only this morning I was thinking of one case in my experience where a goof was enabled to overcome his deplorable malady. It was owing to a girl, of course. The longer I live, the more I come to see that most things are. But you will, no doubt, wish to hear the story from the beginning."

The young man rose with the startled haste of some wild creature, which, wandering through the undergrowth, perceives the trap in his path.

"I should love, to," he mumbled, "only I shall be losing my place at the tee."

"The goof question," said the Sage, attaching himself with a quiet firmness to the youth's coat-button, "was a man of about your age, by name Ferdinand Dibble. I knew him well. In fact, it was to me—"

"Some other time, eh?"

"It was to me," proceeded the Sage, placidly, "that he came for sympathy in the great crisis of his life, and I am not ashamed to say that when he had finished laying bare his soul to me there were tears in my eyes. My heart bled for the boy."

"I bet it did. But—"

The Oldest Member pushed him gently back into his seat.

"Golf," he said, "is the Great Mystery. Like some capricious goddess—"

The young man, who had been exhibiting symptoms of feverishness, appeared to become reigned. He sighed softly.

"Did you ever read 'The Ancient Mariner'?" he said.

"Many years ago," said the Oldest Member. "Why do you ask?"

"Oh, I don't know," said the young man. "It just occurred to me."

Golf (resumed the Oldest Member) is the Great Mystery. Like some capricious goddess, it bestows its favours with what would appear an almost fatheaded lack of method and discrimination. On every side we see big two-fisted he-men floundering round in three figures, stopping every few minutes to let through little shrimps with knock knees and hollow cheeks, who are tearing off snappy seventy-fours. Giants of finance have to accept a stroke per from their junior clerks. Men capable of governing empires fail to control a small, white ball, which presents no difficulties whatever to others with one ounce more brain than a cuckoo-clock. Mysterious, but there it is. There was no apparent reason why Ferdinand Dibble should not have been a competent golfer. He had strong wrists and a good eye. Nevertheless, the fact remains that he was a dub. And on a certain evening in June I realized that he was also a goof. I found it out quite suddenly as the result of a conversation which we had on this very terrace.

I was sitting here that evening thinking of this and that, when by the corner of the clubhouse I observed young Dibble in conversation with a girl in white. I could not see who she was, for her back was turned. Presently they parted and Ferdinand came slowly across to where I sat. His hair was dejected. He had had the boots licked off him earlier in the afternoon by Jimmy Fotherhill, and it was to this that I attributed his gloom. I was to find out in a few moments that I was partly but not entirely correct in this surmise. He took the next chair to mine, and for several minutes sat staring moodily down into the valley.

"I've just been talking to Barbara Medway," he said, suddenly breaking the silence.

"Indeed?" I said. "A delightful girl."

"She's going away for the summer to Marvis Bay."

"She will take the sunshine with her."

was another long silence.

Presently Ferdinand uttered a hollow groan.

"I love her, dammit!" he muttered brokenly. "Oh, golly, how I love her!"

I was not surprised at his making me the recipient of his confidences like this. Most young folk in the place brought their troubles to me sooner or later.

"And does she return your love?"

"I don't know. I haven't asked her."

"Why not? I should have thought the point not without its interest for you."

Ferdinand gnawed the handle of his putter distractedly.

"I haven't the nerve," he burst out at length. "I simply can't summon up the cold gall to ask a girl, least of all an angel like her, to marry me. You see, it's like this. Every time I work myself up to the point of having a dash at it, I go out and get trimmed by some one giving me a stroke a hole. Every time I feel I've mustered up enough pep to propose, I take ten on a bogey three. Every time I think I'm in good mid-season form for putting my fate to the test, to win or lose it all, something goes all blooey with my swing, and I slice into the rough at every tee. And then my self-confidence leaves me. I become nervous, tongue-tied, diffident. I wish to goodness I knew the man who invented this infernal game. I'd strangle him. But I suppose he's been dead for ages. Still, I could go and jump on his grave."

It was at this point that I understood all, and the heart within me sank like lead. The truth was out. Ferdinand Dibble was a goof.

"Come, come, my boy," I said, though feeling the uselessness of any words. "Master this weakness."

"I can't."

"Try!"

"I have tried."

He gnawed his putter again.

"She was asking me just now if I couldn't manage to come to Marvis Bay, too," he said.

"That surely is encouraging? It suggests that she is not entirely indifferent to your society."

"Yes, but what's the use? Do you know," a gleam coming into his eyes for a moment, " have a feeling that if I could ever beat some really fairly good player—just once —I could bring the thing off." The gleam faded. "But what chance is there of that?"

It was a question which I did not care to answer. I merely patted his shoulder sympathetically, and after a little while he left me and walked away. I was still sitting there, thinking over his hard case, when Barbara Medway came out of the club-house.

She, too, seemed grave and pre-occupied, as if there was something on her mind. She took the chair which Ferdinand had vacated, and sighed wearily.

"Have you ever felt," she asked, "that you would like

to bang a man on the head with something hard and heavy? With knobs on?"

I said I had sometimes experienced such desire, and asked if she had any particular man in mind. She seemed to hesitate for a moment before replying, then, apparently, made up her mind to confide in me. My advanced years carry with them certain pleasant compensations, one of which is that nice girls often confide in me. I frequently find myself enrolled as a father-confessor on the most intimate matters by beautiful creatures from whom many a younger man would give his eye-teeth to get a friendly word. Besides, I had known Barbara since she was a child. Frequently—though not recently—I had given her her evening bath. These things form a bond.

"Why are men such chumps?" she exclaimed.

"You still have not told me who it is that has caused these harsh words. Do I know him?"

"Of course you do. You've just been talking to him."

"Ferdinand Dibble? But why should you wish to bang Ferdinand Dibble on the head with something hard and heavy with knobs on?"

"Because he's such a goop."

"You mean a goof?" I queried, wondering how she could have penetrated the unhappy man's secret.

"No, a goop. A goop is a man who's in love with girl and won't tell her so. I am as certain as I am of anything that Ferdinand is fond of me."

"Your instinct is unerring. He has just been confiding in me on that very point."

"Well, why doesn't he confide in *me*, the poor fish?" cried the high-spirited girl, petulantly flicking a pebble at a passing grasshopper. "I can't be expected to fling myself into his arms unless he gives me some sort of a hint that he's ready to catch me."

"Would it help if I were to repeat to him the substance of this conversation of ours?"

"If you breathe a word of it, I'll never speak to you again," she cried. "I'd rather die an awful death than have any man think I wanted him so badly that I had to send relays of messengers begging him to marry me."

I saw her point.

"Then I fear," I said, gravely, "that there is nothing to be done. One can only wait and hope. It may be that in the years to come Ferdinand Dibble will acquire a nice lissom, wristy swing, with the head kept rigid and the right leg firmly braced and—"

"What are you talking about?"

"I was toying with the hope that some sunny day Ferdinand Dibble would cease to be a goof."

"You mean a goop?"

"No, a goof. A goof is a man who—" And I went on to explain the peculiar psychological difficulties which lay in the way of any declaration of affection on Ferdinand's part.

"But I never heard of anything so ridiculous in my life," she ejaculated. "Do you mean to say that he is waiting till he is good at golf before he asks me to marry him?"

"It is not quite so simple as that," I said sadly. "Many bad golfers marry, feeling that a wife's loving solicitude may improve their game. But they are rugged, thick-skinned men, not sensitive and introspective, like Ferdinand. Ferdinand has allowed himself to become morbid. It is one of the chief merits of golf that non-success at the game induces a certain amount of decent humility, which keeps a man from pluming himself too much on any petty triumphs he may achieve in other walks of life; but in all things there is a happy mean, and with Ferdinand this humility has gone too far. It has taken all the spirit out of him. He feels crushed and worthless. He is grateful to caddies when they accept a tip instead of drawing themselves up to their full height and flinging the money in his face."

"Then do you mean that things have got to go on like this for ever?"

I thought for a moment.

"It is a pity," I said, "that you could not have induced Ferdinand to go to Marvis Bay for a month or two."

"Why?"

"Because it seems to me, thinking the thing over, that it is just possible that Marvis Bay might cure him. At the hotel there he would find collected a mob of golfers—I used the term in its broadest sense, to embrace the paralytics and the men who play left-handed—whom even he would be able to beat. When I was last at Marvis Bay, the hotel links were a sort of Sagrasso Sea into which had drifted all the pitiful flotsam and jetsam of golf. I have seen things done on that course at which I shuddered and averted my eyes—and I am not a weak man. If Ferdinand can polish up his game so as to go round in a fairly steady hundred and five, I fancy there is hope. But I understand he is not going to Marvis Bay."

"Oh yes, he is," said the girl.

"Indeed! He did not tell me that when we were talking just now."

"He didn't know it then. He will when I have had a few words with him."

And she walked with firm steps back into the club-house.

It has been well said that there are many kinds of golf, beginning at the top with the golf of professionals and the best amateurs and working down through the golf of ossified men to that of Scotch University professors. Until recently this was looked upon as the lowest possible depth; but nowadays, with the growing popularity of summer hotels, we are able to add a brand still lower, the golf you find at places like Marvis Bay.

To Ferdinand Dibble, coming from a club where the standard of play was rather unusually high, Marvis Bay was a revelation, and for some days after his arrival there he went about dazed, like a man who cannot believe it is really true. To go out on the links at this summer resort was like entering a new world. The hotel was full of stout, middle-aged men, who, after misspent youth devoted to making money, had taken to the game at which real proficiency can only be acquired by those who start playing in their cradles and keep their weight down. Out on the course each morning you could see representatives of every nightmare style that was ever invented. There was the man who seemed to be attempting to deceive his ball and lull it into false security by looking away from it and then making a lightning slash in the apparent hope of catching it off its guard. There was the man who wielded his mid-iron like one killing snakes. There was the man who addressed his ball as if he were stroking a cat, the man who drove as if he were cracking a whip, the man who brooded over each shot like one whose heart is bowed down by bad news from home, and the man who scooped with his mashie as if he were ladling soup. By the end of the first week Ferdinand Dibble was the acknowledged champion of the place. He had gone through the entire menagerie like a bullet through a cream puff.

First, scarcely daring to consider the possibility of success, he had taken on the man who tried to catch his ball off guard and had beaten him five up and four to play. Then, with gradually growing confidence, he tackled in turn the Cat-Stroker, the Whip-Cracker, the Heart Bowed Down, and the Soup-Scooper, and walked all over their faces with spiked shoes. And as these were the leading local amateurs, whose prowess the octogenarians and the men who went round in bath-chairs vainly strove to emulate, Ferdinand Dibble was faced on the eighth morning of his visit by the startling fact that he had no more worlds to conquer. He was monarch of all he surveyed, and, what is more, had won his first trophy, the prize in the great medal-play handicap tournament, in which he had nosed in ahead of the field by two strokes, edging out his nearest rival, a venerable old gentleman, by means of a brilliant and unexpected four on the last hole. The prize was a handsome pewter mug, about the size of the old oaken bucket, and Ferdinand used to go to his room immediately after dinner to croon over it like a mother over her child.

You are wondering, no doubt, why, in these circumstances, he did not take the advantage of the new spirit of exhilarated pride which had replaced his old humility and instantly propose to Barbara Medway. I will tell you. He did not propose to Barbara because Barbara was not there. At the last moment she had been detained at home to nurse a sick parent and had been compelled to postpone her visit for a couple of weeks. He could, no doubt, have proposed in one of the daily letters which he wrote to her, but somehow, once he started writing, he found that he used up so much space describing his best shots on the links that day that it was difficult to squeeze in a declaration of undying passion. After all, you can hardly cram that sort of thing into a postscript.

He decided, therefore, to wait till she arrived, and meanwhile pursued his conquering course. The longer he waited the better, in one way, for every morning and afternoon that passed was adding new layers to his self-esteem. Day by day in every way he grew chestier and chestier.

Meanwhile, however, dark clouds were gathering. Sullen mutterings were to be heard in corners of the hotel lounge, and the spirit of revolt was abroad. For Ferdinand's chestiness had not escaped the notice of his defeated rivals. There is nobody so chesty as a normally unchesty man who suddenly becomes chesty, and I am sorry to say that the chestiness which had come to Ferdinand was the aggressive type of chestiness which breeds enemies. He had developed a habit of holding the game up in order to give his opponent advice. The Whip-Cracker had not forgiven, and never would forgive, his well-meant but galling criticism of his back-swing. The Scooper, who had always scooped since the day when, at the age of sixty-four, he subscribed to the Correspondence Course which was to teach him golf in twelve lessons by mail, resented being told by a snip of a boy that the mashie-stroke should be a smooth, unhurried swing. The Snake-Killer— But I need not weary you with a detailed recital of these men's grievances; it is enough to say that they all had it in for Ferdinand, and one night, after dinner, they met in the lounge to decide what was to be done about it.

A nasty spirit was displayed by all.

"A mere lad telling me how to use my mashie!" growled the Scooper. "Smooth and unhurried my left eyeball! I get it up, don't I? Well, what more do you want?"

"I keep telling him that mine is the old, full St. Andrew swing," muttered the Whip-Cracker, between set teeth, "but he won't listen to me."

"He ought to be taken down a peg or two," hissed the Snake-Killer. It is not easy to hiss a sentence without a single "s" in it, and the fact that he succeeded in doing so shows to what a pitch of emotion the man had been goaded by Ferdinand's maddening air of superiority.

"Yes, but what can we do?" queried an octogenarian, when this last remark had been passed on to him down his ear-trumpet.

"That's the trouble," sighed the Scooper. "What can we do?" And there was a sorrowful shaking of heads.

"I know!" exclaimed the Cat-Stroker, who had not hitherto spoken. He was a lawyer, and a man of subtle and sinister mind. "I have it! There's a boy in my office—young Parsloe—who could beat this man Dibble hollow. I'll wire him to come down here and we'll spring him on this fellow and knock some of the conceit out of him."

There was a chorus of approval.

"But are you sure he can beat him?" asked the Snake-Killer, anxiously. "It would never do to make a mistake."

"Of course I'm sure," said the Cat-Stroker. "George Parsloe once went round in ninety-four.

"Many changes there have been since ninety-four," said the octogenarian, nodding sagely. "Ah, many, many changes. None of these motor-cars then, tearing about killing—"

Kindly hands led him off to have an egg-and-milk, and the remaining conspirators returned to the point at issue with bent brows.

"Ninety-four?" said the Scooper, incredulously. "Do you mean counting every stroke?"

"Counting every stroke."

"Not conceding himself any putts?"

"Not one."

"Wire him to come at once," said the meeting with one voice.

That night the Cat-Stroker approached Ferdinand, smooth, subtle, lawyer-like.

"Oh, Dibble," he said, "just the man I wanted to see. Dibble, there's a young friend of mine coming down here who goes in for golf a little. George Parsloe is his name. I was wondering if you could spare the time to give him a game. He is just a novice, you know."

"I shall be delighted to play a round with him," said Ferdinand, kindly.

"He might pick up a pointer or two from watching you," said the Cat-Stroker.

"True, true," said Ferdinand.

"Then I'll introduce you when he shows up."

"Delighted," said Ferdinand.

He was in excellent humour that night, for he had had a letter from Barbara saying that she was arriving on the next day but one.

It was Ferdinand's healthy custom in the morning to get up in good time and take a dip in the sea before breakfast. On the morning of the day of Barbara's arrival, he arose, as usual, donned his flannels, took a good look at the cup, and started out. It was a fine, fresh morning, and he glowed both externally and internally. As he crossed the links, for the nearest route to the water was through the fairway of the seventh, he was whistling happily and rehearsing in his mind the opening sentences of his proposal. For it was his firm resolve that night after dinner to ask Barbara to marry him. He was proceeding over the smooth turf without care in the world, when there was a sudden cry of "Fore!" and the next moment a golf ball, missing him by inches, sailed up the fairway and came to a rest fifty yards from where he stood. He looked round and observed a figure coming towards him from the tee.

The distance from the tee was fully a hundred and thirty yards. Add fifty to that, and you have a hundred and eighty yards. No such drive had been made on the Marvis Bay links since their foundation, and such is the generous spirit of the true golfer that Ferdinand's first emotion, after the not inexcusable spasm of panic caused by the hum of the ball past his ear, was one of cordial admiration. By some kindly miracle, he supposed, one of his hotel acquaintances had been permitted for once in his life to time the drive right. It was only when the other man came up that there began to steal over him a sickening apprehension. The faces of all those who hewed divots in the hotel course were familiar to him, and the fact that this fellow was a stranger seemed to point with dreadful certainty to his being the man he had agreed to play.

"Sorry," said the man. He was a tall, strikingly handsome youth, with brown eyes and a dark moustache.

"Oh, that's all right," said Ferdinand. "Er—do you always drive like that?"

"Well, I generally get a bit longer ball, but I'm off my

drive this morning. It's lucky I came out and got this practice. I'm playing a match tomorrow with a fellow named Dibble, who's a local champion, or something."

"Me," said Ferdinand, humbly.

"Eh? Oh, you?" Mr. Parsloe eyed him appraisingly. "Well, may the best man win."

As this was the precisely what Ferdinand was afraid was going to happen, he nodded in a sickly manner and tottered off to his bathe. The magic had gone out of the morning. The sun still shone, but in a silly, feeble way; and a cold and depressing wind had sprung up. For Ferdinand's inferiority complex, which had seemed cured for ever, was back again, doing business at the old stand.

Glowing anticipation so often turns out on arrival, flat, cold, and disappointing. For ten days Barbara Medway had been living for that meeting with Ferdinand, when, getting out of the train, she would see him popping about on the horizon with the love-light sparkling in his eyes and words of devotion trembling on his lips. The poor girl never doubted for an instant that he would unleash his pent-up emotions inside the first five minutes, and her only worry was least he should give an embarrassing publicity to the sacred scene by falling on his knees on the station platform.

"Well, here I am at last," she cried gaily.

"Hullo!" said Ferdinand, with a twisted smile.

The girl looked at him, chilled. How could she know that his peculiar manner was due entirely to the severe attack of cold feet resultant upon his meeting with George Pasloe that morning? The interpretation which she placed upon it was that he was not glad to see her. If he had behaved like this before, she would, of course, have put it down to ingrowing goofery, but now she had his written statements to prove that for the last ten days his golf had been one long series of triumphs.

"I got your letters," she said, persevering bravely.

"I thought you would," said Ferdinand, absently.

"You seem to have been doing wonders."

"Yes."

There was a silence.

"Have a nice journey?" said Ferdinand.

"Very," said Barbara.

She spoke coldly, for she was madder than a wet hen. She saw it all now. In the ten days since they had parted, his love, she realized, had waned. Some other girl, met in the romantic surroundings of this picturesque resort, had supplanted her in his affections. She knew how quickly Cupid gets off the mark at a summer hotel, and for an instant she blamed herself for ever having been so ivory-skulled as to let him come to this place alone. Then regret was swallowed up in wrath, and she became so glacial that Ferdinand, who had been on the point of telling her the secret of his gloom, retired into his shell and conversation during the drive to the hotel never soared above a certain level. Ferdinand said the sunshine was nice and Barbara said yes, it was nice, and Ferdinand said it looked pretty on the water, and Barbara said yes, it did look pretty on the water, and Barbara said yes, it did look pretty on the water, and Ferdinand said he hoped it was not going to rain, and Barbara said yes, it would be a pity if it rained. And then there was another lengthy silence.

"How is my uncle?" asked Barbara at last.

I omitted to mention that the individual to whom I have referred as the Cat-Stroker was Barbara's mother's brother, and her host at Marvis Bay.

"Your uncle?"

"His name is Tuttle. Have you met him?"

Ferdinand, his mind returning to the matter nearest his heart. "A fellow named Parsloe."

"Oh, is George Parsloe here? How jolly!"

"Do you know him?" barked Ferdinand, hollowly. He would not have supposed that anything could have added to his existing depression, but he was conscious now of having slipped a few rungs farther down the ladder of gloom. There had been a horribly joyful ring in her voice. Ah, well, he reflected morosely, how like life it all was! We never know what the morrow may bring forth. We strike a good patch and are beginning to think pretty well of ourselves, and along comes a George Parsloe.

"Of course I do," said Barbara. "Why, there he is."

The cab had drawn up at the door of the hotel, and on the porch George Parsloe was airing his graceful person. To Ferdinand's fevered eye he looked like a Greek god, and his inferiority complex began to exhibit symptoms of elephantiasis. How could he compete at love or golf with a fellow who looked as if he had stepped out of the movies and considered himself off his drive when he did a hundred and eighty yards?

"Geor-gee!" cried Barbara, blithely. "Hullo, George!"

"Why, hullo, Barbara!"

They fell into pleasant conversation, while Ferdinand hung himself miserably about the offing. And presently, feeling that his society was not essential to their happiness, he slunk away.

George Parsloe dined at the Cat-Stroker's table that night, and it was with George Parsloe that Barbara roamed in the moonlight after dinner. Ferdinand, after a profitless hour at the billiard-table, went early to his room. But not even the rays of the moon, glinting on his cup, could soothe the fever in his soul. He practiced putting somberly into his tooth-glass for a while; then, going to bed, fell at last into a troubled sleep.

Barbara slept late the next morning and breakfasted in her room. Coming down towards noon, she found a strange emptiness in the hotel. It was her experience of summer hotels that a really fine day like this one was the cue for half the inhabitants to collect in the lounge, shut all the windows, and talk about conditions in the jute industry. To her surprise, though the sun was streaming down from cloudless sky, the only occupant of the lounge was the octogenarian with the ear-trumpet. She observed that he was chuckling to himself in a senile manner.

"Good morning," she said politely, for she had made his acquaintance on the previous evening.

"Hey?" said the octogenarian, suspending his chuckling and getting his trumpet into position. "I said 'Good morning!'" roared Barbara into the receiver.

"Hey?"

"Good morning!"

"Ah! Yes, it's a very fine morning, a very fine morning. If it wasn't for missing my bun and glass of milk at twelve sharp," said the octogenarian, "I'd be down on the links. That's where I'd be, down on the links. If it wasn't for missing my bun and glass of milk."

This refreshment arriving this moment he dismantled the radio outfit and began to restore his tissues.

"Watching the match," he explained, pausing for a moment in his bun-mangling.

"What match?"

The octogenarian sipped his milk.

"What match?" repeated Barbara.

"Hey?"

"What match?"

The octogenarian began to chuckle again and nearly swallowed a crumb the wrong way.

"Take some of the conceit out of him," he gurgled.

"Out of who?" asked Barbara, knowing perfectly well that she should have said "whom."

"Yes," said the octogenarian.

"Who is conceited?"

"Ah! This young fellow, Dibble. Very conceited. I saw it in his eye from the first, but nobody would listen to me. Mark my words, I said, that boy needs taking down a peg or two. Well, he's going to be this morning. Your uncle wired to young Parsloe to come down, and he arranged a match between them. Dibble—" Here the octogenarian choked again and had to rinse himself out with milk, "Dibble doesn't know that Parsloe once went round in ninety-four!"

"What?"

Everything seemed to go black to Barbara. Though a murky mist she appeared to be looking at a negro octogenarian, sipping ink. Then her eyes cleared, and she found herself clutching for support at the back of the chair. She understood now. She realized why Ferdinand had been so distrait, and her whole heart went out to him in a spasm of maternal pity. How she had wronged him!

"Take some of the conceit out of him," the octogenarian was mumbling, and Barbara felt a sudden sharp loathing for the old man. For two pins she could have dropped a beetle in his milk. Then the need for action roused her. What action? She did not know. All she knew was that she must act.

"Oh!"

"Hey?" said the octogenarian, bringing his trumpet to the ready.

But Barbara was gone.

It was not far to the links, and Barbara covered the distance on flying feet. She reached the clubhouse, but the course was empty except for the Scooper, who was preparing to drive off the first tee. In spite of the fact that something seemed to tell her subconsciously that this was one of the sights she ought not miss, the girl did not wait to watch. Assuming that the match had started soon after breakfast, it must by now have reached one of the holes on the second nine. She ran down the hill, looking left and right, and was presently aware of a group of spectators clustered about a green in the distance. As she hurried towards them they moved away, and now she could see Ferdinand advancing to the next tee. With a thrill that shook her whole body she realized that he had the honour. So he must have won one hole, at any rate. Then she saw her uncle.

"How are they?" she gasped.

Mr. Tuttle seemed moody. It was apparent that things were not going altogether to his liking.

"All square at the fifteenth," he replied, gloomily.

"All square!"

"Yes. Young Parsloe," said Mr. Tuttle with a sour look in the direction of that lissom athlete, "doesn't seem to be able to do a thing right on the greens. He has been putting like a sheep with the botts."

From the foregoing remark of Mr. Tuttle you will, no doubt, have gleaned at least a clue to the mystery of how Ferdinand Dibble had managed to hold his long-driving adversary up to the fifteenth green, but for all that you will probably consider that some further explanation of this amazing state of affairs is required. Mere bad putting on the part of George Parsloe is not, you feel, sufficient to cover the matter entirely. You are right. There was another very important factor in the situation—to wit, that by some extraordinary chance Ferdinand Dibble had started right off from the first tee, playing the game of his lifetime. Never had he made such drives, never chipped his chip so shrewdly.

About Ferdinand's driving there was as a general thing a fatal stiffness and over-caution which prevented success. And with his chip-shots he rarely achieved accuracy owing to his habit of rearing his head like a lion of the jungle just before the club struck the ball. But to-day he had been swinging with a careless freedom, and his chips had been true and clean. The thing had puzzled him all the way round. It had not elated him, for, owing to Barbara's aloofness and the way in which she had gambolled about George Parsloe like a young lamb in the springtime, he was in too deep a state of dejection to be elated by anything. And now, suddenly, in a flash of clear vision, he perceived the reason why he had been playing so well to-day. It was just because he was not elated. It was simply because he was so profoundly miserable.

That was what Ferdinand told himself as he stepped off the sixteenth, after hitting a screamer down the centre of the fairway, and I am convinced that he was right. Like so many indifferent golfers, Ferdinand Dibble had always made the game hard for himself by thinking too much. He was a deep student of the works of the masters, and whenever he prepared to plat a stroke he had a complete mental list of all the mistakes which it was possible to make. He would remember how Taylor had warned against dipping the right shoulder, how Vardon had inveighed against any movement of the head; he would recall how Ray had mentioned the tendency to snatch back the club, how Braid had spoken sadly of those who sin against their better selves by stiffening the muscles and heaving.

Consequence was that when, after waggling in a frozen manner till mere shame urged him to take some definite course of action, he eventually swung, he invariably proceeded to dip his right shoulder, stiffen his muscles, heave, and snatch back the club, at the same time raising his head sharply as in the illustrated plate ("Some Frequent Faults of Beginners—No. 3—Lifting the Bean") facing page thirty-four of James Braid's *Golf Without Tears*. To-day he had been so preoccupied with his broken heart that he had made his shots absently, almost carelessly, with the result that at least one in every three had been a lollapalooza.

Meanwhile, George Parsloe had driven off and the match was progressing. George was feeling a little flustered by now. He had been given to understand that this bird Dibble was a hundred-at-his-best man, and all the way round the fellow had been reeling off fives in great profusion, and had once actually got a four. True, there had been an occasional six, and even a seven, but that did not alter the main fact that the man was making the dickens of a game of it. With the haughty spirit of one who had once done a ninety-four, George Parsloe had anticipated being at least three up at the turn. Instead of which he had been two down, and had to fight strenuously to draw level.

Nevertheless, he drove steadily and well, and would certainly have won the hole had it not been for his weak and sinful putting. The same defect caused him to halve the seventeenth, after being on in two, with Ferdinand wandering in the desert and only reaching the green with his fourth. Then, however, Ferdinand holed out from a distance of seven yards, getting a five; which George's three putts just enabled him to equal.

Barbara had watched the proceedings with a beating heart. At first she had looked on from afar; but now, drawn as by a magnet, she approached the tee. Ferdinand was drifting off. She held her breath. Ferdinand held his breath. And all around one could see their respective breaths being held by George Parsloe, Mr. Tuttle, and the enthralled crowd of spectators. It was a moment of the acutest tension, and it was broken by the crack of Ferdinand's driver as it met a mere thirty yards. At this supreme crisis in the match Ferdinand Dibble had topped.

George Parsloe teed up his ball. There was a smile of quiet satisfaction on his face. He snuggled the driver in his hands, and gave it a preliminary swish. This, felt George Parsloe, was where the happy ending came. He could drive as he had never driven before. He would so drive that it would take his opponent at least three shots to catch up with him. He drew back his club with infinite caution, poised it at the top of the swing—

"I always wonder—" said a clear, girlish voice, ripping the silence like the explosion of a bomb.

George Parsloe stared. His club wobbled. It descended. The ball trickled into the grass in front of the tee. There was a grim pause. "You were saying, Miss Medway—" said George Parsloe, in a small, flat voice.

"A little, perhaps. Possibly the merest trifle. But you were saying you wondered about something. Can I be of assistance?"

George Parsloe swallowed once or twice. He also blinked a little feverishly. His eyes had a dazed, staring expression.

"I'm afraid I can't tell you off hand," he said, "but I will make a point of consulting some good encyclopedia at the earliest opportunity."

"Not at all. It will be a pleasure. In case you were thinking of inquiring at the moment when I am putting why greens are called greens, may I venture the suggestion now that it is because they are green?"

And so saying George Parsloe stalked to his ball and found it nestling in the heart of some shrub of which, not being a botanist, I cannot give you the name. It was a close-knit, adhesive shrub, and it twined its tentacles so lovingly around George Parsloe's niblick that he missed his first shot altogether. His second made the ball rock, and his third dislodged it. Playing a full swing with his brassie and being by now a mere cauldron of seething emotions he missed his fourth. His fifth came to within a few inches of Ferdinand's drive, and he picked it up and hurled it from him into the rough as if it had been something venomous.

"Your hole and match," said George Parsloe, thinly.

Ferdinand Dibble sat beside the glittering ocean. He had hurried off the course with swift strides the moment George Parsloe had spoken those bitter words. He wanted to be alone with his thoughts.

They were mixed thoughts. For a moment joy at the reflection that he had won a touch match came irresistibly to the surface, only to sink again as he remembered that life, whatever its triumphs, could hold nothing for him now that Barbara Medway loved another.

"Mr. Dibble!"

He looked up. She was standing at his side. He gulped and rose to his feet.

"Yes?"

There was a silence.

"Doesn't the sun look pretty on the water?" said Barbara.

Ferdinand groaned. This was too much.

"Leave me," he said, hollowly. "Go back to your Parsloe, the man with whom you walked in the moonlight beside this same water."

"Well, why shouldn't I walk with Parsloe in the moonlight beside this same water?" demanded Barbara, with spirit.

"I never said," replied Ferdinand, for he was a fair man at heart, "that you shouldn't walk with Mr. Parsloe beside this same water. I simply said you did walk with Mr. Parsloe beside this same water."

"I've a perfect right to walk with Mr. Parsloe beside this same water," persisted Barbara. "He and I are old friends."

Ferdinand groaned again.

"Exactly! There you are! As I suspected. Old friends. Played together as children, and what not, I shouldn't wonder."

"No, we didn't. I've only known him five years. But he is engaged to be married to my greatest chum, so that draws us together."

Ferdinand uttered a strangled cry.

"Parsloe engaged to be married!"

"Yes. The wedding takes place next month."

"But look here." Ferdinand's forehead was wrinkled. He was thinking tensely. "Look here," said Ferdinand, a close reasoner. "If Parsloe's engaged to your greatest chum, he can't be in love with *you.*"

"No."

"And you aren't in love with him?"

"No."

"Then, by gad," said Ferdinand, "how about it?"

"What do you mean?"

"Will you marry me?" bellowed Ferdinand.

"Yes,"

"You will?"

"Of course I will."

"Darling!" cried Ferdinand.

"There is only one thing that bothers me a bit," said Ferdinand, thoughtfully, as they strolled together over the scented meadows, while in the trees above them a thousand birds trilled Mendelssohn's Wedding March.

"What is that?"

"Well, I'll tell you," said Ferdinand. "The fact is, I've just discovered the great secret of golf. You can't play a really hot game unless you're so miserable that you don't worry over your shots. Take the case of a chip-shot, for instance. If you're really wretched, you don't care where the ball is going and so you don't raise your head to see. Grief automatically prevents pressing and over-swinging. Look at the top-notchers. Have you ever seen a happy pro?"

"No. I don't think I have."

"Well then!"

"But pros are all Scotchmen," argued Barbara.

"It doesn't matter. I'm sure I'm right. And the darned thing is that I'm going to be so infernally happy all the rest of my life that I suppose my handicap will go up to thirty or something."

Barbara squeezed his hand lovingly.

"Don't worry, precious," she said, soothingly. "It will be all right. I am a woman, and, once we are married, I shall be able to think of at least a hundred ways of snootering you to such an extent that you'll be fit to win the Amateur Championship."

"You will?" said Ferdinand, anxiously. "You're sure?"

"Quite, quite sure, dearest," said Barbara.

"My angel!" said Ferdinand.

He folded her in his arms, using the interlocking grip.

Wodehouse on Golf

---

*No man should attempt to play golf who has not good legs
to run with and good arms to throw with,
as well as a modicum of brain power to direct his play.
It is also, by the nature of the game itself,
a most aristocratic exercise,
for no man can play at golf who has not
a servant at command to assist him.
It is probable that no sport exists in the world today
or ever did exist in which the services of a paid assistant
are an essential as in this national game of Scotland.
The truth is that the servant is as essential to the success of the
game as the player himself. . . .*

*The principal qualifications for the game are steady nerve
and eye and good judgment and force with an added
ability to avoid knolls and sandpits which, in the
technical terms of the Scotch game, are called hazards.*

*It is not a game which would induce men of elegance to
compete in, but those who have strong wind and
good muscle may find it a splendid exercise for their abilities.*

PHILADELPHIA TIMES

The "Yips"

GEORGE PLIMPTON

One evening in San Francisco I heard for the first time about the "yips"—a phenomenon talked about rather uneasily by the pros, with wary respect, as one might talk about a communicable disease ravaging the neighboring township. The yips...was the term given the occupational malaise of golf–a nervous affliction that settled in the wrist and hands, finally, after the years of pressure and the money bets and the strain. It was what ultimately drove the pros out of the game to the teaching jobs at the country clubs....

The legs don't give out, as in many other sports, or the wind, or the sense of timing, or the power, but the *nerves*, so that one could see the hands of great golfers beset by the yips tremble visibly on the putting greens, the greatest names in golf completely at the mercy of short putts of 4, 5, 6 feet....

Another older player I talked to about the yips was John Farrell, once the great rival of Bobby Jones and now a teaching professional in Florida. He said that if you play in competition long enough you're sure to get the yips. "Walter Hagen," he said. "If you had to vote for the player with the best temperament, well, you'd *have* to vote for him. Hell, he had such confidence that there wasn't a shot that held any terror for him: they used to say that when he had a particularly tough shot to make, and he'd stepped up and made a great one of it, why then he'd whisper at his caddy, 'Did I make it look hard enough?' and give him a wink, y'see. Well *he* got them. The yips. He got them so bad that he tried strokes and grip styles you could scarcely *believe*: cross-handed putting; or sticking the elbows way out so that the wrist action was throttled down and his whole body moved as stiff as a derrick. He even tried putting in the dark—thought that might cure him. Nothing did. Or look at Ben Hogan. Take a player like him. The 'Iceman' they called him. *He* got the yips. And Bobby Jones. Finally he began to miss putts two feet long, and he quit because he couldn't keep oatmeal in his stomach...."

I asked the question I had put to the others—if there was any connection between the yips and losing one's nerve.

"It's that you lose *nerves*, not nerve," Farrell said. "You can shoot lions in the dark and yet you can quiver like a leaf and fall flat over a two-foot putt."

The Bogey Man

A Humbling Game

NANCY LOPEZ

Golf is, I believe, the only game where the admittedly very best players over a stretch of time hasn't any more than a pretty good chance of winning any individual golf tournament. He or she may be a comparatively strong favorite, and a considerably better bet to win than anyone else, but even the greatest golfer, male or female at any time in history, is not a good risk to bet on at anything less than something like 5-to-1 odds against. There are always too many almost equally talented golfers in the field of a major tournament, any one of whom is capable over a given long weekend of putting together four steady or superb rounds, for even the admittedly dominant player in the long run to be favored strongly. That's not true of other sports. A very good tennis player doesn't beat a player of world championship class, or the best fighter at the local gym doesn't unexpectedly knock out the heavyweight champion. (Even Rocky in the movie didn't!) But in golf tournament after tournament, usually there are half a dozen players right up in the lead or within a stroke or two of the leader, over the final nine holes, and any of them can win. The solid favorite, who will far outstrip the person who beats her over the year in victories and in money earnings, may be quite a way back in that particular tournament and be finishing nowhere. It doesn't take *too* much misfortune to shoot your way out of a tournament with a few unexpected bogeys.

I think Jack Nicklaus made the point best one time. He is quoted as saying that a major golf tournament competitor who wins 20 percent of the events he enters is almost surely the world's best. Think about that rather startling statement. The best performer in this sport of golf is likely *not* to win four out of five times over a 72-hole medal play tournament. No wonder golf has been called "a humbling game"!

The Education of a Woman Golfer

Golf is for Everyone

WALTER SIMPSON

It is a game for the many. It suits all sorts and conditions of men. The strong and the weak, the halt and the maimed, the octogenarian and the boy, the rich and the poor, the clergyman and the infidel, may play every day, except Sunday. The late riser can play comfortably, and be back for his rubber in the afternoon; the sanguine man can measure himself against those who will beat him; the half-crown seeker can find victims, the gambler can bet, the man of high principle, by playing for nothing, may enjoy himself, and yet feel good. You can brag, and lose matches; depreciate yourself, and win them. Unlike the other Scotch game of whisky-drinking, excess in it is not injurious to the health.

The Art of Golf

Golfing Ladies

E. M. Boys

Golfers—I refer to ladies—might be divided into three classes: the Sportswoman; the Enthusiast, or Pot-Hunter; and the Ignorant. Let us try to briefly describe them.

A Sportswoman is one who loves sport for itself, and not for what it will bring. As golfers, sportswomen are a judicious blend of keenness and sense. Content to play once or twice week, their play seldom suffers from staleness; they never play, if they can avoid it, in rain or in a gale of wind, and when they get 'off their game,' wisely refrain altogether from playing for a few days. They take a keen interest in their home club, and are always eager to assist their captain in her efforts to promote inter-club matches and the interests of the club in general; and it is among the ranks of these sportswomen that the best golfers are to be found.

On the other hand, the Enthusiasts, or Pot-Hunters, play, if possible, every day of the week, and in all weathers; in fact, they are quite oblivious of rain, and playing during a gale of wind is only considered good practice, with the result that many of them break down. It is by no means uncommon to hear a lady straining herself, and being obliged in consequence to give up golf entirely for some months, or contracting a bad chill from a thorough wetting, which may settle on her lungs if she is delicate. 'Pot-hunting,' or what has more aptly been termed 'the Cult of the Biscuit Box,' is rapidly ruining golf—and, for that matter, all games—from a sporting point of view. There are a regular set, belonging to this 'Cult,' who go from open meeting to open meeting, 'pot-hunting,' and appear to regard the game only as a means to that end. They will unblushingly try to keep their handicap up to have more chance of achieving their ambition, and I have even heard a golfer of this class regretting that she has been unfortunate enough to win a monthly medal just before a spring or autumn meeting, and in consequence, lowered her handicap, and so reduced her chance of winning 'pots.'

Possibly the worse trait in their character is that they have no genuine esprit de corps, but will unhesitantly throw their captain on the horns of a dilemma by refusing to play in an inter-club match if another engagement of a more fascinating description is suggested to them at the last moment.

We now come to the members of the 'Ignorant' class, or in other words, the beginners, who, one might say, always remain beginners, the despair of professional instructors and the bugbear of every club. They chip along the course, cutting up the grass, day after day, never doing any hole under double figures, and yet cheerfully enter any competition for which they are eligible. Their chief characteristics are unfailing good nature from utter indifference and a dogged determination, which makes them go on, though they never improve.

Badminton Magazine

Iron Tactic

HORACE G. HUTCHINSON

If you find yourself being outplayed by the excellent iron approaches of your adversary, it is sometimes a good plan to say to him, in a tone of friendly interest, "Really you are playing your iron wonderfully well today—better than I ever say you play it before. Can you account for it in any way?" This is likely to promote a slight nervousness when he next takes his iron in his hand; and this nervousness is likely, if the match is at all a close one, to be of considerable service to you. There is no rule to prevent your doing this; only after a time people will cease playing with you.

Hints on Golf

The Ghost of Colonel Bogey

LONG SPOON

There is a "Colonel Bogey" at every Golf links in the kingdom. Some golfers in their ignorance regard him as a mythical personage, who we play against in order that he may play with us—as a cat does with a mouse. Nothing of the kind. He is the spirit of a departed golfer.

Have you ever noticed a golfer whom everyone knows, and yet no one knows? His past history is obscure, but his present and future are painfully patent. He is a golfer who has taken up the game late in life, and has been bitten with the craze in its deadliest form. Some golfers escape his fate because they die, or commit suicide, or are dragged to Bedlam. Better that, than the end waiting for this poor wretch. Sore stricken with the mania, he struggles round the links weekly, daily, hourly. His days are one long foozle, his nights a hideous nightmare. Then a change comes over the scene. The iron has entered his soul. Heaven save the mark! Better a thousand times that he had remained guileless, foozling, Christian old gentleman. His game improves by leaps and bounds. Simple golfers are astounded, but the wise grow fearsome. He becomes, if not the best player in the club, the most deadly. The handicapping committee are nonplused, he carries everything before him. He does not smoke or drink, and he only swears in obscure parts of the course, and in tones deep and guttural and in language strange to human ears. Hanging lies have a fascination for him, and he revels in stymie.

And so he plays on, regardless of the tender feelings of the handicapping committee, winning gold medals galore, scooping the half-crowns of the ardent novice, and breaking records right and left until—until what? Until the end comes and his spirit leaves the clay, to fly to the newest links—inland by preference, where his ghost becomes the "Bogey" of the green. Why do we top our drives, foozle our iron shots, miss ridiculous putts? Because his spirit is always with us annulling our best efforts.

Do you see that irascible-looking golfer on the last green? He has got an eighteen-inch putt, to save the match. If he holes the ball his wife and children will have a week of blissful happiness. If he misses—why heaven help them! His caddie hands him his putter. It is a momentous occasion, and the silence of death falls on the little group. Wise men shake their heads, they recognize that he is fighting with an unseen force. Slowly he squats down and takes his line. Only eighteen inches separate his ball from the hole, and the green is as level as a billiard-table. But he sees a hog's back, four worm casts, and a tricky slope. Back goes the putter and then forward, there is a faint click, the ball speeds forwards towards but (alas! for his wife and children) not into the hole. Both men swear, the loser with savage emphasis, the winner, out of assumed sympathy and softly as if he was pronouncing a benediction. Some men there are who escape the fascination of this demon. These men are dull-witted or imbecile, or men who never drink water, or pray, or go to church, or men possessed of a handy trick of blasphemy.

Golf

"He's not having a good day. He shot his age this morning."

Temper, Temper

H.S.C. EVERARD

From an extremely lofted iron, in the words of Sir Nigel Loring in *The White Company*, 'much honour and advancement may be won.' All *may* go well with you and it, as all ultimately did go well with that paladin of romance just quoted, but even as our nerves are ever kept in extremest tension as each of his adventures in turn unfolds itself, so 'just before the battle', when the hole is to be approached, will the neophyte probably tremble as to the result if he be the owner of a club of this description.

Sooth to say, they are but 'kittle cattle' at the best, one of their peculiarities being that the harder you hit, the less distance will the ball go; it simply rises all the higher in the air, and has all the more underspin—it follows, therefore, that they are of no use, save at very short range, thirty or forty yards, perhaps, from the hole. It is extremely easy to play a villainously bad shot with them; either by cutting into the ground, and moving the ball about the yard, or by topping it with the heavy sole, in which case more run will be imparted to the ball, at the wrong juncture, than could have been coaxed out of any other club in your set; therefore, if the shot happens to be important, assuredly 'shall indignation vex you, even as a thing that is raw'. Of course an iron of this sort has its uses: it is positively invaluable for stymies, which are then robbed of more than half their terrors, or, for instance, if there arise exceptional circumstances, say an approach has to be made over a bunker, down high wind, when the green is like ice, here again is its opportunity, for a ball will run less, if properly played, than off any other club. From what has been said, therefore, it will be apparent,

that if a club of this sort is to be carried at all, the more
it is used, the more practice you have with it, the better.

Golf In Theory And Practice

Golf is Easier Than You Think

ARNOLD PALMER

GOLF IS DECEPTIVELY SIMPLE and endlessly complicated. A child can play it well and a grown man can never
master it. Any single round of it is full of unexpected triumphs and perfect shots that end in disaster. It is almost
a science, yet it is a puzzle without an answer. It is grati-
fying and tantalizing, precise and unpredictable; it
requires complete concentration and total relaxation. It
satisfies the soul and frustrates the intellect. It is at the
same time rewarding and maddening—and it is without
doubt the greatest game mankind has ever invented.

One strange trouble that plagues me, as a professional who has to keep winning to keep eating, is that I
love the game so much that I sometimes forget to play it
as well as I can. Especially in the spring of the year, when
the first warm sun presses down on your shoulders,
when the grass has just been mowed for the first time
and sits there damp and green, with its fresh-cut smell
floating up to your nostrils, when the sky is a deep blue
roof over your head and an occasional cloud drifts by so
white that it dazzles your eyes, a golf course is an intoxicating place.

This was the sort of day, this was the sort of happiness, that we kept waiting for all winter when I was growing up in western Pennsylvania. The winters are long and
hard around Latrobe, my home town; the golf course

where my father was and is the pro usually was frozen over the middle of December; we had to content ourselves with skiing until that first perfect day came along some time toward the end of March. We dreamed about it all winter and went slightly out of our minds when it finally arrived.

I still have trouble keeping my feet on the ground on that kind of day; I want to march right up over the next hill and on and on into the heavens. Life is so wonderful; it is so great to be alive and playing golf; the world is so perfect that my mind sloshes around aimlessly like a baby enjoying a bath. I forget that the ball is there to hit. I stare at it, its white enamel nesting in the grass, as if hypnotized. Physically I am on the golf course but spiritually I am somewhere else, somewhere out in that wild blue yonder, and I have to make a deliberate effort to reach out, pull myself back and get down to business.

What other people may find in poetry or art museums, I find in the flight of a good drive—the white ball sailing up and up into that blue sky, growing smaller and smaller, almost taking off in orbit, then suddenly reaching its apex, curving, falling, describing the perfect parabola of a good hit, and finally dropping to the turf to roll some more, the way I planned it. I even enjoy the mingled pleasure and discomfort of breaking in a new pair of golf shoes. I like the firmness of the leather, the solid feeling against the turf. Sometimes I have changed to a new pair of shoes in the middle of a tournament, have been carried away by the confidence they gave me and the excitement of the play, and have not noticed until I returned to the clubhouse that I had acquired a crop of blisters.

Sometimes, however, I get dead tired of golf. One

tournament has followed another, day in and day out. I am mentally and physically exhausted. My back aches from the constant turning, shot after shot. My shoulders hurt from the constant jar of clubhead biting into hard earth. I cannot sit down, relax and forget there ever was such a game. I sit for an entire day and no thought of golf ever enters my head. The second morning also passes in blissful freedom from the tyranny of the game. But, by the second afternoon, I am downstairs in my shop, fiddling with that 3-wood that felt a little off-balance in the last round. By dinnertime I have unscrewed the bottom plate, added a drop of lead for extra weight, swung the club a dozen times, filed away half the fresh solder, found myself satisfied at last with the 3-wood, and begun to wonder what kind of fraction of an inch alteration would make my putter more accurate.

If you are a golfer, you know what I mean. If you are about to become a golfer, you will soon find out.

Many people—amateurs distressed by their failure to break 100, professionals weary of the travel and the strain of having to break par every day—swear to give up golf. Nobody ever does.

My Game and Yours

A Caddie's Story

H. M. F.

Tim was a caddie at the Highwater Golf Club, and was much sought after by reason of his unswerving interest in the game, his integrity, civility, and general quiet demeanor. He was only twelve years old, and small for his age, though, his old grandmother, with whom he lived, and whom he carefully tended, would say, "There's a power of use in him."

But Tim had a weakness, and it was this. There was another boy, Jack Peterson by name, the smartest caddie on the links, and considered the best player among them. This lad was Tim's hero. He was three or four years Tim's senior, and treated him with the condescending patronage that a retriever might be expected to show to an admiring kitten. That his hero could ever be in the wrong never entered into the little lad's calculations, and to be allowed to fetch and carry for him constituted his highest pleasure in life.

Now, Tim was no mean golfer himself, though he could not drive as far as Jack, with his long slashing drives, and would-be-professional style, yet his neat approaches and steady putting made him a formidable opponent.

A caddies' competition was organized during the summer, and as usual, Jack and Tim played round together. Now, it happened on this occasion that Tim's putting was at fault, and his score mounted up while Jack played a steady as well as a brilliant game, and was doing an excellent score. Tim was in raptures, and could hardly suppress his excitement. All went well till they came to the seventeenth hole, where the green was guarded by a yawning bunker. Here, approaching from a distance, Jack's ball was seen to reach the edge of the bunker and disappear, Tim's ball following in the same direction.

"One of us is in!" cried Jack in an annoyed voice, as they drew nearer and found only one ball visible.

Tim was seized with an inspiration, "It's me," he said, "I saw it go in," and though he had the grace to colour up at what he knew to be a perfectly untrue assertion, he pointed to the other ball lying just to one side of the bunker, and began hammering away at the ball in the sand, as if his very life depended on it. Jack played the other ball without giving it more than a casual glance, as he had no wish to discover the mistake, if such there was.

"Just a bit of lucky" commented he, taking the two balls out of the hole, "I thought as I was done for that time, it 'ud 'ave taken me a week to get out."

Of course Jack proved the winner, and was congratulated and envied by all, except Tim, who rushed off home as soon as he could, the other boys thinking he was annoyed at not winning himself.

But his depression continued the next day, and increased as the week went on, especially when the lad who came in second, and who had always been very kind to him, told him what bad luck he had in losing his ball, which had prevented his coming in first. Jack, too, seemed to avoid him, and was always cross when the competition was mentioned. At last Tim's tender conscience worked him up into such a state of mind that he became quite ill, for worst of all was the harrowing thought that perhaps Jack had known all the time.

Finding how thin and ill he was getting, his grandmother made him stop in bed one day, and seeing the curate of the parish pass she asked him if he would come in and see Tim. The curate, who was a golfer, and Tim's especial patron, willingly complied, and was surprised to see the change in the boy during the last few days. After chatting with him for a little while, he asked if he had anything on his mind, at which Tim burst into tears, and reluctantly confessed the whole of his duplicity. Naturally, the whole tale had to come out, and it transpired that Jack had known perfectly well all the time that he was playing with the wrong ball, and what is more, it turned out, as these things will upon examination, that it was not the first time that he had managed to come in first with the help of a little maneuvering of his own.

The Committee of the Club thought that it was a pity to let the lad continue in the place of his temptation, so they got him a berth at sea, where he proved himself entirely satisfactory. Tim eventually realized the height of his ambition by being apprenticed as a club-maker, and if, as is expected, he becomes a first-class professional, the lesson he learnt as a boy as to the frailty of human nature will not have been wasted.

Golf

Misplaced Modesty

HORACE G. HUTCHINSON

Of course in every match your ultimate success will depend largely upon the terms on which you have arranged to play, before starting. The settling of these conditions is sometimes a nice matter, needing all the wisdom of the serpent in combination with the meekness of the dove. At such times you will perhaps be surprised to hear a person, whom previously you had believed to somewhat overrate his game, now speaking of it in terms of the greatest modesty. These preliminaries once arranged, however, you will find that he soon becomes himself again—till next match making begins.

Hints on Golf

Stay Behind the Ball

HARVEY PENICK

Try to show me a champion who doesn't move his head during his golf swing. You can't do it. Sam Snead comes as close as anyone ever has, but he moves into it too.

However, all these great players move their head slightly backward before and during impact—never forward.

Home-run hitters do the same thing. You'd see Hank Aaron blast one over the scoreboard, and people would say, "He really stayed behind that one."

A golfer also must stay behind the ball.

You couldn't kill a fly with a flyswatter if you lunged your head forward. To get power with a fly swatter you hold your head steady, or pull it back. Byron Nelson dropped his head back nearly a foot coming into the ball.

Before you can stay behind a ball, you must *get* behind it. I mean set up with your head behind the ball and keep your head behind the ball.

If you move your head forward during your downswing or through impact, you will hit a weak, ugly shot, probably a pulled slice.

A student told me about a round of golf he played with Lee Trevino.

On the second tee, a par three, the student hit what he thought was a pretty good shot, about 30 feet short of the pin.

Trevino tossed another ball onto the ground.

"Tee it up and hit again—don't move your head forward this time," Trevino said.

"Lee, I've been trying all my life to stop moving my head forward," the student said. "How can I do it?"

Trevino said, "Read my lips. D-O-N'-T M-O-V-E Y-O-U-R H-E-A-D F-O-R-W-A-R-D. Every time you hit a ball today, I want you to think 'Lee is watching and saying read my lips.'"

The student was deeply impressed. He made another swing, this time without moving his head forward. With an authoritative crack, the ball took off in a slight draw, came down 10 feet past the pin and backed up.

"I have created a monster," Lee said.

The student finished the first nine one under par.

At the turn Lee put his clubs in the trunk of his car and said, "I have to leave now, Frankenstein. Don't forget what I've told you."

I asked the student what happened next.

"By the fourteenth hole my head was moving forward again," he admitted. "I shot my usual forty-one on the back."

Maybe it was the word "don't" that made the suggestion not last long.

A positive way to put it is: *stay behind the ball.*

Harvey Penick's Little Red Book

In any discussion as to the greatest golfer of the past half-century the names of Bob Jones, Ben Hogan and Jack Nicklaus stand alone. To attempt comparison between them, absorbing though it may be, is a purely academic exercise because far too many variables are involved. No man can do more than achieve indisputable supremacy in his own time, and thereby acquire an aura reserved only for those who do something better than anyone else in the world.
Pat Ward-Thomas

Golf Goes On

Arthur Balfour

A tolerable day, a tolerable green, a tolerable opponent, supply, or ought to supply, all that any reasonably constituted human being should require in the way of entertainment. With a fine sea view, and a clear course in front of him, the golfer should find no difficulty in dismissing all worries from his mind, and regarding golf, even it may be indifferent golf, as the true and adequate end of man's existence. Care may sit behind the horseman, she never presumes to walk with the caddie. No inconvenient reminiscences of the ordinary workaday world, no intervals of weariness or monotony interrupt the pleasures of the game. And of what other recreation can this be said? Does a man trust a conversation to occupy his leisure moments? He is at the mercy of fools and bores. Does he put his trust in shooting, hunting, or cricket? Even if he be so fortunately circumstanced as to obtain them in perfection, it will hardly be denied that such moments of pleasure as they can afford are separated by not infrequent intervals of tedium. . . . Moreover, all these games have the demerit of being adapted principally to the season of youth.

Long before middle life is reached, rowing, rackets, fielding at cricket, are a weariness to those who once excelled at them. At thirty-five, when strength and endurance may be at their maximum, the particular elasticity required for these exercises is seriously diminished. The man who has gloried in them as the most precious of his acquirements begins, so far as they are concerned, to grow old; and growing old is not commonly supposed to be so agreeable an operation in itself as to make it advisable to indulge in it more often in a single lifetime that is absolutely necessary. The golfer, on the other hand, is never old until he is decrepit. So long as Providence allows him use of two legs active enough to carry him round the green, and, two arms supple enough to take a 'half swing', there is no reason why his enjoyment in the game need be seriously diminished. Decay no doubt there is; long driving has gone for ever; and something less of firmness and accuracy may be noted even in the short game. But the decay has come by such slow gradations, it has delayed so long, and spared so much, that it is robbed of half its bitterness.

Golf, The Badminton Library

My Caddy

MAURICE NOEL

Who daily comes to meet my trap,
And—touching jerkily his cap—
Seizes umbrella, clubs, and wrap?
    My Caddy.

Who makes a little sandy tee,
And, down upon his bended knee,
Adjusts the Golf-ball carefully?
    My Caddy.

Who, if I make a decent hit,
Is sure to let me hear of it?
Who flatters me a little bit?
    My Caddy.

Who, when the balls erratic fly,
Can always an excuse supply,

"The Stance was bad," or else "the lie"?
      My Caddy.

Who, if to pieces I should fall
And top, and pull and slice the ball,
Knows better than to talk at all?
      My Caddy.

Who, when from hazard blind and bad,
He telegraphs the signal glad—
"All clear," becomes "a clever lad"?
      My Caddy.

But who, if it should come to pass
The ball is lost in whins of grass,
Too frequently becomes "an ass."
      My Caddy.

Who, if I suffer from "a rub,"
Or badly lie in sand and scrub,
Had *better* hand the proper club?
      My Caddy.

Who, when I'm down a hole or two,
Has sometimes all that he can do
A weary task to worry through?
      My Caddy.

Who, though I hurry through the green,
Should ever at my heels be seen,
Attentive, tireless, and keen?
      My Caddy.

Who, when the foe walks proudly in,
Is heard to swear through thick and thin

That luck alone has let him win?
    My Caddy.

Who, ever anxious to defend
My interests from end to end,
Ought to be treated as a friend?
    My Caddy.

Golf

The Links of Leith

TOBIAS SMOLLETT

Hard by, in the fields called the Links, the citizens of Edinburgh divert themselves at a game called Golf, in which they use a curious kind of bats tipped with horn, and small elastic balls of leather, stuffed with feathers, rather less than tennis balls, but of a much harder consistence. These they strike with such force and dexterity from one hole to another, that they will fly to an incredible distance. Of this diversion the Scots are fond, that, when the weather will permit, you may see a multitude of all ranks, from the senator of justice to the lowest tradesman, mingled together, in their shirts, and following the balls with the utmost eagerness. Among others, I was shown one particular set of golfers, the youngest of whom was turned of fourscore. They were all gentlemen of independent fortunes, who had amused themselves with this pastime for the best part of a century, without having ever felt the least alarm from sickness or disgust; and they never went to bed without having each the best part of a gallon of claret in his belly. Such uninterrupted exercise, cooperating with the keen air from the sea, must, without all doubt, keep the appetite on edge, and steel the constitution against all the common attacks of distemper.

The Expedition of Humphrey Clinker

Cooking with Golf Balls

J. D. DUNN

This article is more particularly written for the benefit of golfers in out-of-the-way places where there is no professional or dealer to do the work. And again, some enthusiastic amateurs may come to look upon it as a pleasant pastime for a winter's evening.

Purchase a can of lye, costing fifteen cents. Half a can of lye in a pail of water will take the paint off six dozen balls in about six hours. Ball-makers use a very strong solution of lye, which they put in an apparatus similar to a washing machine. This brings off the paint in short order and does not injure the gutta-percha. Amateurs should stir the balls up in the lye occasionally.

After the balls have been in the lye about six hours, take them out with a vegetable strainer. Place them in some lukewarm water, and then brush off the old paint with a nail-brush.

The balls must now be placed in a pot of water that is almost on the boil. Don't have more or less than half a dozen balls in the pot at one time, and always keep replacing them by others. It is not necessary to let the balls get heated right through. Take the ball out of the pot with a table-spoon and work out the cuts, if any, with your thumb. Roll the ball around in your palms until it is slightly egg-shaped. Do not keep the ball so long in your hands that the outer surface gets cold, or the gutta-percha will not take the impression of the marking. Should the balls be sticky in the hands a little water or linseed oil may be used as a preventive.

When the ball is in the mould squeeze it up in a press. It is not absolutely necessary to have a regular ball press. A book press or vice will do almost as well, and the expedient brings the cost down considerably.

For very little additional cost you can have your initials on the mould. This will save you the trouble of marking your ball before playing in a match, and settles all disputes about ownership.

Allow the ball to remain in the mould about a minute, then put it in a pail of cold water. You can afterwards cut off the "fin" with a sharp knife. On a large scale this is turned off on a machine somewhat like a lathe. The same machine also makes an impression similar to the rest of the marking on the ball. This is not necessary, although it looks better.

The next operation is to paint the ball. This is best done by putting some paint in the palms of one's hands. Rubber gloves may be bought for this work, although they are not nearly so good for the work as the bare skin. The paint does not do any harm and it will wash off easily in warm water. The paint should be put on in four very thin coats. Only the second coat should be rubbed into the marking. After painting, the balls should be stood on a wooden frame to dry.

Bulletin of the USGA

Holes By Accident

George Hibbard

Any golfer playing the average amount, "in his time plays man" shots. He might wish that they were fewer, and the score card did not mount so often toward the hundred point—so often run into a fever heat of disaster above it. But with the best of scores, playing constantly, each player drives, and approaches, and putts a goodly number of times. And when the thousands, and almost hundreds of thousands of present day golfers are taken into account, the strange tales that are told are more readily credible— and golf stories need not necessarily be set down as "fish stories."

In speaking of curious golfing accidents, I have not the intention of speaking of remarkably skillful shots—of the shots that a man remembers with pride for years. I do not wish to say anything of the marvelously accurate work with the lofter, or the putter. These are matters in a certain degree of skill, though in their rarity they might appear matters of accident, or, at least, to be under the control of that tutelar deity of the links—Luck. They are not to be classed with the curious things which happen without the intention of the player.

The following story, which is well-known upon the other side, might be called an example of luck—as it is. Still it is something more, for what happened was not the result of intention, but directly contrary to it. Two golfers in an important match were playing up toward one of the last holes of the course. The man whose turn it was to approach made his shot, and played his ball as near to where the flag was as possible. The ball struck the flag, and bounded off at an angle. When the players came up to the green, they found that the flag was not in the hole, but the ball, in bounding off, had rolled in the direction of the hole and actually rolled into it.

An accident quite as remarkable, and with a touch of that humor which is showing itself ever in this wonderful game, took place in this country. Two well-known players were engaged in a close contest. One of these at an advance hole of the match, was a little down. Both had made equally good drives, but a poor second shot had put the player who was behind with a high board fence between him and the hole. The other man played, and place his ball neatly on the green. He walked onward with all the confidence which comes from lying almost dead, while one's opponent is playing one more in a less advantageous position. suddenly he saw the other ball roll across the grass, and come to rest within a foot of the flag. To play over the fence was almost impossible to do with any accuracy, but his opponent had played and made a poor shot. His ball, however, instead of striking the fence, had passed neatly through a knot hole, and come to rest in a position which enabled him to putt out, winning the hole.

For a long time I believed that the tale of a bird killed by a golf ball was apocryphal.

The first convincing testimony came from the loser of the match last mentioned. A bird had been killed by a golf ball—to his knowledge. And, most remarkable of all, a flying bird by a golf ball also soaring through the air. The driven ball struck the bird fairly, and it fell dead. That there can be no doubt about this, I hasten to give the reasons for my confidence. The fact is attested by a distinguished divine of the Presbyterian Church, and a

Judge of the Court of Appeals of the State of New York, than which, as any one must admit, there could not be better testimony. Usually an historical occurrence does not take place under such fortunate conditions.

Upon the principle of a deluge following a downpour, the writer's mind had no sooner been set at rest upon this hitherto doubtful point, than new proof was added to what was already so satisfactorily proven. With his own eyes he was witness of a golfing accident almost as singular. He was playing a short hole of three hundred and fifteen yards, with the green in a "punch bowl," the hole being in the center of the depression, surrounded by circular enclosing bands. His opponent played with the intention of dropping his ball in the hollow. He topped it, however, and it ran briskly along the ground. As it bounded onward, a number of birds which had been resting in the grass, rose and fluttered upward. At that moment the ball was stopped. The players thought that it had struck a piece of wood, as a dark object was seen to move. Coming up they found, however, that a bird had been hit. The ball had evidently struck the bird on the head, breaking its neck and killing it instantly. The player whose ball had brought down the bird sitting, in this unexpected manner, gave it into the hands of taxidermist. Now in his house it stands to point and adorn another golfing tale.

Speaking of the bird killed on the wing—in a somewhat long golfing experience—the writer has only once seen two balls hit each other in the air. On the links where his happened, the First Hole was parallel with the Home Hole. A ball, sliced by an outgoing player, was hit in mid air by a ball pulled by a player coming in. Both balls broke in wildly different directions, and fell directly to the ground. Fortunately, the matches were not important, or the state of the game critical; as, in spite of the players being friends, the ire which seems so readily excited upon the links might have been aroused, and the eloquence of language, for which golfers are justly celebrated, have quickly followed.

A golfer once met with a singular piece of ill luck when playing the North Berwick Links. He tells the story himself, and even in his own club, where his is known as a most truthful and upright person it was not at first received with the entire confidence which he claimed for it. Knowing the narrator as I do, I have no doubt as to the accuracy and take this occasion to say that I am prepared to believe even a steeper yarn from the same source. As happened, this golfer playing a hole of the famous old Scottish links, and coming up to the place where he thought his ball was, could not find it. He and his caddie searched for some time. Near the line of the course, was an excavation; into this they looked, but could not find what they sought. Looking closer, he saw that a large drain pipe led from the hole. Investigating still more, he discovered, at the opening of the pipe, a trap set to catch some small animal. Examining further, he found that his ball had rolled into the trap, spring it, and was safely held there. Of course he lost the hole.

This might appear to the "Ultima Thule" of golfing credulity—the outer limit to which belief cannot reach. Some might consider it the last straw to break the back of confidence. But as has been said before, the golfer who tells it has never been found wanting.

The present writer and golfer has seen a ball, played out of bounds, fall in a large tin can. The player was obliged to play the tin can. To write that the can was played to the green, and the ball then fell in the hole would be pleasant. As was the fact, however, the ball, when the can was hit, bounded out of it, and was then played in the regular manner.

There are many legends of the links—as mythical as the old Greek Legends, and as wonderful. Perhaps, as was possibly the case with the Greek Legends, there was once in the dim past some foundation of fact, but there has been so much added to me original material, that the facts of the case can no longer be recognized. The story of the man who played a ball into the wool of a sheep on the course, may be true. Things quite as remarkable have happened. That the sheep walked to the green, and shook the ball off on it must be, however, doubted. That something the same story is told of a mythical raven, which picked up the ball and deposited it in the hole, gives the tale more of the true mythical character; the same story often appearing in various changing forms.

However, at the risk of having his own word doubted, the present scribe must relate something which actually happened to himself. He was playing on the private links in the extensive property surrounding one of the famous country houses of the East. In one of the fields through which the course passed, some cows were pastured. Driving from the tee, he saw his ball carry a respectable distance—roll on a little farther—only to be caught up in the mouth of a small calf, which had been feeding a short way off. If he could say that the animal carried the ball on, and dropped in near the flag, the story would be better. Alas, truth compels the statement that the calf, after curveting along for at most a hundred yards, let it fall. Even in its incomplete state—lacking finish and climax— there would be hesitation in advancing this tale if there were not three witnesses whose testimony could be produced on occasion.

Indeed, "The queer things we do, and the queer things we see"—to quote from the popular song once so well-known—in golf are very numerous. A ball that has dropped directly from the tee shot into the four and a quarter inch orifice of an eighty-yard hole, only, however, to bound out again, is a minor happening that may be attested from personal knowledge. And at the same hole —a short shot across an old disused quarry—a strange golfing incident occurred, which, if not an accident, was singular enough to merit narration.

A man who was a scratch player, was giving another man a stroke a hole. The man who was receiving these heavy odds, having won the preceding hole, had the honor and played first. As happened, by wonderful fortune—and this was a curious accident—his ball rolled into the hole in one. The other man had lost the hole before he had played a shot.

The rolling of a ball into a hole in one is not an uncommon enough thing to need particular mention. There are, however, records of such very long holes made in one, that a list of such happenings might very well be place among curious golfing accidents. But every golfer knows of such, or has heard of such.

There is another golfing story having something of the mythical tone, which is yet so possible as to be almost credible. On a very rainy day—upon a very soft and clay covered course—a golfer swung his club down on a ball resting on the side of a bunker. Watching to see the flight of the ball, he saw nothing. Looking at the ground he could not see it. But, happening to notice the head of his club, he saw a large clot of clay clinging to it, in which the ball was imbedded. The story goes on to say that he walked up to the hole, shook the ball out of the clay into it, claimed the hole, and it was given to him. That the first could happen is highly probably, but the climax may be questioned. Still, this is not beyond the bounds of possibility, as far as the Rules are concerned, and with such strange things occurring, if not true, it is *ben trovato.*

As the writer remember what he has written, he is suddenly assailed with certain doubts. either he may seem a person of quite wonderful credulity himself, or else one who seeks to make great demands upon the credulity of others. But, indeed, neither one nor the other is the case. Truth is, in fact, often stranger than fiction, and there is no place where this is more clearly shown than on the golf links.

The illustration which sneers a little at the head of this article may seem to be looking in cynical doubt. But even the illustration itself is a case of a singular accident, the proof of what curious things can happen.

In a mixed foursome, a ball was driven with a top from the tee by a fair but inexperienced golfer. Her partner made a clean shot. Again the lady topped the ball. Her partner played once more, hitting the ball fairly. Once more the lady made a poor shot, the ball, however, rolling on the green. After holing out, the ball was found in the state presented in this illustration, which is a direct photographic reproduction. The three strokes of the fair performer had neatly cut eyes and mouth as well as if it had been done on purpose. That this happened the writer knows, for he was of the foursome. He picked up the ball. He had kept it, and he has it now.

He who has penned these lines asks for charity. That he has not allowed himself to be misled, he hopes. That he has no intention to mislead, he is sure. Indeed, he assures the reader that the most of what he has said may be accepted unquestionably. However, he gives his assurance on his word and honor—and he believes that what he has said proves it—that many strange golfing accidents have happened, and will continue to happen to give even more interest to what is one of the best of honest old games.

The Hands of Fate

HORACE G. HUTCHINSON

If you are one of the many golfers who overrate their game, and, when constantly beaten by those they imagine to be their inferiors, are in the habit of ascribing their ill success to indisposition, the state of the atmosphere, or even to the Government's foreign policy or the spots on the sun, you really must not be surprised at finding some ill-natured persons disposed to accept the issue of a large number of matches as a tolerably conclusive test of your powers, in preference to attributing the result to any agency in the field of politics or astronomy.

Hints on Golf

Golf gives you an insight into human nature, your own as well as your opponent's. Eighteen holes of match or medal play will teach you more about your foe than will 18 years of dealing with him across a desk. A man's true colors will surface quicker in a five-dollar "Nassau" than in any other form of peacetime diversion that I can name.

GRANTLAND RICE

Early Master

BYRON NELSON

Though the Masters was already considered a major tournament in the golf world in '37, none of us had any idea it would get to be as popular as it is today. To think of all these people today trying every way to get tickets, when back then they maybe charged $3 and hardly had enough gallery to count—well, it sure is quite a change. And in most ways I think it's good.

Getting back to that 66, though, it was the best I'd ever played any golf course in my life, tee to green. I hit every par 5 in two, every par 4 in two, and every par 3 in one, for 32 strokes. Add 34 putts to that—pretty average putting, really—and you have an easy 66. I was paired with Paul Runyan that round. He called himself Pauly, and I remember he'd talk to himself quite a bit. "Hit it Pauly," or "Pauly, you sure messed up on that one." But I wasn't really paying a whole lot of attention to him. I was concentrating real well that day. . . .

In the second round, I shot even par 72, and in the third, 75. I'd now lost the lead. In the fourth round, I was still faltering—shot a 38 on the front nine, leaving me three strokes behind Ralph Guldahl. Walking down to the tenth hole, someone in the gallery told me Guldahl had already birdied the tenth. That meant I had to birdie it too, or I'd be 4 back with eight holes to go. I put my second shot on the green about fifteen feet from the hole and made it. I was paired with Wiffy Cox, the pro at Congressional in Washington, D. C. When I sank that putt, he said, "Kid, I think that's the one we needed."

I parred 11, and next was the wonderful, difficult 12th hole, one of the most famous par threes in the country. Rae's Creek runs diagonally across the front of the green—on television, it looks like it's straight across, but it's not. If the pin's on the right, it plays one club longer. And with that Amen Corner wind, it's always a tricky shot, no matter where the pin is.

Standing on the tee, I saw Guldahl drop a ball short of the creek, which meant he'd gone in the water from the tee. If he got on and 2-putted, he'd have a 5. Watching his misfortunes, I suddenly felt like a light bulb went off in my head, like the fellow you see in the cartoons when he gets a brilliant idea. I realized then that if I could get lucky and make a 2, I'd catch up with Guldahl right there. Fortunately, I put my tee shot six feet from the hole with a 6-iron into the wind, and holed it. So now I was caught up, with six holes to go.

The 13th hole is a very famous par 5. I hit a good drive down the center of the fairway, just slightly on the upslope. I saw Ralph fooling around on the front of the green, and learned he'd made a 6. There was water in a ditch that runs just in front of the green, and there were a lot of rocks in it. Once in a while, if your ball landed in the right place, you could play out of it, but that day, Ralph didn't have any luck.

The green then had a real high left side, up on a ridge, making the left side much higher than the right. It's been changed since then. The pin that day was on that high left side. Waiting to play my shot, I knew I'd have to play a 3-wood to reach the green. If I played safe and got on in three I'd probably make a 5, or could even make a 4. That would put me in the lead by one shot, but I knew that wasn't enough. So I said to myself, "The Lord hates a coward," and I simply tried to make sure my ball didn't go off to the right and into the water. I pulled it slightly, and it stopped just off the green, about twenty feet from the hole. I chipped in for a 3, which made me feel pretty good, because I was now three strokes ahead of Ralph.

I parred fourteen, then got on fifteen in 2 and tree-putted for par. Guldahl had made a 4 at fifteen, and we both parred in after that, so I won by two shots, with a 32 on the back nine. That 32 did more for my career at that time than anything, because I realized my game could stand up under pressure, and I could make good decisions in difficult circumstances.

There was no green jacket then, but I got a great thrill out of winning, especially after leading, losing a lead, and finishing strong. The other thing that pleased me was having Bob Jones present me with the gold medal. He was the "King of Golf" then, so that was a real thrill. As I recall, Clifford Roberts and Jones made a few remarks each, and then presented medals to the first- and second-place players. And that was it.

I still have that medal, and when my playing career was over, I looked back and realized that was the most important victory of my career. It was the turning point, the moment when I realized I could be a tough competitor. Whenever someone asks me which was the most important win of all for me, I never hesitate. It was the 1937 Masters, the one that really gave me the confidence in myself.

How I Played the Game

A day spent in a round of strenuous idleness.
WILLIAM WORDSWORTH

Jungle Golf

C. E. Bechhofer Roberts

My uncle was stationed in the Central Provinces. He was the civil magistrate of a small district and, having learned to play golf during his leaves in England, he was keen to keep it up. The nearest course however was about four hundred miles away, and this was rather far for a busy man to go except at week-ends and occasionally in the middle of the week, so he decided to lay out a course of his own.

He enlisted the support of a young subaltern who had just arrived there; they chose a nice bit of jungle only a short ride from town, and, with the assistance of the Government grass-farm superintendent, they laid out a passable nine-hole course.

Anyone who could go round it in seventy strokes and not lose more than half a dozen balls on the fairway had nothing to fear when he came to England and met the scratch men.

The worst drawback was the shortage of players. There were only six or seven other white men in the district, including a German missionary eighty years old, and of these only an elderly major wanted to play. So they were three.

The first week the course was open the Major was mauled in the rough by a tiger that was lying there after a kill. He was looking for his ball, and while knocking the grass aside with his club he inadvertently struck the tiger in the face and woke it. It knocked him senseless with one blow of its paw, and he was rescued only by my uncle running up and shooting the brute with one of the rifles which he had always carried with his clubs for such emergencies.

After this there remained only my uncle and the subaltern, and then the latter went home on leave. So my uncle used to have to play round by himself.

One day he was standing on the seventh tee, which was in a particularly desolate part of the course. It was a blind hole, and he had sent his caddie on ahead to mark the ball.

He was finishing what was perhaps his thirteenth waggle and was just about to take his swing when he suddenly saw something move in the grass some few yards away.

At first he took no notice; he thought probably it was only a baby giraffe or zebra or something of that kind caught in the rough. But it put him off his swing, and he started to waggle again.

Judge of his surprise when, as he was in the middle of his second bout of waggling, the thing in the grass took shape and, as it rose up, he saw that it was an enormous king cobra, the largest snake he had ever seen, nearly thirty feet long, he guessed, from head to tail! It was the most dangerous and bloodthirsty snake in the district and was notorious for having killed as many as eight men—white, black and intermediate—in a single week a little time before.

There was a price on its head, but there were few men bold enough to wish to hunt for it, for it was as cunning as it was murderous.

My uncle thought his last hour had come. The caddie was far ahead along the course with the rifle, and he himself was unarmed.

Out of sheer fright he continued to waggle his club over the ball, glancing out of the corner of his eye at the monster.

Then he noticed with astonishment that the cobra's eyes seemed dulled and that it was swaying rapidly from side to side. Instead of striking at him, the brute continued this extraordinary movement.

Still nervously waggling his club, my uncle tried to think what was the matter with the cobra. Its appearance and behaviour reminded him of something familiar, but he could not remember what it was.

Gaining confidence from the brute's delay, he stopped waggling and prepared to run for his life. But the moment the head of his club grew still the brute's eyes began to clear and a dreadful hungry light blazed up in them. At the same time the swaying of its body ceased and its head drew back for a spring.

Suddenly my uncle knew what he was trying to recall. The dull eyes and swaying body were exactly like those of a charmer's snake when its master has hypnotized it. My uncle realized that the continued waggling of his club had charmed the cobra. That was why it had not struck him.

The only course indicated was to start waggling his club again. Imagine his relief when he saw the hunger begin to fade out of those deadly eyes as the cobra resumed its rhythmical swaying in time with the head of the club! He was saved for the time being.

He dared not call his caddie or do anything that might break the spell he had cast upon the snake. So he stood there waggling, with the animal swaying beside him, its eyes fixed upon the club.

You would think that after a while my uncle's caddie

would have come back to see what was happening and why the ball did not come over. For there was, of course, no question of my uncle's attempting to strike the ball. That would have been fatal. But unfortunately the caddie, an Indian boy of low caste, was new in the game; he reasoned that, if my uncle liked to send him out of his sight to wait for him, it was his duty to stay there until the sahib came.

So my uncle had to stay there waggling and waggling with never a pause or an opportunity to change his position. He did once or twice try to straighten his back, but each time a growing wakefulness in the cobra's eyes warned him to desist.

The afternoon was nearing to a close. He feared that, when dusk fell, the snake would no longer be able to see the head of the club and so would come out of its trance and bite him. Moreover there was no hope of any other player coming along, for the major was still in the hospital and the subaltern in England.

'Is he still there then?' you will ask.

He is not. This was nearly twenty years ago. No, he was saved by a most extraordinary piece of good luck. An Indian cultivator happened to come by just before nightfall, saw what was happening and gave the alarm to the caddie. The latter rushed up with the rifle, leveled it at the cobra and fired. The sideways movement of the beast saved it, but, scared by the shot, it came out of its stupor and rustled away into the long grass. Ten minutes later the sun set and darkness covered the earth.

My uncle was a man of considerable physical strength. But after four or five hours' uninterrupted waggling he was more dead than alive and had to be taken home in an ox-cart and put to bed.

As for the cobra, my uncle killed it in the end. He baited that same tee with a young elephant—the snake was too vicious to be tempted by anything smaller except perhaps a juicy human baby. When it started to devour the bait my uncle shot it dead. Before he skinned it he measured it and found it was thirty-five feet in length, not counting the protruding fangs!

After this terrifying experience my uncle decided to give up golf and take to chess problems.

The Vardon Grip

Harry Vardon

Now comes the all-important consideration of the grip. This is another matter in which the practice of golfers differs greatly, and upon which there has been much controversy. I use what is known as the overlapping grip, believe in it very firmly, and advise every golfer to try to accustom himself to it. It makes the two hands work as one, and the game is far easier and steadier with it. I adopted it only after a careful trial of all the other grips of which I had ever heard, and in my opinion it has contributed materially to the attainment of such skill as I possess. The favour which I accord to my method might be viewed with suspicion if it had been my natural or original grip, which came naturally or accidentally to me which I first began to play as a boy, so many habits that are bad being contracted at this stage and clinging to the player for the rest of his life. But this was not the case, for when I first began to play golf I grasped my club in what was until recently regarded as the orthodox manner, that is to say, across the palms of both hands separately, with both thumbs right round the shaft (or the left one, at all events), and with the joins between the thumbs and first fingers showing like two Vs over the top of the shaft. This is usually described as the two–V grip. Of course it is beyond question that some players achieve very fine results with this grip, but I abandoned it many years ago in favour of one that I consider to be better. My contention is that the overlapping is sounder in theory and easier in practice, tends to make a better stroke and to secure a straighter ball, and that players who adopt it from the beginning will stand a much better chance of driving well at an early stage than if they went in for the old-fashioned two–V. My grip is an overlapping, but not an interlocking one. I use it for all my strokes, and it is only when putting that I vary it in the least, and then the change is so slight as to be scarcely noticeable.

It will be seen at once that I do not grasp the club across the palm of either hand. The club being taken in the left hand first, the shaft passes from the knuckle joint of the first finger across the ball of the second. The left thumb lies straight down the shaft—but the following are the significant features of the grip. The right hand is brought up so high that the palm of it covers over the left thumb, leaving very little of the latter to be seen. The firs and second fingers of the right hand just reach round to the thumb of the left, and the third finger completes the overlapping process, so that the club is held in the grip as if it were a vice. The little finger of the right hand rides on the first finger of the left. The great advantage of this grip is that both hands feel and act like one, and if, even while sitting in his chair, a player who has never tried it before will take a stick in his hands in the manner I have described, he must at once be convinced that there is a great deal in what I say for it.

The Complete Golfer

Spoons, Niblicks and Stymies

ANON

What chess is to draughts, what billiards is to bagatelle, what cricket is to trap-and-ball, so is golf to hockey. It is a game of skill, judgment, and science. It takes the player to breezy moors and healthful commons; it exhilarates without fatiguing him.

I well remember that inspiring day when I accompanied those two friends, members of the renowned and ancient club of St. Andrews, to witness their sport and to receive a few practical lessons on the art of avoiding hazards and getting out of a bunker. I well remember the smile of the attendant caddie as I swung the play-club as if I was going to send the ball the famed ten score yards, and only succeeded in "topping" it after all. It requires practice and patience to acquire the "far and sure" stroke which is the motto of the best golf players.

Come, then, to the sandy links, as they are called. Their fellows in England are the undulating downs and grassy commons, a plain of fine green turf, diversified by knolls, furze-bushes, tufts of grass, hollows, and, maybe, car ruts or pools of water. These form on any golfer's parlance hazards, which are to be avoided if possible. The caddie is but the Scotch term for club bearer, and he carries the somewhat miscellaneous appliances which the game demands.

Before, however, the game can be understood, some idea must be formed of the implements with which the game is played.

The Ball is made of gutta-percha, about two inches in diameter, and painted white, so as to be easily seen. Formerly it was made of leather, stuffed hard with feathers. The price is about a shilling.

The Clubs are, however, the most important portion of the golfer's outfit. They are as various as the days in the week, and no good player would begin without a set of at least half a dozen. A fastidious player on an unknown ground would at least have half as many more, and would display with pride his (1) *play-club*, (2) *long spoon*, (3) mid-spoon, (4) *short spoon*, (5) baffing-spoon, (6) driving-putter, (7) *putter*, (8) *sand-iron*, (9) *cleek*, (10) *niblick*, or track-iron. Those most useful in ordinary play are printed in italics: indeed, the ground must be very difficult and full of hazards to require them all.

These clubs—for they all come under that generic name—are put to a variety of uses. The play-club is used for swiping, or driving the ball off the tee at the commencement of a game.

If the ball rests on a hollow, amidst rough grass or on uneven ground, then the long spoon is used. The mid-spoon is used for the same purpose, for short distances only. When near the hole, the short spoon comes into play: indeed it and the shorter baffing-spoon are used to elevate the ball for short distances only. As the cleek answers the purpose of the latter, it is generally used in preference.

The putter is more like a club that the croquet-player would appreciate, for it comes into use when the ball lies on the putting-green within, say, eighteen or twenty yards of the hole.

If the player could insure the ball falling in pleasant green places, the foregoing clubs would suffice; but balls will fall at times in bunkers, as sand-holes are called, or fall in the whin-bushes, among the rushes and long bents, or among the rough stones of a road. Then the sand-iron is required.

The cleek is useful for driving balls over intervening obstacles lying between the ball and the hole near the putting-green. The niblick, sometimes called the track-iron is used to drive the balls from deep hollows, cart-ruts, or from among the stiff coarse stems of the furze or whin-bushes.

On reaching your ball, if it lies on the open turf, you may repeat the long swipe with advantage if you are not too ambitious. If in a sand-hole, you will require your sand-iron, if in a hollow of the turf, the long spoon; if in a rut, the niblick. You will find the bunker, or sand-hole, a hazard to be avoided rather than courted. It will require patience and perseverance ere the ball can be driven from its snug retreat on to the turf at one stroke.

At length your ball lies on the green itself, and the hole is temptingly near. You now want judgment and nicety of touch. You have to consider, not only the distance between your ball and the hole, but the possibility of a stymie.

A stymie is an ugly affair for a beginner, and it occurs when your antagonist's ball lies in a direct line between your hole and the ball, so that putting is out of the question. There is no other course open but to take the sand-iron and "loft" your ball over the stymie into the hole if you can. Stymies are sometimes play purposely, but it is not considered exactly fair to play them; but, whether played purposely or not, they often occur, and the young player should practice "lofting" with a view to overcoming stymies when they occur. Even without this obstruction, he has to consider the necessary strength to drive his ball safely in. He must also consider the nature of the intervening ground, whether up-hill or otherwise, and the best way of overcoming the difficulty.

"To putt" well ought to be the aim of every beginner; and, as he can practice it on any greensward, it is his own fault if he does not succeed.

The Game of Golf

Why Women Should Play Golf

SANDRA HAYNIE

No two people are built exactly alike. Some people are long-legged and others have short legs with a long trunk. It's the same way with feet; the shoe size may be the same, but each person has a distinctive walk, a way of putting her feet down that sets her off as an individual.

Warren Cantrell, the first golf teacher I had, used to say that he could tell whether a person is a golfer by the way he or she walks toward him. There are other people who say that they can tell policemen, ex-fighters, wrestlers, mailmen, etc., by the way they walk, but I'm not one of them. I say regardless of how you walk, you can learn to play golf naturally and easily without accepting dogma or following rules that will make you uncomfortable or self-conscious.

Besides being the director of golf for the city of Lubbock, Texas, Warren Cantrell is a professional engineer and builder. Perhaps his training as an engineer gives him an insight into planes of motion and stresses that escapes other people, but at any rate I guess that I owe my start to golf to him.

One day, when I was eleven years old, I accompanied my father to the golf course. Dad was a very good amateur player and he was getting some instructions from Warren on the practice tee when I walked up to see what was going on.

"Do you know that girl?" Warren asked my father. Later he said that my walk had fulfilled all the requirements of a potential golfer—balance, ease and natural grace.

"That's my daughter, Sandra Jane," Dad said. "Sandy, come over here and say hello to Mr. Cantrell."

"Do you mind if she hits a few balls for me?" Warren asked, interested, I guess, in testing his theory.

"Not at all, go right ahead," Dad said. "I'll meet you back in the clubhouse." I guess he didn't want to be embarrassed, but at any rate he left.

Warren gave me an old No. 6 iron and 30 practice balls. I had watched Dad and the golfers around the course quite a bit, so I just did what was natural for me. I hit the balls, and Warren's eyes seemed to become bigger as I went through the whole lot without a miss. Usually, I found out later, even good golfers muff a shot or two when they are practicing. That convinced Warren that his instant analysis was right and he spent 45 minutes with me before rejoining Dad in the clubhouse. He left me on the practice tee and I continued to hit with that old No. 6 iron. Even today, the iron game is my strong point and I often wonder if that groove wasn't established the first time I picked up a club.

A Natural Course for Women

The Appliance of Science

At an ordinary meeting of the Royal Society of Edinburgh, held on June 5th, Professor Sir Douglas MacLagan presiding, Professor Tait read a paper on the "Approximate determination of the path of a rotating spherical projectile," The point which he discussed, and which he demonstrated by means of a model, was that a rotating spherical body moving through the air is deflected in the direction towards which its front rotates. Thus if a ball is thrown to a distance, with a rotary motion along a vertical axis in the direction of the hands watch, the ball, instead of following a strait path, will curve away to the right, the explanation being…same initial velocity, but with a slight amount of rotation, the range of the ball, at a tangent of one in four, would be about 500 feet, and at a tangent of one in eighty over 400 feet.

Finally, if they gave a large amount of rotation, and started the ball with an initial velocity of 400 feet per second, at a tangent of one to eight, it would, at the outset of its flight, follow a path which was concave up, and reach its greatest height at a distance of three-fourths of its total range, dropping with greater amount of inclination at a distance from the starting point of about 560 feet. If it were started off without any inclination at all, it would gradually achieve a height, and have a range of 520 feet. In reply to Lord M'Laren, Professor Tait said that his impression was that the rotation of the ball was only slightly diminished in the course of its flight, and after landing it might still be seen spinning with extreme rapidity.

Golf

The Putt

A. J. BALFOUR

While, on the whole, playing through the green is the part of the game most trying to the temper, putting is the most trying to the nerves. There is always hope that a bad drive may be redeemed by a fine approach shot, or that a "foozle" with the brassy may be balanced by some brilliant performance with the iron. But when the stage of putting-out has been reached, no further illusions are possible—no place for repentance remains: to succeed in such a case is to win the hole; to fail, is to lose it. Moreover, it constantly happens that the decisive stroke has to be made precisely at a distance from the hole such that, while success is neither certain nor glorious, failure is not only disastrous but ignominious. A putt of a club's length which is to determine not merely the hole but the match will try the calmness even of an experienced performer, and many there are who have played golf all their lives whose pulse beats quicker when they have to play the stroke. No slave ever scanned the expression of a tyrannical master with half the miserable anxiety with which the performer surveys the ground over which the hole is to be approached. He looks at the hole from the ball, and he looks at the ball from the hole. No blade of grass, no scarcely perceptible inclination of the surface, escapes his critical inspection. He puts off the decisive moment as long, and perhaps longer, than he decently can.

If he be a man who dreads responsibility, he asks the advice of his caddie, of his partner, and of his partner's caddie, so that the particular method in which he proposes to approach the hole represents not so much his own individual policy as the policy of a Cabinet. At last the stroke is made, and immediately all tongues are loosened. The slowly advancing ball is addressed in tones of menace or entreaty by the surrounding players. It is requested to go on or stop; to turn this way or that, as the respective interests of each party require. Nor is there anything more entertaining than seeing half a dozen faces bending over this little bit of moving gutta-percha which so remorselessly obeys the laws of dynamics, and pouring out on it threatenings and supplications not to be surpassed in apparent fervour by the devotions of any fetish worshippers in existence.

Golf

In golf the contest is not with your fellowman.
The foe in golf is not your opponent,
but great Nature herself, and the game is to see who will
overreach her better, you or your opponent.
In almost all other games you pit yourself against a mortal foe;
in golf it is yourself against the world, no human being
stays your progress as you drive your ball over the face of the globe.
It is very like life in this, is golf. Life is not an internecine strife.
We are all here fighting, not against each other for our lives,
but against Nature for our livelihoods.

ARNOLD HAULTAIN

Summer Golf in Georgia

Berry Fleming

I used to think that golf was played in the same general way the world over, I admitted, of course, that there would probably be a few local rules in Siberia that wouldn't apply in Philippines, but I thought that there would always be holes and balls and clubs, and that any group of people would be satisfied with that and play the game pretty much as it was played anywhere else.

But golf is a different game in Georgia. While it includes the game played by the rest of the world it adds to it several other fundamental pleasures. The cause of the difference is undoubtedly the climate.

Last year Will and I, having met a gentleman from Georgia who was passing through New York on the way to Europe, and having learned from him that Georgia in the summer-time was the pleasantest place in the known world, decided to go there in August and dry out.

'Isn't it terribly hot?' Will asked him.

'It's hot, sir,' said the gentleman from Georgia, 'but you don't notice it.'

We didn't understand this for a long time; indeed our eagerness to understand it was one of the reasons we went to Georgia.

When we got there Georgia was dry. They hadn't seen rain down there since the hot weather had set in, and the hot weather had set in so long before that nobody seemed to have any recollection of a time when the hot weather had not been in. It was, of course, the hottest weather they had had in twenty years; the State appeared to be located that year close to the edge of the Gulf Stream and about three miles north of the Equator, and the temperature struggled continually to get into three figures, and not infrequently got there. It was so hot that all my joints seemed to have been too profusely lubricated and my knees tended, without warning, to bend in any direction whatever. It was not the sort of weather that I like to use for golf.

Will said he understood perfectly how I felt, but we had encountered again the irresistible force of Southern hospitality and there was nothing to do but give way.

We met our three hosts at the Country Club at four o'clock in the afternoon. (The hottest section of the day in these parts is supposed to be near three o'clock, but this is about an hour and a half or two hours fast, though it takes a person of keen sensibilities to note the error.) They were garbed in wide linen trousers which, back in those days before the hot weather had set in, had probably been white, shirts with the collars open and the sleeves torn off above the elbow and cork helmets. When one of the gentlemen sat down I noticed that he had neglected to put the customary garments between himself and his shoes; but the other two gentlemen had neglected it too, and I thought I began to understand.

Will and I wore white knickerbockers and coats. We had planned to take off the coats, but our hosts would not hear of such minor modification; they took us into the locker-room and shouted for 'Robert'. Robert was told to see if he couldn't run down some suitable clothes for these gentlemen. He returned in a few minutes, having run down a pair of thin trousers, a helmet and the principal parts of a shirt for each of us.

One of our solicitous hosts was known to his friends as Colonel Dan. He had one of those non-committal figures which if seen without feet or head would seem to lead in both directions. He was standing by when Will began to put on the shirt Robert had brought him.

'Sakes, sir,' said the Colonel, 'you ain't going to wear an undershirt, are you?'

So we left off our undershirts. In fact when we walked out on the first tee we were clad in five pieces of clothes, counting our shoes as two pieces and our helmets as one.

We drove five balls in the general direction of the fairway and set out. I had seen a large black cloud of caddies overshadowing the first tee, but I rather thought they had come down as a compliment to Will and me and paid no attention to them. Half-way to the hole I looked back; they were following us. I counted nine of them. They were laden in a peculiar way: five of them carried the bags as usual in a fivesome, but the others carried thermos bottles, umbrellas, glasses, boxes, towels, buckets and such things, and Colonel Dan's caddie carried a large palmetto fan.

'We are apparently going to spend the night,' I remarked to Will.

Will said he hoped they hadn't brought a radio set.

The second hole took us off down a hill into the heart of a pine forest. We played our second shots towards the green, then Colonel Dan said, 'We gen'ally rest a bit here, gentlemen.' This was to Will and me, for the other players had already thrown their clubs to the caddies and were walking towards the shade of the pine-trees. The four caddies carrying the thermos bottles, umbrellas, glasses, boxes, towels, buckets and so forth went to the side of a small spring and unloaded themselves. The other caddies sauntered towards the green and picked up our balls.

'Now, gentlemen,' said Colonel Dan, sitting down on the grass and casting aside his helmet, 'what'll you have? Here, Mule, open the White Rock. Gentlemen you can have Scotch or Rye. Crack us a little ice, Boll-weevil.'

'How long are you going to be down?' one of the other golfers asked Will.

'Probably all summer,' said Will.

'Half an hour later towels were passed round and we left the caddies at the spring and walked slowly through the pines for about a hundred yards. There we came suddenly upon a new explanation of why we wore only five pieces of clothing, counting our shoes as two pieces; it was a small pool of water with a sandy bottom.

'Is this the third hole?' asked Will.

'Yes, sir,' said Colonel Dan, 'at the third hole we have a water-hazard. But you can go in without penalty.'

'I don't want to lose my ball,' said Will, looking back towards the spring where the bottles were.

'There's plenty more where that one came from,' said Colonel Dan.

And such pleasantries.

When we got back to the spring the sun had dropped behind the trees.

'Let's have that box of cigars, Boll-weevil,' said the Colonel, and he passed them round. 'Now, gentlemen, if you had Scotch and Rye before, you'd better have Rye and Scotch after, just to undo whatever ill effects you may have suffered.'

This sounded logical and we followed his advice.

But it didn't seem to help Will any, and he tried to

undo the ill effects with two of Scotch. After this he asked the Colonel how far it was back to the club-house.

'Over three hundred yards,' said the Colonel.

'I believe a good man could jump that far,' said Will.

'I doubt it,' said the Colonel, 'it's farther than it looks; we'll have to ride. My car will be here at six-forty-five.'

'Well,' said Will, 'just to do what I can towards lightening the load of those tired caddies—'

'Exactly, sir,' said the Colonel. 'Mule, that bottle of White Rock.'

When the car came the caddies were loaded with the empty equipment and sent back on foot; we climbed into the seats and drove slowly back through the woods.

On arriving at the Club Will told the Colonel that he had never enjoyed a game of golf so much in his life.

'It's a good game,' said the Colonel. 'That element of uncertainty in it is what fascinates us.'

'Yes,' said Will,'and it gets you out into the open air. We'd like to challenge you to a return match.'

'Delighted,' said the Colonel.

And so it was arranged.

Fatalists and Optimists

H.S.C. EVERARD

[In golf] a sneaking belief in fatalism is not to be reprehended; everybody lays approaches dead, or holes good putts sometimes; and if they are destined for you today, so much the better; that is not a bad frame of mind; better this than trying for something which may land you in disaster; for, as Sir Walter Simpson aptly says: "Your forcing shot sends the ball from bad to worse, and what might have been won in five is lost in seven. A secret disbelief in the enemy's play is very useful for match play." To persevere while there is a shadow of hope is of course necessary, though in the interests of players who may be waiting behind it is not desirable to carry it to an extreme, as in an instance within the writer's knowledge. The match was a foursome; one side were well on towards the hole, and lying clear; and the others were in hopeless trouble, in a cross ditch, against a high turf bank. After strokes numerous as blackberries in autumn, it occurred to one partner that the time had arrived when, as far as that hole was concerned, they might as well accept the inevitable. "Hadn't we better pick up," he said, "we've played nine more." "Not a bit," was the unexpected answer, "we'll make it up on the green."

Golf in Theory and Practice

Bicycle Skirts and Sailor Hats

E. M. Boys

There are some members of all three classes who bring lady golfers into ridicule by wearing as 'mannish' clothes as possible. They are to be seen with soft hunting ties, loose red shapeless coats, and the shortest and narrowest of bicycling skirts. Why bicycling skirts for golf? the reader may be moved to ask. Why, indeed? After giving the subject much thought, the only obvious explanation is that bicycling skirts are made to open at the sides, and are thus very adaptable for side pockets.

I must endeavor to draw a thumb-nail sketch of a golfer of this description attired in complete armour.

Her hair is dragged up into a knot on the top of her head, on to which a man's cap is fixed (how, is not apparent); underneath is a tan-coloured face, from constant exposure to the elements without any of the protection which an ordinary sailor hat affords. A soft white hunting tie, fastened with a pin (an emblem of the game in some form or other), a loose red coat and a narrow bicycling skirt, into the pockets of which the wearer rams both hands when they are not required for golfing purposes; then, as a fitting climax, a pair of thick, clumsily made boots. It is needless to add that the attitudes and manners are quite as 'mannish' as the clothes.

Now, as no picture of this kind can be thoroughly appreciated without its antithesis, let me draw another. A neat sailor hat, surmounting a head 'beautifully coiffeured,' every hair of which is in its place at the end of the round. A smart tight-fitting red coat, a spotless linen collar and tie, an ordinary tailor-made skirt, and a pair of well-made walking boots with nails in the soles.

Golf is by this time as much a woman's game as a man's, and ladies can and do look perfectly graceful when playing the game as it ought to be played. Let us all, then, take pride in raising golf as a game over our own, rather than in depreciating it ourselves, by making it appear as if we were merely imitating man.

> To play at golf beneath the sea,
> Is just as hard as it can be.
> One cannot put, or drive, or tee
> With very much facility;
> The hazards are so hard you see.

Badminton Magazine

Long-Winded Winners

HORACE G. HUTCHINSON

Never, if you can possibly help it, allow yourself to be beaten by a man from whom you generally win. If you do so, you are likely to find that this one particular round, which appears to you of such peculiarly little importance, is more talked of by your opponent than the score or so of matches in which you have previously defeated him.

Hints on Golf

Tommy's Master-Stroke

RALPH HENRY BARBOUR

Tommy was feeling sore. Dickie had beaten him badly that afternoon and Tommy didn't like being beaten at golf, especially by Dickie. Tommy—Tommy Winslow, you know—is quite a dab at golf; he won from Travis once at Garden City; the Duke says Travis wasn't feeling well that day, but Tommy denies it. Dickie isn't much at the game; I downed him once myself, and I'm considered about as rotten as they make 'em. That's what made Tommy rather hot; that and the way Dickie rubbed it in. Tommy's the best-natured chap in the world, but Dickie Boswell was certainly beastly exasperating that night.

We were sitting around in the Duke's room drinking mint juleps. We were all in our pajamas, for it was an awfully warm night; when it *is* hot at Island Lake, it's— worse than that We'd all four of us been up there three days, staying at the Medford Arms, the big, long hotel on the hill back of the links; you know the joint I mean, the one with the big verandah all around it and red chimneys sticking up here and there through the roof. The boy had just brought up fresh drinks, and we were smoking the last of my Egyptians.

"You see, Tommy, it was that long drive to the tenth hole that queered you, my boy." Dickie took a straw out of his glass and swept it through the air.

"Here, quit sprinkling me with juice!" growled the Duke. He isn't really a duke, you know. That's just his nickname; his real name's Hastings.

"I made the tenth in two and you took four," continued Dickie. "If it hadn't been for that you might have done better, Tommy. It was my master-stroke that beat you."

"Master-stroke be blowed," sputtered Tommy. "It was a bally fluke, that's what it was!"

"That's envy speaking," replied Dickie, wagging his head sadly, "that's not you Tommy."

"Bally fluke, I said!" reiterated Tommy, sitting up suddenly and spilling his julep on the pillow. "Why, you were the worst surprised man in the country when you found you'd hit the ball! It was the first clean swipe you'd made; you'd been topping and slicing all afternoon! Master-stroke—!" Tommy gulped—"master-stroke thunder!"

"Then how did I happen to beat you?" asked Dickie sweetly.

"Fool luck!" cried Tommy. "You had fool luck all the way; no one can win against luck! But I'll play you tomorrow for any money you like and give you a handicap; that's what I'll do!"

"Cut it out, you two," groaned the Duke, nibbling his orange peel and looking disgusted. "Neither of you really knows a golf ball from a hen's egg."

"I'll take you," Dickie cried, "but I don't want your handicap. I'll play you for fifty a side going out and fifty more coming back! And what's the good of waiting until to-morrow? I'll play you right now, Tommy!"

"Ah, that's a sporting proposition for you," said the Duke, looking interested. "Annie, see if Bill the moon's up."

I slid off the bed and went to the window.

"No, darker than Egypt; you couldn't see a ball ten feet away."

"Hard luck," said the Duke, going back to his julep. "I suppose, though, we might get lanterns," he added grinning.

"Poppycock!" said Dickie. He was silent a minute, but the light battle still shone in his eyes.

"Just wait until to-morrow," threatened Tommy, "and I'll give you a chance to make all the master-strokes you want!"

"I'll tell you what I'll do with you, little Tommy," cried Dickie explosively, "I'll play you from here to the office for fifty dollars a side, loser to pay for damages!"

Tommy stared; then he put his glass on the floor and dropped his cigarette into it.

"Done!" he said; The Duke applauded loudly.

"But isn't it a bit late?" I ventured.

"Late nothing," said Dickie, "it's only half-past eleven. What if it is late?"

"The halls are dark, aren't they?"

"Well, we'll light 'em up then."

"Now, hold on," said the Duke, "let's understand this proposition. I'll act as referee. You're to play from here to the office; the one holding out in the least number of strokes wins the match and takes the money; is that it?"

"Yes," chimed Tommy and Dickie.

"All right. And if you lose a ball you may drop another, eh? And the loser's to put up for breakage. Where are you going to hole out?"

We all thought intensely; at least I did. Finally I said:

"The ink-well on the office desk!"

"Good eye!" said the Duke. "Only we'll have to put it on the floor. Anise-seed, you be caddie."

My name is Annismead; but nobody ever calls me that; it's generally Annie, sometimes Anise-seed; that's the trouble with having a name that sounds like something else. I got the clubs and the Duke armed himself with a rule book.

"This match is going to be played right," he said.

Dickie put a bath gown on and so did I; but Tommy and the Duke said it was too warm. So Tommy got into a red golf jacket with green sleeves, and the Duke went in his pajamas. We went out into the hall and Tommy teed. Our rooms were about twelve feet broad, but there were more than twenty trunks between us and the first corner, and that made it difficult. Tommy got away with a long, low drive that put the ball pretty near the full length of the hall and beyond the turn. Dickie followed and went high, rolling behind a big trunk.

"You'll need a lofter to get out of there," chuckled the Duke. But Dickie swore a little and got back onto the carpet in three. The carpet, by the way, was green, and the Duke said that helped out the illusion. On the next stroke Dickie banged the ball against the door of Number 68 and it flew behind another trunk.

"Well, aren't you coming?" jeered Tommy, who was sticking his head out around the corner.

Dickie swore more and pushed his ball out into the

open, the Duke pretending not to see. Then he banged away at it again and got a good lie just where the hallway turned toward the stairs. Tommy had to make a short approach here, and the score was 2 to 5. From the corner to the stairway was about twenty yards and Dickie called for a wooden putter. He had fine luck and landed right at the head of the stairs. Tommy got his ball about half way, when it rolled up onto a door sill. It took him three to get it away again. Of course, he banged the door a good deal, and pretty soon it opened and a man's head popped out.

"What in thunder's the row?" he asked calmly.

But Tommy was swinging for his next stroke and so we merely told him to shut up. He came out into the hall then and looked on. Tommy's ball rolled against the banisters.

"A good lie, Tommy, my boy," said the Duke. I took up the two bags and started after.

"Say, what's up?" asked the man we had disturbed. I told him; match for fifty a side to the office ink-well.

"Good stuff," said he; and went in and put on a bathrobe. When he returned he brought cigarettes and we all lighted up, all except Tommy; he said he never smoked while playing; it was bad for the wind. We were making a good deal of a rumpus, I fancy, about this time; anyhow, doors began to open and people put their heads out and asked silly questions. One old lady wanted to know if it was a fire. We told her no, it was golf, and she went back to bed. But a chap down the hall yelled up to ask if we thought that was a links, and the Duke said:

"Sure, Bill; don't you see the green?" He pointed to the carpet and we all laughed; and the man swore a lot and threatened to have us put out of the house. We could hear the bell ringing down in the lower hall and pretty soon a bellboy came crawling up stairs. The Duke caught him half way up.

"Nothing doing, Bill," he said. "Go back to sleep and tell me about it in the morning when I have money with me."

The boy said "Yes, sir," and went back.

A young chap whose room was at the head of the stairway looked on for awhile and then crawled into a box coat and joined us. It was Dickie's play and he dropped his ball neatly down onto the first landing. Tommy followed and did better yet, for his ball went to that landing and then rolled half way down the next. But Dickie was after him and reached the next floor below in one. The score was 8 all. The chap in the bath robe and the one in the box coat made a wager of ten dollars a side, the bath robe taking Tommy and the box coat Dickie.

Tommy had a lot of trouble finishing the flight and reaching the second floor; when he got a good lie close to the banisters at the head of the next flight the score was 8 to 11 in favor of Dickie, and Tommy was swearing like a trooper.

"I'll raise the stakes another fifty," said Dickie, grinning.

"Take you," said Tommy, like a little man.

"Can't be done," the Duke said. "But you can make a side bet." So they did; and the ink-well meant a hundred to the one who made it in the best score. The excitement was getting intense. Doors were opening and closing all over the shop and bells were ringing and folks were asking what in something was up. We told them the truth, but, generally, they didn't believe it and had to come and see for themselves. So pretty soon we had about a dozen spectators, all making suggestions and laying wagers. Dickie was a prime favorite now and the best odds were ten dollars to six; I took some of that myself, getting the Tommy end without trouble. You see, I knew that Tommy was better at putting than Dickie and knew besides that he was feeling sore about the "master-stroke" and was resolved to win out. About that time the man in the bath robe began backing Tommy for all he could get. He laid about fifty dollars and then took Tommy aside and whispered to him. No one noticed it except me, I fancy, for the rest of the bunch was watching Dickie. The bellboy crawled upstairs again and said he was going to rooms 28, 36, 42, 61, and a lot more. We sent him back for ice water; told him the occupants of the rooms were thirsty, and promised him a dollar if he'd take twenty minutes to get it. He was a sensible kid and did it.

Dickie slammed his ball hard with the idea of hitting the wall at the turn and rolling. But it didn't work and he got no farther than the first landing. Downstairs some one was thumping the office gong to beat the symphony orchestra and a stout, baldheaded man on the floor above was dancing up and down and talking a blue streak. We told him to go back to bed and be good, but he wouldn't; wanted to know how in smoke he could sleep with a lot of damphools raising Ned around the place. The Duke told him that he didn't know what the answer was and offered to lay him two to one in fivers that there wasn't any. The baldheaded chap was a sport all through and took the Duke for twenty. That calmed him down and he sat at the top of the stairs and tried to think what the answer was.

The score was 9 to 11 now, and Tommy's play. His

gutty was right alongside the railing. He took an iron putter and gave the ball a little tap that sent it between the spindles and down the well; we heard it hit the floor below and bounce around. Everybody stared; everybody except the bath robe chap; he grinned; so did every one else after a moment; everybody except Dickie.

"You can drop another ball there, you know," he said to Tommy. Tommy shook his head.

"No, thanks," he replied sweetly.

"But you have to!"

"Not a bit of it, Dickie; it's your play."

"What—what—?" Dickie stuttered.

"It's all right," answered Tommy; "that's my masterstroke."

"But you can't do that!" shouted Dickie. "I'll leave it to the Duke! He can't do that, can he, Duke?"

The Duke opened his rule book and stood under the light, pretending to search the pages. Everybody was laughing except Dickie, and Tommy, and the Duke. Dickie was frothing at the mouth; Tommy was merely grinning pleasantly; the Duke was frowning while he turned the leaves. Finally he said:

"There appears to be no rule bearing on the point of dispute. It is very thoughtless of the committee, but it can't be helped. As there is nothing forbidding the play, I presume it to be allowable, and so decide."

We all howled, and Dickie ranted and went on terribly. But we shut him up and the play went on. Dickie was mad clean through, and as a result he slammed around for five minutes. Of course, he followed Tommy's example and dropped his ball down the well, but he had a lot of trouble getting it through between the spindles, and when he did the score was in Tommy's favor, 12 to

13. The Dickie chaps tried to hedge, but there was nothing much doing. We all trooped down the last flight and met a sleepy-looking man in his shirt sleeves who said he was the night clerk and what was the trouble?

We explained the matter to him at some length, as he was a very dense sort of chap; and even when he got it through his head he tried to make objections; said we were disturbing the whole house and a lot of poppycock like that. But the duke called him "dear Bill," and smoothed him down, and we went on. The two balls were lying side by side between the stairs and the elevator. No one knew which was which, but, as the Duke pointed out, it didn't matter. From there to the desk was about sixty feet. We got the ink-well down and placed if half way between the desk and the other side of the lobby and built up around it with the register and a lot of cards, blotters, and paper. The night clerk turned in and helped and proved to be a very accommodating sort. When we had finished we had a very decent hole.

Tommy got to work with a putter and rolled his ball to within ten feet. Dickie managed a better lie, a foot or so nearer, and where he had a nice ascent to the ink-well by way of the blotting papers. Then we all made a big circle around the two and watched. The night clerk wanted to pour the ink out of the well first; said it might get on the floor. But we reminded him of the blotting papers and refused to have the green disturbed.

The score was 13 to 14 in favor of Tommy. Every one smoked hard. The annunciator began to buzz again, so the night clerk went over and did something to it. Dickie was viley nervous and on the first put went two feet wide, and swore.

"Better make that in two and be sure of holing,"

some one suggested. But Dickie thought he couldn't spare two and tried again from a distance of about four feet. The ball started up the ascent all right but was stopped by the edge of the register, about six inches from the ink-well.

"Sixteen," said the Duke.

Dickie straddled the book and blotters and things and shortened his grip. "Remarkable stance, eh?" murmured the chap in the box coat. Then the ball rolled and the ink spurted out.

"Seventeen," said the Duke; and every one clapped loudly.

Dickie fished the gutty out of the ink-well with a toothpick and stood aside, watching Tommy anxiously. Tommy went to work very carefully, picking a piece of lint out of the path and finding the line by means of a dark spot in one of the oak boards. Then he tapped the ball gently and it rolled straight for the hole. Every one held his breath. When the ball reached the foot of the little hill it was going so slowly that it didn't seem as though it could get half way toward the top. But it did; it went over the strewn cards and made the writing paper, going slower and slower, seeming always on the point of stopping but not doing it. Straight for the ink-well it rolled and right on the very edge came to a pause. Tommy went forward to drop it in when, presto, over it went of itself!

Then every one clapped and shouted and shook hands with Tommy. Dickie was feeling pretty well cut up, but there's nothing mean about him, so up he marched with the rest of them. Tommy shook hands and clapped him on the shoulder.

"It was that master-stroke of mine beat you, Dickie," he said grinning.

"The match goes to Mr. Winslow," announced the Duke, "the score, 14 to 17." Then we all cheered some more, and the chap in the bath gown went over and talked to the night clerk. At first the latter shook his head; but in the end he led the way down the corridor.

"Gentlemen," said the bath robe chap, "we are going to have liquid refreshments in honor of the victor in the most unique golf match of history. After you, gentlemen!"

So we all trooped into the bar and turned on the lights and sat around in pajamas and dressing gowns and blankets and drank Tommy's health. And just when the bath robe chap, who had won about ninety dollars, had finished a speech of congratulation the door was quietly opened and in walked the old codger with the bald head.

"Hello, Bill," said Duke, "you're just in time."

"Thank you, with all the pleasure in the world," said the other. "And I'll thank you, too, for that twenty, sir."

"Which twenty is that?" asked the Duke, who had forgotten the wager.

"Why, sir, you bet me twenty to ten that there was no answer to the question."

"What question, Bill?"

"The question, sir, as nearly as I recall it was this: How in blazes can I sleep while a lot of damned idiots are raising Ned in the corridors?"

"Ah, to be sure," replied the Duke. "I recollect. And there is an answer?"

"Yes, sir, and I have found it."

"And what is it?"

"The answer, sir," replied the old chap soberly, "is, Take a narcotic!"

"The money is yours, Bill," answered the Duke laughing. "Now have a drink."

The old chap joined us, and the night clerk opened some more bottles. When the glasses were filled the Duke got up.

"Gentlemen, to the Master-Stroke!"

We drank standing.

Hall of Fame

LEE TREVINO

When I was inducted into the World Golf Hall of Fame in September 1981 I passed another milestone. Now I know that someday I can officially become a has-been. And I'd much rather be a has-been than a never-was.

It means that when I'm sixty-two and sitting at the bar and I meet some guy who never saw me play, he may ask me, "How good were you?" "Well," I'll tell him, "I'm in the Hall of Fame."

It's a rare honor, one that means so much to me that I passed up $50,000 appearance money at the Bob Hope Classic in England to go to Pinehurst, North Carolina, for my induction. I was voted by the media, and if the media think you belong there, then you must have been pretty good.

A great many golfers, football players and baseball players never will get into their Hall of Fame, guys who contributed a tremendous amount to their sport. When I look back on my U. S. Open, British Open and PGA championships and about three dozen other tournaments I've won around the world, the perfect topping is the Hall of Fame. . . .

A lot of people were disturbed that I wasn't elected earlier, once I had become eligible by playing the tour for ten years, but it didn't bother me. I thought there were more deserving players who should have made it before I did.

Billy Casper was as great a player as any of us but he was overlooked simply because he was at his peak during the Jack Nicklaus–Gary Player–Arnold Palmer era in the 1960s. He won a lot of big tournaments but he never received the attention he deserved. He was elected a year before I was.

I was honored to have Gary Player induct me because we have become very close through the years. He came from a tough background, too. If he hadn't worked his way to the top as a world-class golfer he might have spent his life in the mines of South Africa.

I told him once, "I'm very lucky. If it wasn't for golf I don't know what I'd be doing."

"If my IQ had been two points lower," I said, "I'd have been a plant somewhere."

Well, he thought that was so funny he opened my induction with it. Gary knows me so well that he can stand up and say anything about me and it won't bother me. And, what the hell, it got a big laugh. . . .

In my acceptance speech at Pinehurst I said, "When you play a sport you have two things in mind. One is to get into the Hall of Fame and the other is to go to Heaven when you die." I looked up to the sky and said, "I hope He doesn't need me up there any time soon."

They Call Me Super Mex

The Prestwick Links

J. M'Bain

As a centre of Golf, Ayrshire occupies in the West of Scotland the position that Fifeshire does in the East. It is now, and likely to remain, the chief seat of Golf in the West, and it contains more Golf links and more golf clubs than all that remains of the West of Scotland placed together. And what St. Andrews is to Fifeshire and the East, Prestwick is to Ayrshire and the West, the richest in incident and the most important in the recent annals of Golf. In respect of historical records within the last thirty years Prestwick with its premier club occupies a place not second even to St. Andrews and the Royal and Ancient. As compared with the antiquity of the Royal and Ancient it is, of course, a comparatively modern institution, but during three of the four decades of its existence it has kept pace with its elder and larger rival in maintaining, promoting, and encouraging the game of Golf. St. Andrews is the Mecca of the golfer, but Prestwick is the Medina, and no enthusiast would consider his pilgrimage complete who had not visited the last named placed as well as the former.

It is invidious to make comparison sometimes, and I am not anxious to set off Prestwick against St. Andrews, especially to the disadvantage of the latter. But everything in this objective world is comparative, and one must have some approximate equivalent to set one's comparisons against. There is one circumstance that gives Prestwick the advantage over St. Andrews, the circumstance that a considerable portion of the links is the property of the club. Lord Wellwood has aptly written that "A fine day, a good match, and clear green make up a golfer's dream of perfect happiness." The last essential here is always a feature of Prestwick links. The familiar "Fore" is a word that is almost unknown there. The club has the exclusive rights in an arbitrary way. Needless to say that they are not in the habit of warning pedestrians off the ground, or of refusing the use of the greens to applicants for a day's Golf, still the private character of the links is a guarantee against any outside interference, and the casual pedestrian, aware that he is on the ground by the goodwill of the club, takes care not to interfere with their game.

Prestwick Golf club came early to the front as a promoter of the game. In 1860, it instituted the Open Championship, an institution which has lasted till the present day, and is now likely to be permanent. For eleven years this important event was played over Prestwick alone; but in 1878, as is well known, young Tom Morris by winning the championship belt three times in succession became its possessor; and after being a year in abeyance the meeting was reconstituted under its present conditions, these conditions providing for the event taking place in rotation over Prestwick, St. Andrews and Musselburgh.

Prestwick has always taken a leading part in the settlement of important professional matches. The links are as eminently adapted in every way for these contests, and provide as good a test of Golf, as the best links in the kingdom. There is no living golfer of repute among the professionals who has not played in important matches over the ground. Old Tom Morris was custodian of the green for thirteen years, till he was transferred to St. Andrews.

Many of Tom's most important triumphs were won over Prestwick, including the winning of the championship four times. Young Tommy, who was brought to Prestwick from St. Andrews when he was only a few weeks old, was initiated into the mysteries of the game at Prestwick, and when at the early age of thirteen he left it he was beginning to make his mark as a player. His subsequent career brought him often back to Prestwick, and his most important laurels were won over the ground where he first began to handle the clubs.

The links are situated on the Ayrshire coast at Prestwick, a well-known West of Scotland watering place three miles north of Ayr. So far as convenience in the matter of being easily got at is concerned, Prestwick is the most favourably situated links in the Kingdom. The town is for all practical purposes situated on the main line, and all the expresses north and south pick up and set down passengers there. The club-house door is within thirty yards of the station platform, and the first tee is within the same distance. The club has a private entrance from the station, so that in this respect the links could not be more favourably situated. As originally laid out, the round consisted of twelve holes, the space within which they were included forming a compact area with clearly defined boundaries. The boundaries were the railroad on the east, the Pow Burn and "The Wall" on the north, the Sandhills on the margin of the sea on the west, and the public road on the south. The enclosure constitutes what may be called the classic portion of the present links, that portion over which some of the most memorable contests in modern golf took place. More recently the links expanded to the north, over "The Wall," the burn was crossed, and the club strayed into "meadows green and pastures new."

When "The Wall" is crossed the Golf is a somewhat different character from what it is on the older portion, not unlike the new ground that was added to North Berwick, though a good deal more varied. Indeed the links is one of the most diversified I know, and contains every species of hazard, with the exception of rabbit holes. There is not a rabbit on the whole ground nor the signs of one, although the never portion was at one time a warren, and so styled in the title deeds of the property.

Golf

In the Springtime

I. A. MONKHOUSE

Come and see the Golf links
On an April day,
Hawthorns are in blossom,
Lambs, too are at play.

Scarlet coats are flying
In the balmy air
Sailor hats are nodding
Over faces fair.

Old and young have turned out,
Wielding club and ball,
Some for competition,
For enjoyment all.

On the green are old men
Busy holing out,
Golf is their elixir,
Warding off the gout.

By a silv'ry streamlet
Wander "he and she,"
Other links, they dream of
In futurity.

Naught we feel beyond us
On a day of Spring,
E'en to break the record,
Seems an easy thing.

Golf

A Sight for the Gods

The man "wot" golfs is as well satisfied with himself as a newly feathered turkey. He likes to be though an ardent player and continually interlards his conversation with such words as "Bunkers," "Tees," "Click," and other dreadful sounding things. His costume consists of a tweed coat and knickerbockers of an alarming pattern, with stockings conspicuous a mile off, a shirt loud enough to startle a township, and new orange-yellow boots. A sight for the gods, he fussily lugs towards the links a bright leather bag —on which his initials are painted, about a foot or two a letter—full of curious looking implements, the bulk of whose names he doesn't even know, but which appear to him to be the correct thing to carry. He strides over the turf as though all Southampton belonged to him, shouts out your name across the field, wanting to know "'ow many you've made," swears volubly and "muffs" everything. The men avoid him; the ladies keep a respectful distance, whilst the "caddie" with visible difficulty suppresses an emphatic opinion concerning his skill. He is single, and has a keen desire to move society.

Some People We Meet

Ill-Fated Shots

HORACE G. HUTCHINSON

When you hear a golfer enlarging upon the cruel ill-treatment which his ball suffered after "one of the finest shots that ever was played," you need not hastily conclude that the stroke was one of any really very transcendent merit. This is generally a mere golfing *façon de parler*, and should be taken to imply no more than that the stroke in question was not a noticeably bad one.

Hints on Golf

Eight Hints on How to Lower Your Score

BEN HOGAN

1) *PRACTICE.* Almost always club members familiar with the course have a higher score on the front nine than they have on the back nine and the reason is that they are just getting "warmed up" when they play the back nine. If you will practice only as long as it will take you to hit five balls before you start it will help you to lower your score on the front nine. Furthermore, it is just a case of "warming up" your muscles. You have to start thinking golf right from the start in order to score.

2) *COMMON SENSE.* Many players throw away strokes because they don't take the time to think about a

shot before they attempt it. For instance, in playing over a bunker make sure to put your ball on to the green. Play your shot so as to make allowances for the margin of error to be on the far side of the cup rather than risk being short because of the danger of landing in the bunker. *USE YOUR COMMON SENSE.*

3) *USE A CLUB WITH ENOUGH LOFT.* A novice golfer is inclined to neglect to use enough loft when playing on the green. Consequently, he doesn't get the ball into the air high enough and is short. On the next hole the fact that he was short is fresh in his mind, but once again he takes the wrong club. This time he attempts to make an adjustment by hitting the ball too hard in seeking to insure himself enough distance. As a result his mistakes in club selection have cost him two strokes.

4) *PLAY SAFE IF YOU CAN'T GET A CLEAN SHOT.* Don't take any unnecessary chances in the rough because you'll probably lose two or three strokes just trying to get the ball out. It is better to concede the loss of one stroke than it is to take a chance and sacrifice three or four.

5) *LEARN TO PLAY THE SAND WEDGE.* Most novices neglect to learn to use this club because they don't appreciate what a utility club really is.

6) *LET YOUR CLUB DO THE JOB.* Instead of trying to maneuver the ball with your body, arms and hands, trust your swing and the club you select to do the job.

7) *PLAY FOR THE GREEN NOT THE PIN.* Never play for the pin when it is cut in a corner of the green that is severely bunkered. In this instance it is better for you to rely on your putting ability rather than your second shot. Take chances only after you have your game under control at all times.

8) *DON'T BE AFRAID.* Fear will influence your mus-

cular reactions so dismiss all ideas and fears of shooting over water off the tee, at a green with water around it, or any other hazards. It is foolish to be frightened by hazards because most players have the club range to miss those hazards if they just swing freely.

Power Golf

New Golf Accessories

Ring Lardner

Nearly every body now days is playing golf or at lease thinking about it and this is the best time in the yr. to try and decide what is the matter with your game and how to improve same wile I don't make no pretences of knowing nothing about form, style and etc., still I am going to give my readers a few suggestions in regards to new accessorys which it looks to me like they are worth a trial at lease and they don't none of them cost much money so if they work good so much the better and vica versa.

I suppose my readers will think that they can't possibly be no accessorys that ain't been thought of before because golf has all ready got more accessorys than anything except those little automobiles that grows wild in Detroit, and the last one I heard about seemed like they had reached the limit, namely a stroke register which you fastened on to your arm and every time you swung at the ball the stroke was recorded on the register and when you had played around you would just half to look at the register and it would tell you whether you had made a 80 or 110 or what not.

This one doesn't seem to of had much of a sale though it certainly should ought to, on acct. of there being so many of the boys who can't seem to recall how many strokes they have had on one hole let alone a complete rd. but of course they was one trouble with it, namely that it registered practice swings the same like when you was in ernest and I guess I'm about the only golfer in the world that don't use at least 18 practice swings per rd. and the reason I don't its because I never seem to have time on acct. of people behind me being in a hurry.

But these accessorys which I am going to tell you about is some which I never heard of them being on the market and if any of them are I apologize to the inventor of the same and no harm done.

No.1 is a invention of Octavus Roy Cohen, of Birmingham, Alabama. This invention is a human being and should either ought to be a pastor or a lay reader.

If he is also a golfer himself so much the better as you can probably get him to go along with you just for the pleasure of playing but anyway the idear is that every time you start to shoot, he starts to pray and the result is that you have to keep your head down.

No.2 is a simple contrivance namely a empty bbl. and is recommended to golfers like Irvin S. Cobb and James J. Montague who ain't no sooner than hit the ball than they are off down the field after it like it was a punt and they was ends.

The bbl. is placed side ways right ahead of their left ft. and as soon as they have swang and start their dash they fall over the bbl. and more than likely light on their nose and hurt themselfs. About a wk. of the bbl. cure will make a new man out of these kinds of boys.

No.3 is another simple device namely a extra direction flag which the caddy carrys along and places it where it will do the most good. Like for inst. the golfers has got the sliceing habit and they ain't nobody can cure him of same. Well he comes to a blind hole and they's a regular direction flag right out in the middle of the course but if our hero was to aim at it he would land way over in the ruffles at the right.

So before he shoots the caddy takes this extra direction flag and sticks it in the ground on the edge of the rough on the left. Then the caddy hollers here is the direction flag and the man aims at it and the ball lands in the middle of the fairways. In the case of he who hooks the direction flag placed on the opp. or right side of the fair ways.

No.4 is the common smoke screens used dureing what I have dubbed the great war. The screen is made by a kind of a bomb which you set fire to it and nothing happens only great big clouds of smoke comes out of the bomb and you can't see through them. As a golf accessory these bombs would be carried by the caddy till the golfer come to a place where he had to shoot over a mound or a valley or a water hazard.

The caddy would set off one of the bombs about 10 ft. ahead of where the player was going to make his shot and when the smoke was so thick that the player couldn't see what happened to him if he topped his shot, why he could then go ahead and shoot without no nervous break down.

No.5 is a pocket compass and is used in connection with putting. Like suppose for inst. you land on the green about 10 ft. from the cup, why the next thing is to find out in what direction the hole is at and this can't be done and done right without a compass.

At least I have seen a whole lot of golfers try and putt without no compass and their ball has went from 10 to

45 ft. degrees to the right or left of where the hole is actually located. This is because they was just guessing where as with a compass they's no guess work about it. If you miss a putt with a compass to tell you just where a hole is at, why it's because you can't putt so good.

No.6 and last is like No. 1 namely it's a human being only this time it's a man who is in the sand and gravel business and he goes along with you around the course driveing a empty sand wagon till your ball lands in a sand trap and then you make a deal with him that he can have all the sand in the trap provided he removes it off the premises. You would be surprised how much easier it is to shoot out of a sand trap after the wagon has drove off with the sand.

The undersigned is now prepared to answer any questions my readers may wish to ask in regards to golf.

The Ring Lardner Reader

©1996 John Jonik from The Cartoon Bank™, Inc.

"What's this I hear about you giving up golf photography?"

your shotmaking. An interesting illustration that comes to mind concerns Harry Vardon. Around the turn of the century when Vardon was in his heyday, he was so much straighter off the tee than any other golfer of that era that a group of golf scholars decided that some tests should be made with Vardon from which they might be able to deduce, in semi-scientific fashion, the secrets of his accuracy. One of the experiments they set up was for Vardon to hit a series of drives from a dirt tee: on each drive, they charted the position of Vardon's feet in relation to the ball, and then, after he had driven, they erased his footprints so that there would be nothing to guide him when he stepped on the tee again and addressed the next ball. Vardon hit about two dozen drives and split the fairway with every one of them. And what did the scholars find when they studied the charts they'd made? They found out that Vardon's stance had varied slightly each time. On one drive his left foot was angled a shade more open; on another, the distance between his heels are wider; on another, the right toe was nearer the ball than usual; and so on. Their conclusion, necessarily, was that the variations in Vardon's stance didn't seem to have any effect on how he hit the ball.

In general terms, the same thing is true of *some* other aspects of the golf swing: you can vary your execution of certain moves and continue to play well, providing you are blessed with the athlete's instinctive coordination of hand and eye—and providing that the basic components of your swing remain sound. Those basic components, of course, are what the best golf minds have arrived at as the true fundamentals. While a golfer now and then can get away with a shot, or even with a series of shots, on which some fundamental is faulty, he won't be able to get away with it for long. This is why nearly all top-flight golfers, when they fall into a really bad swing pattern, retreat to the practice tee, return to the fundamentals, and start to reconstruct their swing from the ground up.

The Greatest Game of All

An Exhibition Golf-Lesson

L. B. GULLICK

It was a sultry August evening when at Thompson's request I went round to the Golf Club with him and gave him a lesson. I took him on the sixteenth tee, which is conveniently near the club-house and provides an ideal spot for practice, there being a nice wide stretch of fairway in front of it and a good-sized cross-bunker just reasonable distance away. With us we took twenty balls, which Thompson had acquired for the purpose of practicing, and a caddie, whom we sent on in front.

'Well,' I said, 'let's have a look at your swing.'

Thompson swung. It was a most horrible sight: a parody of all the vices known to the golfer.

'Ah,' I said, 'that'll never do. You'll have to start from the very beginning and learn the swing bit by bit.'

I showed him the grip, stance, back-swing, downswing, follow-through—all very carefully and slowly, telling him to imitate me, as I did so. And then I showed him the whole swing in one. I teed up a ball and drove it over the cross-bunker.

'Like that, you see,' I said: and I did it again. Both shots were perfect, and Thompson was of course deeply impressed.

'My word,' he exclaimed, 'I wish I could do that.'

'You will,' I said, 'in time. It's just a matter of getting accustomed to swinging the right way. Like this—' And I started to show him again. But Thompson had got out of his place, and the head of my driver caught him on the shin as I was swinging back, and he went hopping round the tee muttering angrily and holding on to his leg.

'I'm awfully sorry,' I said, 'but I hadn't the slightest idea you were standing there.' And I explained to him the proper place to stand when anyone was making a shot. 'In front,' I said, 'always in front: and, when you're on a tee, always the other side of the tee-box.'

Thompson went to the other side of the tee-box. I then showed him some more drives, and when I had hit all the twenty balls and we were waiting for the caddie to bring them back I had a chat with him about the iron shot, explaining the need for a shorter and slightly compacted swing. But he took no interest in the iron. All he wanted was to begin slogging away with a driver: and when the boy returned he teed a ball up with the idea of making a drive.

'One moment,' I said: 'first let's see how you're going to swing at it.'

He showed me. It was absolutely hopeless.

'No good at all,' I said, 'You can't possibly hope to do any good like that. You simply must get away from that horrible scything action before you attempt to hit a ball.'

I took him off the tee again and pointed him out a dandelion to swing at.

'Now,' I said, 'measure your distance from that dandelion, swing slowly back, keeping your head stock-still and your shoulders on the same level right through the swing: and be sure you've got your eye on the dandelion at the moment when your club-head meets it.'

I addressed the ball which he had teed up.

'Watch me before each stroke,' I said. 'We will drive alternately.'

My first drive was a real beauty. Thompson's was as bad as ever. He hit the air some inches above the dandelion, and, without waiting for me to play my next one, he had another shot, this time thumping the ground behind it. He really did not appear to be making any serious effort.

I drove again—and again—all beauties. Then I topped one: but this was because Thompson was swishing about too close to me just as I was driving. I told him to keep a little further away.

'But,' he said, 'I've ruined that dandelion and there aren't any more over there.'

'Anything'll do,' I told him. 'Find a weed or a worm-cast or something. It's only a matter of having something to swing at, so as to get the feeling of the proper swing.'

He moved a little farther away.

I made another shot. My swing was feeling simply fine, and I was conscious of a sense of complete freedom and confidence. I was putting more 'snap' into the shots than I could remember ever have done before, and almost every drive went sailing far over the bunker and straight as a dart. I am certain that anyone watching would have said I was as good a model as the beginner could want. Out of the twenty shots there was only one that didn't carry the bunker (not counting the one I duffed through Thompson putting me off) and only two that weren't on the fairway. It was a jolly good perfor-mance for me and I was particularly glad to bring it off for the benefit of a pupil.

'There!' I said, as my twentieth shot went fizzing

through the air: and I looked up to where Thompson was standing. But Thompson was not there. He had disappeared. I looked all around for him: he was nowhere to be seen.

Exhausted with so much effort and disappointment at the strange behaviour of Thompson, I walked back to the club-house, and there, believe me, lying full-length on a sofa, was Thompson; beside him a whisky-and-soda and in his hands a book, *How to Play Golf*, by Harry Vardon.

Turning Point

Horace G. Hutchinson

In wellnigh every golf match which is at all a close one there is almost inevitably some one notable turning point, a crisis at which the golfing quality is put to its severest test. In the case of two golfers evenly pitted, it is most interesting to watch. After the first few holes are over there will be a ding-dong, give-and-take contest, in which the luck of the green will give now one and now the other a quickly passing advantage. They fight neck and neck, the match draws nearer its conclusion, and still the balance hangs even. The excitement grows constantly; they are passing through the crucial test, then one or the other, in the expressive golfing parlance, 'cracks'. He plays badly, just because it is the moment at which he most wants to play his best; it has become a test of *morale*, rather than of mere eye and muscle. And the moment the one 'cracks' he is done for, the other gains confidence; the intensity of the strain has passed for him and it is scarcely in human nature that the golfer who has

'cracked' at the crucial moment can pull himself together, even if there were yet time.

Golf, The Badminton Library

The Golfers Blend

THE Tobacco for the links.
Does not fritter away in the wind.
Does not burn the tongue.
Does not fall to ashes half-way through your
    pipe.
Does help you to keep that calm temper
    without which you will be useless at the tee,
    and worse than useless on the green.

The Manchester Golfer

Driving to Destruction

J. C. LAW

If a good golfing temperament were not a *sine qua no´n* to
success on the links, there would be many more players
of first rank. Golfers there are by the score who are capable of playing the game with accuracy and power, and
when things are going well of doing brilliant deeds; and
yet they somehow or other fail when we most hope and
expect that they will succeed. And this failure may, I
fancy, not infrequently be laid at the door of mental
rather than physical causes. The flesh is able, the muscles are fit, the eye is keen, the knowledge is sufficient,
but the mind cannot control and govern the whole man.
It has been said by one well able from experience both of

life and golf to give a good judgment, that golf is a game which is always fighting against the player.

That golf is an irritating game anyone who has played it seriously knows, and recognizes also that the man who loses his temper as a rule loses also the match. "I know it's only a damned game," shouted an eminent legal luminary as he snapped his croquet mallet over his knee and then hurled its head through the drawingroom window, but even games require some mastering or they will get the upper hand.

Nothing is more annoying than, after a good drive, to find one's self hampered for the next stroke by an unfortunate lie. Among the many ways of improving golf that have been suggested, a proposal that every ball should be "teed" seemed to me, at the time it was made, to be the most destructive. It was argued that this would make the game fairer and eliminate luck; and certainly the idea should have been welcomed by all bad-tempered golfers. But to overcome bad luck and come out triumphant in the end is the most satisfactory of enjoyments, the greatest of glories. Remove luck from the game and it loses one of its chief recreative qualities, and becomes, in fact, a game no longer.

If it be the bad lies that bring out the qualities of the player it will be found that it is the even-minded golfer who will overpower circumstances and surmount difficulty with success. The ball lies badly, then tackle the situation with all the ability you possess, and do not waste time and mind in thinking how different it would have been reached had a wooden club shot been possible. But the ball does not lie well, so the best thing to be done is to make the most of the possibilities of the situation, to master within limits the work that has actually been done.

And yet this is easy to say, and hard to do; for the golfing mind is hard to concentrate, though concentration is vital.

If we think we are doing well success will probably follow; if we regard every misfortune as a catastrophe, every small failure as only one of many others sure to follow, then we are playing a losing game.

I like not the partner who assures me, after I have missed a short putt at the first hole that it is unlucky to win on the first green. I like better the man who says "Never mind, there are other holes to play." For this is true golfing philosophy, namely, not to look back on the milk on the ground, but rather go forward with a determination to observe more care.

There will probably happen in the course of a golf match things that may either be taken humorously or in anger, and the former attitude of mind will be found to answer the better. A lady may allow her parasol to be blown across the putting green just when a stroke is about to be made; a spectator may audibly ask the name of the player who is addressing the ball.

But what is most important, from the player's point of view, is that he should treat such incidents in a friendly way and not as pointed and premeditated insults to himself. Let him laugh at the matter for a moment, and then return with fixed mind to the business on hand.

The man who can fix his whole will power on every shot he play, who is unconscious of what others are thinking of him, who cheerfully is determined to make the best use of every chance, be it ill-looking or fair, that man is not far from the perfection of golfing temperament.

The Golfer

Over-Golfing

HORACE G. HUTCHINSON

Remember that it is always possible to "over-golf" yourself. Two rounds a day is enough for any man with a week or more of solid golf before him—I am speaking of eighteen hole rounds, of course—and even then your game will probably be improved by your indulging yourself in another *dies non* besides the Sabbath. Two rounds, moreover, occupy most of the ordinary man's day, and leaves but little spare time for the lighter matters of life.

Hints on Golf

How to Go About Buying a Putter

JOHN L. LOW

If you wish a good putter, you will hardly expect to find one in a clubmaker's ready-made stock, far less in a toyshop or a tobacconist's window. The putter must be sought for with care and not hastily, for she is to be the friend, be it hoped, for many years. First, then, find out a workman of repute as a make of putters—and in these days of "reach-me-down" clubs there are few such artists —and, having found him, proceed warily. It will never do to go and order him to make you a first-class club for your match next morning; you would probably receive only the work of an apprentice. Wait your time and you will find the great man about his shop, or on his doorstep at the dinner hour, and you may remark to him that the day is fine; this will be a safe opening even though rain be falling in torrents, for it will give him the idea that you are a simple fellow and so throw him off his guard.

○ **224** ○

If a half-empty pipe lies beside him, offer him a cigar, and mention that you are afraid that it is not as good as you would have wished, being the last of the box, at the same time giving him to understand that another box is expected that evening. The cigar having been accepted and lighted, you may, in course of conversation, allude to a very fine putter made by a rival clubmaker which, you will tell your friend, is being much talked about and copied. This will be almost certainly a winning card to play, for there is much jealousy among the profession, and as likely as not the remark will be made that So-and-so—naming the rival maker—has about as much idea of fashioning a putter as he has of successfully solving the problem of aerial navigation. Do not press the matter to a conclusion, but meet your man again in similar manner, this time carelessly holding in your hand the club which you have long felt was the cause of the success of some distinguished player. Almost seem to hide it from the clubmaker, and he will be sure to ask to see it, and probably volunteer to make you one on the same lines with slight improvement of his own.

In time you will get your putter, and it will probably be a good one; in any case it will be good enough to resell if it does not suit you, which is always a point to be considered.

Concerning Golf

---

*Golf is a game whose aim is to hit a very small ball
into an even smaller hole,
with weapons singularly ill-designed for the purpose.*
Sir Winston Churchill

An Old Friend

I. A. MONKHOUSE

Years ago I bought this driver
Which you hold now in your hand.
Dear it seemed at seven shillings;
    Golf I did not understand.

Time, alas! has spoilt the varnish,
Cracked the head in pieces twice,
Worn away the marker's trade-mark;
    On the shaft there is a splice.

Yet was ever club so supple?
Give it just one gentle swing,
Whizz! the ball went swiftly flying,
    Clearing walls and everything.

True, its working days are over,
But it hangs still on the wall—
Souv'nir sweet of days long vanished,
    Gone forsooth beyond recall.

Golf

Visualization and Your Swing

JOHNNY MILLER

When you first start off in golf, you have literally no visual image of how to execute the golf swing. So, the only thing to do is pick out model golf swings and try to emulate them, When I started off, my dad showed me pictures of Hogan and Snead, and even today you couldn't get better models. However, of the current tour stars I would certainly recommend two for particular study—Al Geiberger and Tom Weiskopf.

Al's swing looks upright because he's tall, but in reality he takes it back on the line in a perfect plane. Tom's swing is also just about as good as any I've seen. To me that's the kind of swing to have—one where you don't have to work 100 per cent to get the ball out there for good distance. Both Al and Tom have excellent balance, keeping themselves perfectly centered over the ball. There are not many people who do that.

You should use every chance you get to formulate good mental images of the swing. Watch your professional, watch the really low handicap players at your course, study sequence pictures of great players in books and magazines, and study the swings of the best players on TV. Compare some of the best players with some of the less talented players on the tour. A particularly good time to learn is when a tour hits your area. Go to the practice tee and look down the line of players practicing. Slowly, you will learn to pick out what the great players do that the lesser don't. All of this sharpens your perceptions of the swing and makes for sharp, clear mental images for your own use.

Little by little you'll compile a list of fundamentals of your own swing; these are the mental images that get the job done for you. However, at this point in your career, you will find that much of what you have learned is ingrained—it's in your subconscious. Because of this, changes in your swing do become more difficult. For example, if you have been swinging a certain way for three years and all of a sudden change and offer your subconscious a new method of swinging, be prepared to spend considerable time working on it. Major change cannot be made overnight.

There is one caution here: If you have an established swing, don't try to feed too many conscious images into your subconscious mind at once. It just won't work. You'll give your subconscious a case of indigestion. Feed new images in one at a time preferably, and certainly no more than two.

Lastly, . . . Mental pictures are the way you program your subconscious, but no amount of visualization is any good if the mental pictures used aren't accurate. Make use of every visual aid you can lay your hands on, be it a full-length mirror, still pictures and movies of your swing, or TV replay machines. In this way, you will be able to "see" your swing honestly at all times.

Pure Golf

A Golf Pipe

This is the latest novelty which has been brought out for the benefit of the golfing community. The wonder is that the thing has not been attempted before, seeing how readily the implements of the game lend themselves to miniature reproduction, not only in jewellery but in other forms of ornamental and decorative art. The golf Pipe is elegant in appearance and practical in use, as it can be smoked with or without the long stem, and the Golfer who indulges in the fragrant weed will be able to enjoy a long pipe while reading, or a short one at cards or billiards. The stem of the pipe is an exact reproduction of the club, but of course, proportionately smaller, and the bowl, which is made of briar or meerschaum, resembles a Golf ball, both in size and appearance.

The pipe can be obtained through any tobacconist from the makers of the well-known brand of Pipes. Judging from the specimen now before us, the makers seem to have produced this interesting novelty in material of excellent quality and high finish of workmanship. We cannot imagine a more suitable prize for competition than the long Golf Pipe with meerschaum bowl, and handsome case covered with Russia leather. The short briar pipe will be found a useful addition to the Golfer's outfit.

Golf

The Ooley-Cow

CHARLES E. VAN LOAN

AFTER THE EXPLANATION, and before Uncle Billy Poindexter and Old Man Sprott had been able to decide just what had hit them, Little Doc Ellis had the nerve to tell me that he had seen the fuse burning for months and months. Little Doc is my friend and I like him, but he resembles many other members of his profession in that he is usually wisest after the post mortem, when it is a wee bit late for the high contracting party.

And at all times Little Doc is full of vintage bromides and figures of speech.

"You have heard the old saw," said he. "A worm will turn if you keep picking on him, and so will a straight road if you ride it long enough. A camel is a wonderful burden bearer, but even a double-humped ship of the desert will sink on your hands if you pile the load on him a bale of hay at a time."

"A worm, a straight road, a camel and a sinking ship," said I. "Whither are we drifting?"

Little Doc did not pay any attention to me. It is a way he has.

"Think," said he, "how much longer a camel will stand up under punishment if he gets his load straw by straw, as it were. The Ooley-cow was a good thing, but Uncle Billy and Old Man Sprott did not use any judgment. They piled it on him too thick."

"Meaning," I asked, "to compare the Ooley-cow with a camel?"

"Merely a figure of speech," said Little Doc; "but yes, such was my intention."

"Well," said I, "your figures of speech need careful auditing. A camel can go eight days without a drink—"

Little Doc made impatient motions at me with both hands. He has no sense of humor, and his mind is a one-way track, totally devoid of spurs and derailing switches. Once started, he must go straight through to his destination.

"What I am trying to make plain to your limited mentality," said he, "is that Uncle Billy and Old Man Sprott needed a lesson in conservation, and they got it. The Ooley-cow was the easiest, softest picking that ever strayed from the home pasture. With care and decent treatment he would have lasted a long time and yielded an enormous quantity of nourishment, but Uncle Billy and Old Man Sprott were too greedy. They tried to corner the milk market, and now they will have to sign tags for their drinks and their golf balls the same as the rest of us. They have killed the goose that laid the golden eggs."

"A minute ago," said I, "the Ooley-cow was a camel.

Now he is a goose—a dead goose, to be exact. Are you all done figuring with your speech?"

"Practically so, yes."

"Then," said I, "I will plaster up the cracks in your argument with the cement of information. I can use figures of speech myself. You are barking up the wrong tree. You are away off your base. It wasn't the loss of a few dollars that made Mr. Perkins run wild in our midst. It was the manner in which he lost them. Let us now dismiss the worm, the camel, the goose and all the rest of the menagerie, retaining only the Ooley-cow. What do you know about cows, if anything?"

"A little," answered my medical friend.

"A mighty little. You know that a cow has hoofs, horns and a tail. The same description would apply to many creatures, including Satan himself. Your knowledge of cows is largely academic. Now me, I was raised on a farm, and there were cows in my curriculum. I took a seven-year course in the gentle art of acquiring the lacteal fluid. Cow is my specialty, my long suit, my best hold. Believe it or not, when we christened old Perkins the Ooley-cow we builded better than we knew."

"I follow you at a great distance," said Little Doc. "Proceed with the rat killing. Why did we build better than we knew when we did not know anything?"

"Because," I explained, "Perkins not only looks like a cow and walks like a cow and plays golf like a cow, but he has the predominant characteristic of a cow. He has the one distinguishing trait which all country cows have in common. If you had studied that noble domestic animal as closely as I have, you would not need to be told what moved Mr. Perkins to strew the entire golf course with the mangled remains of the two old pirates before mentioned. Uncle Billy and Old Man Sprott were milking him, yes, and it is quite likely that the Ooley-cow knew that he was being milked, but that knowledge was not the prime cause of the late unpleasantness."

"I still follow you," said Little Doc plaintively, "but I am losing ground every minute."

"Listen carefully," said I. "Pin back your ears and give me your undivided attention. There are many ways of milking a cow without exciting the animal to violence. I speak now of the old-fashioned cow—the country cow—from Iowa, let us say."

"The Ooley-cow is from Iowa," murmured Little Doc.

"Exactly. A city cow may be milked by machinery, and in a dozen different ways, but the country cow does not know anything about new-fangled methods. There is one thing—and one thing only—which will make the gentlest old mooley in Iowa kick over the bucket, upset the milker, jump a four-barred fence and join the wild bunch on the range. Do you know what that one thing is?"

"I haven't even a suspicion," confessed Little Doc.

Then I told him. I told him in words of one syllable, and after a time he was able to grasp the significance of my remark. If I could make Little Doc see the point, I can make you see it too. We go from here.

Wesley J. Perkins hailed from Dubuque, but he did not hail from there until he had gathered up all the loose change in Northeastern Iowa. When he arrived in sunny Southern California he was fifty-five years of age, and at least fifty of those years had been spent in putting aside something for a rainy day. Judging by the diameter of his bankroll, he must have feared the sort of a deluge which caused the early settlers to lay the ground plans for the Tower Of Babel.

Now it seldom rains in Southern California—that is to say, it seldom rains hard enough to produce a flood—and as soon as Mr. Perkins became acquainted with the climatic conditions he began to jettison his ark. He joined an exclusive downtown club, took up quarters there and spent his afternoons playing dominoes with some other members of the I've-got-mine Association. Aside from his habit of swelling up whenever he mentioned his home town, and insisting on referring to it as "the Heidelberg of America," there was nothing about Mr. Perkins to provoke comment, unfavorable or otherwise. He was just one more Iowan in a country where Iowans are no novelty.

In person he was the mildest-mannered man that ever foreclosed a short-term mortgage and put a family out in the street. His eyes were large and bovine, his mouth dropped perpetually and so did his jowls, and he moved with the slow, uncertain gait of a venerable milch cow. He had a habit of lowering his head and staring vacantly into space, and all these things earned for him the unhandsome nickname by which he is now known.

"But why the Ooley-cow?" someone asked one day. "It doesn't mean anything at all!"

"Well," was the reply, "neither does Perkins."

But this was an error, as we shall see later.

It was an increasing waistline that caused the Ooley-cow to look about him for some form of gentle exercise. His physician suggested golf, and that very week the board of directors of the Country Club was asked to consider his application for membership. There were no ringing cheers, but he passed the censors.

I will say for Perkins that when he decided to commit golf he went about it in a very thorough manner. He had himself surveyed for three knickerbocker suits, imported stockings and spiked shoes, and he gave our professional *carte blanche* in the matter of field equipment. It is not a safe thing to give a Scotchman permission to dip his hand in your change pocket, and MacPherson certainly availed himself of the opportunity to finger some of the Dubuque money. He took one look at the novice and unloaded on him something less than a hundred weight of dead stock. He also gave him a lesson or two, and sent him forth armed to the teeth with wood, iron and aluminum.

Almost immediately Perkins found himself in the hands of Poindexter and Sprott, two extremely hard-boiled old gentlemen who have never been known to take interest in a financial proposition assaying less than seven per cent, and that fully guaranteed. Both are retired capitalists, but when they climbed out of the trenches and retreated into the realm of sport they took all their business instincts with them.

Uncle Billy can play to a twelve handicap when it suits him to do so, and his partner in crime is only a couple of strokes behind him; but they seldom uncover their true form, preferring to pose as doddering and infirm invalids, childish old men, who only think they can play the game of golf, easy marks for the rising generation. New members are their victims; beginners are just the same as manna from heaven to them. They instruct the novice humbly and apologetically, but always with a small side bet, and no matter how fast the novice improves he makes the astounding discovery that his two feeble old tutors are able to keep pace with him. Uncle Billy and Old Man Sprotts are experts at nursing a betting proposition along, and they seldom win any sort of a match by a margin of more than two up and one to go. Taking into account the natural limitations of age they play golf very well, but they play a cinch even better—and harder. It is common scandal that Uncle Billy has not bought a golf ball in ten years. Old Man Sprott bought one in 1915, but it was under the mellowing influence of the third toddy and, therefore, should not count against him.

The Ooley-cow was a cinch. When he turned up, innocent and guileless and eager to learn the game, Uncle Billy and his running mate were quick to realize that Fate had sent them downy bird for plucking, and in no time at all the air was full of feathers.

They played the Ooley-cow for golf balls, they played him for caddie hire, they played him for drinks and cigars, they played him for luncheons and they played him for a sucker—played him for everything, in fact, but the locker rent and the club dues. How they came to overlook these items is more than I know. The Ooley-cow would have stood for it; he stood for everything. He signed all the tags with a loose and vapid grin, and if he suffered from writer's cramp he never mentioned the fact. His monthly bill must have been a thing to shudder at, but possibly he regarded this extra outlay as part of his tuition.

Once in a while he was allowed to win, for Poindexter and Sprott followed the system practiced by other confidence men; but they never forgot to take his winnings away from him the next day, charging him interest at the rate of fifty per cent for every twenty-four hours. The Ooley-cow was so very easy that they took liberties with him, so good-natured about his losses that they presumed upon that good nature and ridiculed him openly; but the old saw sometimes loses a tooth, the worm turns, the straight road bends at last, so does the camel's back, and the prize cow kicks the milker into the middle of next week. And, as I remarked before, the cow usually has a reason.

One morning I dropped into the downtown club which Perkins calls his home. I found him sitting in the reception room, juggling a newspaper and watching the door. He seemed somewhat disturbed.

"Good morning," said I.

"It is not a good morning," said he. "It's a bad morning. Look at this."

He handed me the paper, with his thumb at the head of the Lost-and-Found column, and I read as follows:

LOST—*A black leather wallet, containing private papers and a sum of money. A suitable reward will be paid for the return of same, and no questions asked. Apply to W. J. P., Argonaut Club, City.*

"Tough luck," said I. "Did you lose much?"

"Quite a sum," replied the Ooley-cow. "Enough to make it an object. In large bills mostly."

"Too bad. The wallet had your cards in it?"

"Have you an idea where you might have dropped it? Or do you think it was stolen?"

"I don't know what to think. I had it last night at the Country Club just before I left. I know I had it then, because I took it out in the lounging room to pay a small bet to Mr. Poindexter—a matter of two dollars. Then I put the wallet back in my inside pocket and came straight here—alone in a closed car. I missed it just before going to bed. I telephoned to the Country Club. No sign of it there. I went to the garage myself. It was not in the car.

Of course it may have been there earlier in the evening, but I think my driver is honest, and—"

At this point we were interrupted by a clean-cut looking youngster of perhaps seventeen years.

"Your initials are W. J. P., sir?" he asked politely.

"They are."

"This is your ad in the paper?"

"It is."

The boy reached in his pocket and brought out a black leather wallet. "I have returned your property," said he, and waited while the Ooley-cow thumbed a roll of yellow-backed bills.

"All here," said Perkins with a sigh of relief. Then he looked up at the boy, and his large bovine eyes turned hard as moss agates. "Where did you get this?" he demanded abruptly. "How did you come by it?"

The boy smiled and shook his head, but his eyes never left Perkins' face. "No questions were to be asked, sir," he said.

"Right!" grunted the Ooley-cow. "Quite right. A bargain's a bargain. I—I beg your pardon, young man— Still, I'd like to know—Just curiosity, eh?—No?—Very well then. That being the case"—he stripped a fifty-dollar note from the roll and passed it over—"would you consider this a suitable reward?"

"Yes, sir, and thank you, sir."

"Good day," said Perkins, and put the wallet into his pocket. He stared at the boy until he disappeared through the street door.

"Something mighty queer about this," mused the Ooley-cow thoughtfully. "Mighty queer. That boy—he looked honest. He had good eyes and he wasn't afraid of me. I couldn't scare him worth a cent. Couldn't bluff him —Yet if he found it somewhere, there wasn't any reason why he shouldn't have told me. He didn't steal it—I'll bet on that. Maybe he got it from someone who did. Oh, well, the main thing is that he brought it back—Going out to the Country Club this afternoon?"

I said that I expected to play golf that day.

"Come out with me then," said the Ooley-cow. "Poindexter and Sprott will be there too. Yesterday afternoon I played Poindexter for the lunches today. Holed a long putt on the seventeenth green, and stuck him. Come along, and we'll make Poindexter give a party— for once."

"It can't be done," said I. "Uncle Billy doesn't give parties."

"We'll make him give one," chuckled the Ooley-cow. "We'll insist on it."

"Insist if you want to," said I, "but you'll never get away with it."

"Meet me here at noon," said the Ooley-cow. "If Poindexter doesn't give a party, I will."

I wasn't exactly keen for the Ooley-cow's society, but I accepted his invitation to ride out to the club in his car. He regaled me a dreary monologue, descriptive of the Heidelberg of America, and solemnly assured me that the pretty girls one sees in Chicago are all from Dubuque.

It was twelve-thirty when we arrived at the Country Club, and Uncle Billy and Old Man Sprott were there ahead of us.

"Poindexter," said Perkins, "you are giving a party today, and I have invited our friend here to join us."

Uncle Billy looked at Old Man Sprott, and both laughed uproariously. Right there was where I should have detected the unmistakable odor of a rodent. It was surprise number one.

"Dee-lighted!" cackled Uncle Billy. "Glad to have another guest, ain't we, Sprott?"

Sprott grinned and rubbed his hands. "You bet! Tell you what let's do Billy. Let's invite everybody in the place —make it a regular party while you're at it!"

"Great idea!" exclaimed Uncle Billy. "The more the merrier!" This was surprise number two. The first man invited was Henry Bauer, who has known Uncle Billy for many years. He sat down quite overcome.

"You shouldn't do a thing like that, Billy," said he querulously. "I have a weak heart, and any sudden shock—"

"Nonsense! You'll join us?"

"Novelty always appealed to me," said Bauer. "I'm forever trying things that nobody has ever tried before. Yes, I'll break bread with you, but—why the celebration? What's it all about?"

That was what everybody wanted to know and what nobody found out, but the luncheon was a brilliant success in spite of the dazed and mystified condition of the guests, and the only limit was the limit of individual capacity. Eighteen of us sat down at the big round table. and sandwich-and-milk orders were sternly countermanded by Uncle Billy, who proved an amazing host, recommending this and that and actually ordering Rhine wine cup for all hands. I could not have been more surprised if the bronze statue in the corner of the grill had hopped down from its pedestal to fill our glasses. Uncle Billy collected a great pile of tags beside his plate, but the presence of so much bad news waiting at his elbow did not seem to affect his appetite in the least. When the party was over he called the head waiter. "Mark these tags paid," said Uncle Billy, capping the collection with a yellow-backed bill, "and hand the change to Mr. Perkins."

"Yes sir," said the head waiter, and disappeared.

I looked at the Ooley-cow, and was just in time to see the light of intelligence dawn in his soft eyes. He was staring at Uncle Billy, and his lower lip was flopping convulsively. Everybody began asking questions at once.

"One moment, gentlemen," mooed the Ooley-cow, pounding on the table. "One moment!"

"Now don't get excited, Perkins," said Old Man Sprott. "You got your wallet back, didn't you? Cost you fifty, but you got it back. Next time you won't be so careless."

"Yes," chimed in Uncle Billy, "you oughtn't to go dropping your money round loose that way. It'll teach you a lesson."

"It will indeed." The Ooley-cow lowered his head and glared first at one old pirate and then at the other. His soft eyes hardened and the moss-gate look came into them. He seemed about to bellow, paw up the dirt and charge.

"The laugh is on you," cracked Poindexter, "and I'll leave it to the boys here. Last night our genial host dropped his wallet on the floor out in the lounging room. I kicked it across under the table to Sprott and Sprott put his foot on it. We intended to give it back to him today, but this morning there was an ad in the paper—reward and no questions asked—so we sent a nice bright boy over to the Argonaut Club with the wallet. Perkins gave the boy a fifty-dollar note—very liberal, I call it—and the boy gave it to me. Perfectly legitimate transaction. Our friend here has had a lesson, we've had a delightful luncheon party, and the joke is on him."

"And a pretty good joke, too!" laughed Old Man Sprott.

"Yes," said the Ooley-cow at last, "a pretty good joke. Ha, ha! A mighty good joke." And place it to his credit that he managed a very fair imitation of a fat man laughing, even to the shaking of the stomach and the wrinkles round the eyes. He looked down at the tray in front of him and fingered the few bills and some loose silver.

"A mighty good joke," he repeated thoughtfully, "but what I can't understand is this—why didn't you two jokers keep the change? It would have been just that much funnier."

The Ooley-cow's party was generally discussed the next ten days, the consensus of club opinion being that someone ought to teach Poindexter and Sprott the difference between humor and petty larceny. Most of the playing members were disgusted with the two old skinflints, and one effect of this sentiment manifested itself in the number of invitations that Perkins received to play golf with real people. He declined them all, much to our surprise, and continued to wallop his way round the course with Uncle Billy and Old Man Sprott, apparently on as cordial terms as ever.

"What are you going to do with such a besotted old fool as that?" asked Henry Bauer. "Here I've invited him into three foursomes this week—al white men, too—and he's turned me down cold. It's not that we want to play with him, for as a golfer he's a terrible thing. It's not that we're crazy about him personally, for socially he's my notion of zero minus; but he took his stinging like a dead-game sport and he's entitled to better treatment than he's getting. But if he hasn't any better sense than to pass his plate for more, what are you going to do about it?"

"'Ephraim is joined to idols,'" quoted Little Doc Ellis. "Let him alone!"

"No, it's the other way around," argued Bauer. "His idols are joined to him—fastened on like leaches. The question naturally arises, how did such a man ever accumulate a fortune? Who forced it on him, and when, and where, and why?"

That very afternoon the Ooley-cow turned up with his guest, a large loud person, also from Heidelberg of America, who addressed Perkins as "Wesley" and lost no time in informing us that Southern California would have starved to death but for Iowa's capital. His name was Cottle—Calvin D. Cottle—and he gave each one of us his card as he was introduced. There was no need. Nobody could have forgotten him. Some people make an impression at first sight—Calvin D. Cottle made a deep dent. His age was perhaps forty-five, but he spoke as one crowned with Methuselah's years and Solomon's wisdom, and after each windy statement he turned to the Ooley-cow for confirmation.

"Ain't that so, Wesley? Old Wes knows, you bet your life! He's from my home town!"

It was good as a circus to watch Uncle Billy and Old Man Sprott sizing up this fresh victim. It reminded me of two wary old dogs circling for position, maneuvering for a safe hold. They wanted to know something about his golf game—"what was his handicap? for instance."

"Handicap?" repeated Cottle. "Is that a California idea? Something new, ain't it?"

Uncle Billy explained the handicapping theory.

"Oh!" said Cottle. "You mean what do I go round

in—how many strokes. Well, sometimes I cut under a hundred; sometimes I don't. It just depends. Some days I can hit 'em, some days I can't. That's all there is to it."

"My case exactly," purred Old Man Sprott. "Suppose we dispense with the handicap?"

"That's the stuff!" agreed Cottle heartily. "I don't want to have to give anybody anything; I don't want anybody to give me anything. I like an even fight, and what I say is, may the best man win! Am I right, gentlemen?"

"Absolutely!" chirped Uncle Billy. "May the best man win!"

"You bet I'm right!" boomed Cottle. "Ask Old Wes her about me. Raised right in the same town with him, from a kid knee-high to a grasshopper! I never took any the best of it in my life, did I, Wes? No, you bet not! Remember that time I got skinned out of ten thousand bucks on the land deal? A lot of fellows would have hollered for the police; but I just laughed and gave 'em credit for being smarter than I was. I'm the same way in sport as I am in business. I believe in giving everybody credit. I win if I can, but if I can't—well, there's never any hard feelings. That's me all over. You may be able to *lick* me at this golf thing—likely you will; but you'll never scare me, that's a cinch. Probably you gentlemen play a better game than I do—been at it longer; but then I'm a lot younger than you are. Got more strength. Hit a longer ball when I do manage to land on one right. So it all evens up in the long run."

Mr. Cottle was still modestly cheering his many admirable qualities when Perkins party went in to luncheon, and the only pause he made was on the first tee. With his usual caution Uncle Billy had arranged it so that Dubuque was opposed to Southern California, and he had also carefully neglected to name any sort of a bet until after he had seen the stranger drive.

Cottle teed his ball and stood over it, gripping his driver until his knuckles showed white under the tan. "Get ready to ride!" said he. "You're about to leave this place!"

The clubhead whistled through the air, and I can truthfully say that I never saw a man of his size swing any harder at a golf ball—or come nearer cutting one completely in two.

"Topped it, by gum." ejaculated Mr. Cottle, watching the maimed ball until it disappeared in a bunker. "Topped it! Well, better luck next time! By the way, what are we playing for? Balls, or money, or what?"

"Whatever you like," said Uncle Billy promptly. "You name it."

"Good! That's the way I like to hear a man talk. Old Wes here is my partner, so I can't bet with him, but I'll have a side match with each of you gentlemen—say, ten great, big, smiling Iowa dollars. Always like to bet what I've got the most of. Satisfactory?"

Uncle Billy glanced at Old Man Sprott, and for an instant the old rascals hesitated. The situation was made to order for them, but they would have preferred a smaller wager to start with, being petty larcenists at heart.

"Better cut that down to five," said Perkins to Cottle in a low tone. "They play a strong game."

"Humph!" grunted his guest. "Did you ever know me to pike in my life? I ain't going to begin now. Ten dollars or nothing!"

"I've got you," said Uncle Billy. "It's against my principles to play for money; but yes, this once."

And then those two old sharks insisted on a four-some bet as well.

"Ball, ball, ball," said the Ooley-cow briefly, and proceeded to follow his partner into the bunker. Poindexter and Sprott popped conservatively down the middle of the course and the battle was on.

Battle, did you say? It was a massacre of the innocents, a slaughter of babes and sucklings. Our foursome trailed along behind, and took note of Mr. Cottle, of Dubuque, in his fruitless efforts to tear the cover off the ball. He swung hard enough to knock down a lamppost, but he seldom made proper connections, and when he did the ball landed so far off the course that it took him a dozen shots to get back again. He was hopelessly bad, so bad that there was no chance to make the side matches close ones. On the tenth tee Cottle demanded another bet—to give him a chance to get even, he said. Poindexter and Sprott each bet him another ten dollar note on the last nine, and this time Uncle Billy did not say anything about his principles.

After it was over Cottle poured a few mint toddies into his system and floated an alibi to the surface.

"It was those confounded sand greens that did it," said he. "I'm used to grass, and I can't putt on anything else. Bet I could take you to Dubuque and flail the ever-lasting daylights out of you!"

"Shouldn't be surprised," said Uncle Billy. "You did a lot better on the last nine—sort of got into your stride. Any time you think you want revenge—"

"You can have it," finished Old Man Sprott, as he folded a crisp twenty-dollar note. We believe in giving a man a chance—eh, Billy?"

"That's the spirit!" cried Cottle enthusiastically. "Give a man a chance; it's what I say, and if he does anything, give him credit. You beat me today, but I never saw this course before. Tell you what we'll do: Let's make a day of it tomorrow. Morning and afternoon both. Satisfactory? Good! You've got forty dollars of my dough and I want it back. Nobody ever made me quit betting yet, if I figure to have a chance. What's money? Shucks! My country is full of it! Now then, Wesley if you'll come out on the practice green and give me some pointers on this sand thing. I'll be obliged to you. Ball won't run on sand like it will on grass—have to get used to it. Have to hit 'em a little harder. Soon as I get the hang of the thing we'll give these Native Sons a battle yet! Native Sons? Native Grandfathers! Come on!" Uncle Billy looked at Old Man Sprott and Old Man Sprott looked at Uncle Billy, but they did not begin to laugh until the Ooley-cow and his guest were out of earshot. Then they chuckled and cackled and choked like a couple of hysterical old hens.

"His putting!" gurgled Uncle Billy. "Did he have a putt to win a hole all the way round?"

"Not unless he missed count of his shots. Say, Billy!"

"Well?"

"We made a mistake locating so far west. We should have stopped in Iowa. By now we'd have owned the entire state!"

I dropped Mr. Calvin D. Cottle entirely out of my thoughts; but when I entered the locker room shortly after noon the next day something reminded me of him. Possibly it was the sound of his voice.

"Boy! Can't we have 'nother toddy here? What's the matter with some service? How 'bout you, Wes? Oh, I forgot—you never take anything till after five o'clock. Think of all the fun you're missing. When I get to be an old fossil like you maybe I'll do the same. Good rule— You gentlemen having anything? No? Kind of careful, ain't you? Safety first, hey?—Just one toddy, boy, and if that mint ain't fresh, I'll—Yep, you're cagey birds, you are, but I give you credit just the same. And some cash. Don't forget that. Rather have cash than credit any time, hey? I bet you would! But I don't mind a little thing like that. I'm a good sport. You ask Wes here if I ain't. If I ain't a good sport I ain't anything—Still, I'll be darned if I see hoe you fellows do it! You're old enough to have sons in the Soldiers' Home over yonder, but you take me out and lick me again—lick me again and I like it! A couple of died-up mummies with one foot in the grave, and I'm right in the prime of life! Only a kid yet! It's humiliating, that's what it is, humiliating! Forty dollars apiece you're into me—and a flock of golf balls on the side! Boy! Where's the mint toddy? Let's have a little service here!"

I peeped through the door leading to the lounging room. The Dubuque-California foursome was grouped at a table in a corner. The Ooley-cow looked calm and placid as usual, but his guest was sweating profusely, and as he talked he mopped his brow with the sleeve of his shirt. Uncle Billy and Old Man Sprott were listening politely, but the speculative light in their eyes told me that they were wondering how far they dared go with this outlander from the Middle West.

"Why," boomed Cottle, "I can hit a ball twice as far as either one of you! 'Course I don't always know where it's going, but the main thing is I got the *strength*. I can throw a golf ball farther than you old fossils can hit one with a wooden club, yet you lick me easy as breaking sticks. Can't understand it all—Twice as strong as you are— Why, say, I bet I can take one hand and outdrive you! *One hand!*"

"Easy, Calvin," said the Ooley-cow reprovingly. "Don't make wild statements."

"Well, I'll bet I can do it," repeated Cottle stubbornly. "If a man's willing to bet his money to back up a wild statement, that shows he's got the right kind of heart anyway. I ought to be able to stick my left hand in my pocket and go out there and trim two men of your age. I ought to, and I'll be dammed if I don't think I can!"

"Tut, tut!" warned the Ooley-cow. "That's foolishness."

"Think so?" Cottle dipped his hand into his pocket and brought out a roll of bills. "Well, this stuff here says I can do it—at least I can *try*—and I ain't afraid to back my judgment."

"Put your money away," said Perkins. "Don't be a fool!"

Cottle laughed uproariously and slapped the Ooley-cow on the back.

"Good old Wes!" he cried. "Ain't changed a bit. Conservative! Always conservative! Got rich at it, but me I got rich taking chances. What's a little wad of bills to me, hey? Nothing but chicken-feed! I'll bet any part of this roll—I'll bet *all* of it—and I'll play these sundried old sports with one hand. Now's the time to show whether they've got any sporting blood or not. What do you say, gentlemen?"

Uncle Billy looked at the money and moistened his lips with the tip of his tongue.

"Couldn't think of it," he croaked at length.

"Pshaw!" sneered Cottle. "I showed you too much—I scared you!"

"He ain't scared," put in Old Man Sprott. "It would be too much like stealing it."

"I'm the one to worry about that," announced Cottle. "It's my money, ain't it? I made it, didn't I? And I can do what I damn please with it—spend it, bet it, burn it up, throw it away. When you've worried about everything else in the world, it'll be time for you to begin worrying about Mr. Cottle's money! This slim little roll—bah! Chicken-feed! Come get it if you want it!" He tossed the money on the table with a gesture which was an insult in itself. "There it is—cover it! Put up or shut up!"

"Oh, forget it!" said the Ooley-cow wearily. "Come in and have a bite to eat and forget it!"

"Don't want anything to eat!" was the stubborn response. "Seldom eat in the middle of the day. But I'll have 'nother mint toddy—Wait a second, Wes. Don't be in such a rush. Lemme understand this thing. These—these gentlemen here, these two friends of yours, these dead-game old Native Sons have got eighty dollars of my money—not that it makes any difference to me, understand, but they've got it—eighty dollars that they won from me playing golf. Now I may have a drink or two in me and I may not, understand, but anyhow I know what I'm about. I make these—gentlemen a sporting proposition. I give 'em a chance to pick up a couple of hundred apiece, and they want to run out on me because it'll be like stealing it. What kind of a deal is that, hey? Is it sportsmanship? Is it—"

"But they know you wouldn't have a chance," interrupted the Ooley-cow soothingly. "They don't want a sure thing."

"They've had one so far, haven't they" howled Cottle. "What are they scared of now? 'Fraid I'll squeal if I lose? Tell 'em about me, Wes. Tell 'em I never squealed in my life. I win if I can, but if I can't—'s all right. No kick coming. There never was a piker in the Cottle family, was there, Wes? No, you bet not! We're sports, every one of us. Takes more than one slim little roll to send us up a tree! If there's anything that makes me sick, it's a cold-footed, penny-pinching, nickel-nursing, sure-thing player!"

"Your money does not frighten me," said Uncle Billy, who was slightly nettled by this time. "It is against my principles to play for a cash bet—"

"But you and your pussy-footed old side-partner got into me for eighty dollars just the same!" scoffed Cottle. He was looking at the roll of bills on the table.

"If you are really earnest—" began Poindexter, and glanced at Old Man Sprott.

"Go ahead, Billy," croaked that aged reprobate. "Teach him a lesson. He needs it."

"Never mind the lesson," snapped Cottle. "I got out of school a long time ago. The bet is that I can leave my left arm in the clubhouse safe—stick it in my pocket—and trim you birds with one hand."

"We wouldn't insist on that," said Old Man Sprott. "Play with both hands if you want to."

"Think I'm a welsher?" demanded Cottle. "The original proposition goes. "'Course I wouldn't really cut the arm off and leave it in the safe, but what I mean is, if I use two arms in making a shot, right there is where I lose. Satisfactory?"

"Perkins," said Uncle Billy, solemnly wagging his head, "you are a witness that this thing has been forced on me. I have been bullied and browbeaten and insulted into making this bet—"

"And so have I," chimed in Old Man Sprott. "I'm almost ashamed—"

The Ooley-cow shrugged his shoulders.

"I am a witness," said he quietly. "Calvin, these gentlemen have stated the case correctly. You have forced them to accept your proposition—"

"And he can't blame anybody if he loses," finished Uncle Billy as he reached for the roll of bills.

"You bet!" ejaculated Old Man Sprott. "He was looking for trouble, and now he's found it. Count it, Billy, and we'll each take half."

"That goes, does it?" asked Cottle.

"Sir?" cried Uncle Billy.

"Oh, I just wanted to put you on record," said Cottle with a grin. "Wesley, you're my witness too. I mislaid a five-hundred-dollar note the other day, and it may have got into my change pocket. Might as well see if a big bet will put these safety-first players off their game! Anyhow, I'm betting whatever's there. I ain't sure how much it is."

"I am," said Uncle Billy in a changed voice. He had come to the five-hundred-dollar bill, sandwiched in between two twenties. He looked at Old Man Sprott, and for the first time I saw doubt in his eyes.

"Oh, it's there, is it?" asked Cottle carelessly. "Well, let it all ride. I never backed out on a gambling proposition in my life—never pinched a bet after the ball started to roll. Shoot the entire works—'s all right with me!"

Uncle Billy and Old Man Sprott exchanged significant glances, but after a short argument and some more abuse from Cottle they toddled over to the desk and filled out two blank checks—for five hundred and eighty dollars apiece.

"Make 'em payable to cash," suggested Cottle. "You'll probably tear them up after the game. Now the next thing is a stakeholder—"

"Is that necessary?" asked Old Man Sprott.

"Sure!" said Cottle. "I might run out on you. Let's have everything according to Hoyle—stakeholder and all the other trimmings. Anybody'll be satisfactory to me; that young fellow getting an earful at the door; he'll do."

So I became the stakeholder—the custodian of eleven hundred and sixty dollars in coin and two checks representing a like amount, I thought I detected a slight nervousness in the signatures, and no wonder. It was the biggest bet those old petty larcenists had ever made in their lives. They went in to luncheon—at the invitation of the Ooley-cow, of course—but I noticed that they did not eat much. Cottle wandered out to the practice green, putter in hand, forgetting all about mint toddy which, by the way, had never been ordered.

"You drive first, sir," said Uncle Billy to Cottle, pursuing his usual system. "We'll follow you."

"Think you'll feel easier if I should hit one over into the eucalyptus trees yonder?" asked the man from Dubuque. "Little nervous, eh? Does a big bet scare you? I was counting on that—Oh, very well, I'll take the honor."

"Just a second," said Old Man Sprott, who had been prowling about in the background and fidgeting with his driver. "Does the stakeholder understand the terms of the bet? Mr. Cottle is playing a match with each of us individually—"

"Separately and side by each," added Cottle.

"Using only one arm," said Old Man Sprott.

"If he uses both arms in making a shot," put in Uncle Billy, "he forfeits both matches. Is that correct, Mr. Cottle?"

"Correct as hell! Watch me closely, young man. I have no mustache to deceive you—nothing up my sleeve but my good right arm. Watch me closely!"

He teed his ball, dropped his left arm at his side, grasped the driver firmly in his right hand and swung the club a couple of times in tentative fashion. The head of the driver described a perfect arc, barely grazing the top of the tee. His two-armed swing had been a thing of violence—a baseball wallop, constricted, bound up, without follow-through or timing, a combination of brute strength and awkwardness. Uncle Billy's chin sagged as he watched the easy, natural sweep of that wooden club —the long graceful follow-through which gives distance as well as direction. Old Man Sprott also seemed to be struggling with an entirely new and not altogether pleasant idea.

"Watch me closely, stakeholder," repeated Cottle, addressing the ball. "Nothing up my sleeve but my good right arm. Would you gentlemen like to have me roll up my sleeve before I start?"

"Drive!" grunted Uncle Billy.

"I'll do that little thing," said Cottle, and this time he put the power into the swing. The ball, caught squarely in the middle of the clubface, went whistling toward the distant green, a perfect screamer of a drive without a suspicion of hook or slice. It cleared the cross-bunker by ten feet, carried at least a hundred and eighty yards before it touched grass, and then bounded ahead like a scared rabbit, coming to rest at least two hundred and twenty-five yards away. "You like that?" asked Cottle, moving off the tee. "I didn't step into it very hard or I might have had more distance. Satisfactory, stakeholder?" And he winked at me openly and deliberately.

"What—what sort of game is this?" gulped Old Man Sprott, finding his voice with an effort.

"Why," said Cottle, smiling cheerfully, "I wouldn't like to say offhand and so early in the game, but you might call it golf. Yes, call it golf, and let it go at that."

At this point I wish to go on record as denying the rumor that our two old reprobates showed the white feather. That first tee shot, and the manner in which it was made, was enough to inform them that they were up against a sickening surprise party; but, though startled and shaken, they did not weaken. They pulled themselves together and drove the best they knew how, and realized that for once I was to see their true golfing from uncovered.

Cottle tucked his wooden club under his arm and started down the course, and from that time on he had very little to say. Uncle Billy and Old Man Sprott followed him, their heads together at a confidential angle, and I brought up the rear with the Ooley-cow, who had elected himself a gallery of one.

The first hole is a long par four. Poindexter and Sprott usually make it in five, seldom getting home with their seconds unless they have a wind behind them. Both used brassies and both were short of the green. Then they watched Cottle as he went forward to his ball.

"That drive might have been a freak shot," quavered Uncle Billy.

"Lucky fluke, that's all," said Old Man Sprott, but I knew and they knew that they only hoped they were telling the truth Cottle paused over his ball for an instant, examined the lie and drew a wooden spoon from his bag. Then he set himself, and the next instant the ball was on its way, a long, high shot, dead on the pin.

"He's got the green on it!"

From the same distance I would have played a full mid-iron and trusted Providence, but Cottle had used his wood, and I may say that never have I seen a ball better placed. It carried to the little rise of turf in front of the putting green, hopped once, and trickled close to the cup. I was not the only one who appreciated that spoon shot.

"Say," yapped Old Man Sprott, turning to Perkins, "what are we up against here? Miracles?"

"Yes, what have you framed up on us?" demanded Uncle Billy vindictively.

"Something easy, gentlemen," chuckled the Ooley-cow. "A soft thing from my home town. Probably he's only lucky."

The two members of the Sure-Thing Society went after their customary fives and got them, but Cottle laid his approach putt stone dead at the cup and holed out in four. He missed a three by the matter of half an inch. I could stand the suspense no longer. I took Perkins aside while the contestants were walking to the second tee.

"You might tell a friend," I suggested. "In strict confidence, what are they up against?"

"Something easy," repeated the Ooley-cow, regarding me with his soft, innocent eyes. "They wanted it and now they've got it."

"But yesterday, when he played with both arms—" I began.

"That was yesterday," said Perkins. "You'll notice that

they didn't have the decency to offer him a handicap, even when they felt morally certain that he had made a fool bet. Not that he would have accepted it—but they didn't offer it. They're wolves, clear to the bone, but once in a while a wolf bites off more than he can chew." And he walked away from me. Right there I began reconstructing my opinion of the Ooley-cow.

In my official capacity as stakeholder I saw every shot that was played that afternoon. I still preserve the original score card of that amazing round of golf. There are times when I think I will have it framed and present it to the club, with red-ink crosses against the thirteen and fourteen holes. I might even set a red-ink star against the difficult sixth hole, where Cottle sent another tremendous spoon shot down the wind, and took a four where most of our Class-A men are content with five. I might make a notation against the tricky ninth, where he played a marvelous shot out of a sand trap to halve a hole which I would have given up as lost. I might make a footnote calling attention to his deadly work with his short irons. I say I think of all these things, but perhaps I shall never frame that card. The two men most interested will never forget the figures. It is enough to say that Old Man Sprott, playing such golf as I had never seen him play before, succumbed at the thirteenth hole, six down and five to go. Uncle Billy gave up the ghost the fourteenth green, five and four, and I handed the money and the checks to Mr. Calvin D. Cottle, of Dubuque. He pocketed the loot with a grin.

"Shall we play the bye-holes for something?" he asked. "A drink—or a ball, maybe?" And then the storm broke. I do not pretend to quote the exact language of the losers. I merely state that I was surprised, yes, shocked at Uncle

Billy Poindexter. I had no idea that a member of the Epis-copal church—but let that pass. He was not himself. He was the biter bitten, the milker milked. It makes a differ-ence. Old Man Sprott also erupted in an astounding man-ner. It was the Ooley-cow who took the center of the stage.

"Just a minute, gentlemen," said he. "Do not say any-thing which you might afterward regret. Remember the stakeholder is still with us. My friend here is not, as you intimate, a crook. Neither is he a sure-thing player. We have some sure-thing players with us, but he is not one of them. He is merely the one-armed golf champion of Dubuque—and the Middle West."

Imagine an interlude here for fireworks, followed by pertinent questions.

"Yes, yes, I know," said Perkins soothingly. "He can't play a lick with two arms. He never could. Matter of fact, he never learned. He fell off a haystack in Iowa—how many years ago was it, Cal?"

"Twelve," said Mr. Cottle. "Twelve next July."

"And he broke his left arm rather badly," explained the Ooley-cow. "Didn't have the use of it for—how many years, Cal?"

"Oh, about six, I should say."

"Six years. A determined man can accomplish much in that length of time. Cottle learned to play golf with his right arm—fairly well, as you must admit. Finally he got the left arm fixed up—they took a piece of bone out of his shin and grafted it in—new-fangled idea. Decide there was no sense in spoiling a one-armed star to make a dub two-armed golfer. Country full of 'em already. That's the whole story. You picked him for an easy mark, a good thing. You thought he had a bad bet and you had a good one. Don't take the trouble to deny it. Gentlemen, allow me to present the champion one-armed golfer of Iowa and the Middle West!"

"Yes," said Cottle modestly, "when a man does anything, give him credit for it. Personally I'd rather have the cash!"

"How do you feel about it now?" asked the Ooley-cow.

Judging by their comments, they felt warm—very warm. Hot, in fact. The Ooley-cow made just one more statement, but to me that statement contained the gist of the whole matter.

"This," said he, "squares us on the wallet proposition. I didn't say anything about it at the time, but that struck me as a scaly trick. So I invited Cal to come out and pay me a visit—Shall we go back to the clubhouse?"

I made Little Doc Ellis see the point; perhaps I can make you see it now.

Returning to the original simile, the Ooley-cow was willing to be milked for golf balls and luncheons and caddie hire. That was legitimate milking, and he did not resent it. He would have continued to give down in great abundance, but when they took fifty dollars from him, in the form of a bogus reward, he kicked over the bucket, injured the milkers and jumped the fence.

Why? I'm almost ashamed to tell you, but did you ever hear a country cow—an Iowa cow—that would stand for being milked from the wrong side?

I think this will be all, except that I anticipate a hard winter for the golfing beginners at our club.

If you're a golfer and you're on your game, life is a bowl of cherries.
JACK NICKLAUS

How to Get Out of Trouble in Golf

WILLIE TUCKER

A Scotch proverb says, "He who plays with a thistle must expect to get pricked," and he who plays golf must expect to get into trouble. Indeed, a golfer's life is one continuous series of problems, "How to get out of trouble." Trouble he will have, willy-nilly. This may at first blush seem a somewhat dispiriting view to take of so fascinating a game, but it is the very variety of the points of the game, ever occurring yet scarcely ever duplicated, that give it its unique position. It is this that renders it so exhilarating to the devotee, both mentally and physically.

I have not especially in my mind the troubles which beset beginners, for the reason that no amount of precept has for the beginner half the value of a very small quantity of example, and nowhere except upon the links can anything really worth learning be taught. Even there, however, there are troubles special to golf besetting the beginner. The main of these is not so much in the acquisition of the knowledge of how to perform this or that motion, as it is in overcoming the habits of childhood or youth acquired in the wielding of the baseball bat, the cricket bat or the polo stick. The novitiate who comes to golf from any of these field sports has tendencies and instinctive habits of holding the club and striking the ball that are indeed hard to eradicate; they are habit that have become second nature; they have become imbedded, as it were, in the bone, and nothing but the most determined and long-continued efforts can eradicate these very troublesome tendencies.

When, however, these have been overcome on the links, there yet remains a crop of troubles upon which hypothetical and written advice is nearly as valuable as example, for the reason that the experience gained in early play enables the novitiate to understand what is written an impossibility in the very earliest stages of the game. Just as it is useless to explain higher arithmetic to a pupil who has never heard of the multiplication table, so it is useless to expect a pupil who has never held a club in his hands to comprehend terms relating to "slicing," "drawing," "following on." Yet the bulk of the instructors who have favored the world with their practical hints flood their writings with what, to the beginner, must be jargon. I propose these observations only for those who have, by practice on the links, discovered how much more there is yet to learn, and what an infinite variety of trouble and pleasure lies before them.

Let me illustrate: We will suppose that a player is fairly experienced in all the lesser minutiæ of the game; that he has command of his club; that he can drive with accuracy and putt with fair precision, and that he can traverse a course of eighteen holes in, say one hundred strokes. Still, giving all these qualifications in, there will only be thirty-six strokes—two strokes for each hole, the drive-off and the holding—which may be counted upon with anything like certainty. He may be able to drive with fair accuracy an estimated number of yards from each tee and *putt* an estimated number of feet on each green, but, between the anchorage of the tee and the port of the green, what uncertainties will arise? Ah, there's the rub! The power of the wind may be misjudged, or its direction miscalculated; he may drive too high, and his ball fall without an inch of *run* in it, or he may drive too low, and a long run may take it into the much-dreaded long grass. It may strike an unseen tree-limb, or get into the intricacies of a stone wall; it may glide into a ditch or fly off at a tangent and overshoot the aimed-at mark. All these and a thousand other posers will meet the golfer, golf he never so wisely.

The main purpose of all advice to the golfer must, therefore, be "how to get out of trouble," what club to use under certain general conditions, why to use it, what it will effect, what it will not effect, and the method of getting the most out of the club and of the player's physique.

Vanishing Acts

HORACE G. HUTCHINSON

If your adversary is a hole or two down, there is no serious cause for alarm in his complaining of a severely sprained wrist, or an acute pain, resembling lumbago, which checks his swing. Should he happen to win the next hole, these symptoms will in all probability become less troublesome.

Hints on Golf

. . . And how beautiful the vacated links at dawn,
when the dew gleams untrodden beneath the pendant flags
and the long shadows lie quiet on the green;
when no caddie intrudes upon the still and silent lawns,
and you stroll from hole to hole and drink in
the beauties of a land to which you know
you will be all too blind when the sun
mounts high and you toss for the honor!
ARNOLD HAULTAIN

Putting the Ladies Right

E. M. BOYS

There is a theory extant that the 'weaker sex' is (if one may use such a paradox) the stronger at putting; but, after some years' experience, I must candidly confess that I have always found women painfully erratic putters. Of course, there are brilliant exceptions; but, speaking collectively, I have not found women to be much superior in this respect to men. The few really good putters are, curiously enough, generally weak in their play through the green or in their driving, and one rarely meets a player who is proficient in all three. 'Putting is an Inspiration,' we are told, but I am more inclined to agree with the man who so sapiently said, 'Putting is the Devil!' On days when every putt goes down, no matter how remote you may be from the hole, you are ready to say proudly, 'Putting is an Inspiration,' but on other days, when you are losing hole after hole through atrocious putting, you would fain proclaim aloud the other sentiment.

Badminton Magazine

The Double Bogey Golfer's Manifesto

HOLLIS ALPERT, IRA MOTHNER AND HAROLD SCHONBERG

"If God had meant man to golf," argued Peter Piper the Elder before the Aberdeen presbytery, back when Scotland first sanctioned Sunday sports, "the Almighty would have made man's right side shorter than his left. Thus, he could not but strike the ball out fair and high." Besides using the word "golf" as a verb for the very first time and revealing greater knowledge of the game (if little kinesiology) than any other 17th-century divine, old Peter put his finger on golfing's number one problem. Few men (and women) are naturally designed to play it well.

Indeed, the "classic" golf swing—that illusory arc, pivot, and push—is perhaps the most unnatural of all athletic movements. God simply could not have intended man to play par golf. If He had, then a perfect swing would be as automatic as the movement of fork to face. Since it is not, golfers must struggle against their divine- ly programmed inclination to handle a driver as though it were an ax, sledge, or mallet. "Golf," declared piper's great-hearted contemporary MacTeague, the Sage of Frither Glen, "was sent to test mankind."

The testing can be heard on tee and green, in rough and bunker throughout the land, particularly on warm Sabbath mornings, as golfers rant and bend their clubs in distress, resisting a fate that has nailed their handicaps somewhere north of 20. They resist double bogeydom, their natural condition, for lack of spirit and the strength of character to accept it. By far the most tortuous part of the test is to view without rancor those happy few with perfect or nearly perfect golfing motions. They exist, as do others who can accomplish *pirouettes en pointe* and four-minute miles or traverse Olympian swimming pools, butterfly fashion, in 26 seconds flat. "Many are called, but few to greatness," as MacTeague has said. Only a select number are given the means to control the raising and lowering of their golfing utensils so as to speed balls hole- ward in booming drives and pitches of majestic precision. Plainly, they are freaks.

Thorvald MacDougal, a high-handicap contem- porary of Young Tommy Morris (four times the Births

Open champion, winning first in 1868) has written wisely on the proper attitude to take toward scratch or near-scratch golfers. "Courtesy, decency and simple right-thinking instruct us to ignore the deformities of others. Yet, good and kindly souls, who would not dream of starting at a cripple or making sport of a midget, will peer and ogle and make a great show over golfers whose skills are so at odds with normal abilities as to be market eccentric or unnatural." To MacDougal is credited golf's great social doctrine. It was he who said, "All golfers are peers."

If indeed all golfers are peers or equals, then the Double Bogey Golfer is most equal of all. No golf club of 250 playing members can have many more than a score of championship class players and two score of straight bogeymen. Of course, we are counting *every* member—matron, maid, stripling, and codger—and every stroke, not just those the prideful post on their good days. Clearly, the vast majority of golfers follow the Almighty's design and round the course in man's natural relationship to pat—double bogey.

This is not badness. It is the golden mean of golf, for the sad truth is that there are subdouble bogey inadequates just as there are near-scratch freaks. Not everyone has the skill and rhythm to break the 110-stroke barrier that is the bottom line of double bogeydom.

It was MacDougal, the first great champion of the "natural" (i.e., high handicap) golfer, who declared: "Let the governance of great golf rest with the greatest group of golfers."

Obviously, he was speaking out for his own, raising a challenge to the tyranny of excellence that dominated the game in his day as in ours. Low-handicap golfers have always been a pushy and puffed-up lot. They have never perceived that their abilities do not make them *better* than other players. They make them *different*, strange, queer, peculiar, and certainly unsuitable to determine what is best for all of golfing mankind.

The authors do not go so far as MacDougal, who considered a low handicap to be as desirable an attribute as wens or warts. We say there is a place for the low handicapper on the course (though they are an impatient crew) and room for them in the clubhouse (boastful and loutish lot though they may be). But there is no more room for them on golf, greens, rules and tournament committees, save in proportion to their numbers. It is not for such as them to determine the placement of pins, the length of holes, thickness of rough, prizes, paintings and when winter rules may be played. "We will not," as Mac-Dougal protested, "be ground under the mashies of sweaty semi-professionals and exhibitionists."

Why have MacDougal's words fallen on deaf ears? Why has not the mass of golfing humanity risen to claim its rightful dominance of the game? It is because the lesson of MacTeague, Sage of Frither Glen, has been lost. "Golf was sent to test mankind." And we have, thus far, failed the test. We have to a man (and increasingly to a woman) scorned our natural state, struggled to pervert double bogeydom into something rigid and artificial, in direct violation of the Almighty's genius.

The test of golf is not athletic, but spiritual. It is not our game that must improve; it is ourselves. We must be at peace with the duffer within us. Only then will we grow in spirit, and growth of spirit is what golfing is all about.

How To Play Double Bogey Golf

The Follow-Through

HARRY VARDON

A hint I give to all my pupils to encourage their follow-through is that when they are bringing the club down on to the ball, they should imagine that they have not only to hit the ball that they see, but another one about six inches in front of it also. This induces the club to go forward in the line of the flight of the ball, and is one of the most effectual hints I know.

I like to see the arms finish well up, with the hands level with the head. This generally means a properly hit ball and a good follow-through.

The Complete Golfer

The Golfer's Alphabet

K. V. KENEALY

A is for Andrew, the Saint of the game,
B for the Bunker that made him profane.
C is for Caddie, inscrutable Sphinx,
D for a bad word they use on the links.
E for the Expert by whom links are laid,
F for the Fluke that the *other* man made!
G is for Golf, the game "Ancient and Royal,"
H is for Hazard, the golfer to foil.
I th'Infatuation when once you've begun,
J is the Joy when you've "holed out" in one.
K is the Kilt which weather defies,
L is for Lofter to make the ball rise.
M is for Morris, the famous Golf Veteran,
N must be Novice, I can't find a better 'un!

O's the opponent, on winning so keen,
P is the Putter he wields on the green.
Q for the Queries to drive editors wild,
R the Replies so kindly and mild.
S is the Score that you make on the Links,
T is for Tee (*not* the kind that one drinks!)
U the Ubiquitous "Bogey" we fear,
V is for Vardon, the "crack" of the Year.
W is the Drink which to Scotch Golf conduces,
X the 'Xpletive a "Foozle" produces!
Y is the Yell in which you cry "Fore,"
Z is the Zenith of joy when you score
　　Has beaten the record of "Bogey" by four!

Golf

Trouble Shots

Julius Boros

At one time or another every golfer finds himself off the fairway, faced with a difficult shot. Sometimes you can't avoid having to accept the loss of a stroke or two to get you back into play. If that's the story, accept it and consider yourself lucky it wasn't worse. What can make it worse is to try to get back into play by means of a miraculous shot, often leading to three or four extra strokes. This rarely happens to a smart golfer. He knows his game and what he can and cannot do.

On the other hand, situations that often look like trouble are really not trouble at all. A flat lie in the rough isn't any different from a flat lie in the fairway. Don't get the jitters just because it's the rough. Should conditions be such that you cannot swing or stand normally, then you must make the necessary adjustments. Take the most comfortable stance you can find, grip down on the shaft if necessary, swing back with deliberate control and *stroke* the ball out. Don't tighten up and pound the ball viciously. The main thing to remember on these shots is to relax and stroke the ball. In "playing safe" to get out of trouble, you must still use your head to avoid going from one trap to another or coming out of the woods and crossing to the woods on the other side. Hit just hard enough to get the ball back into play.

Here are two dependable rules to follow when you're in a difficult situation: (1) Decide whether the penalty is worth taking, especially within the limits of your shot-producing capabilities. (2) If you decide to play the shot, use your ingenuity. For example, if you have to play a left-handed shot away from a tree, fence, etc., your putter might be just the club to turn the trick.

Not long ago, I had an interesting dilemma. I hit a shot which landed green high but off to one side, about six inches from an out-of-bounds stone wall. Because I couldn't get a club between the ball and the wall, I played my shot into the wall and bounced it onto the green. Admittedly they're usually not that dramatic but a more extensive use of your imagination might solve some of those troublesome situations.

Swing Easy, Hit Hard

The game is not as easy as it seems. In the first place, the terrible inertia of the ball must be overcome.
LORD WELLWOOD

The Importance of Style

WILLIE PARK

It is of the first importance that a golfer should have a good style of play, these words being here used as including grip of club, stance, and swing. One frequently hears this said, "What does my style signify provided I can play a good game?" To this I would reply, "It is also said that if the best golfers be closely watched no two of them have the same style, and which among all these styles is the correct one?" My answer to this is that there are few crack players who have not a good style, and that although there may be, and undoubtedly are, many whose styles are different in detail, they are fundamentally the same—they are all modeled on the recognized lines. There are, however, among the followers of every game men whose play can hardly be excelled, and who yet violate the canons of style. Such players have been termed geniuses, and a few are to be found among the ranks of golfers; but I would further say that these are the exceptions that prove the rule. The imitators of geniuses seldom attain to any perfection, and generally find it difficult to reach mediocrity. For geniuses no rules can be laid down—their success justifies their play, but only their success. Failure would heap on their heads deserved ridicule.

I would recommend all golfers to model their styles upon the recognized lines that have stood the test of decades of play at the hand of the best amateurs and professionals. If anyone finds himself to be a genius, he can easily carve out his own particular style, and will be none the worse, but probably much the better, for having begun upon the orthodox lines.

The Game Of Golf

A Little Bit

HARVEY PENICK

THE GOLF SWING is one swing, but it is made up of little things all working together.

Dutch Harrison said, "A little bit is a little bit."

This means that the club hitting the ball just a little bit off angle is going to grow into a large error by the time the ball flies out there. If the clubface is two or three degrees off at impact, the ball will be 29–30 yards off at 200 yards.

There are four things that make a good shot—angle of clubface, path of club, clubhead speed at impact and hitting the ball in the center of the clubface.

We talk so much about the swing that we forget the angle of face at impact is just as important.

Many golfers look at the so-called slice slashes on the bottoms of their woods and think they are swinging across the ball from the outside.

But it could just as easily be an open clubface that causes the marks.

Square your clubface at address to give yourself a better chance to keep it square at impact. Some students insist on opening their clubface at address, and a very few feel better with it closed. When I show them a square clubface, they can hardly believe it.

There is no other feeling quite like the euphoria of hitting a golf ball with a square clubface and connecting on what is called the sweet spot. Actually the sweet spot is the "no-roll" spot, where the ball comes off absolutely straight, not spinning to one side or the other. This shot is usually hit accidentally, even though you are trying.

The average player will hit maybe three shots on the sweet spot in 18 holes. Ben Hogan said by his high standards he hit the sweet spot maybe once in a round. "If I hit the sweet spot four or five times, I would shoot in the fifties," he told me.

The important question is not how good your good shots are—it's how bad are your bad ones?

Even beginners hit one of these sweet-spot shots now and then. The rush of thrill and excitement resulting from it is what inspires learners to want to get better, so they can have this wondrous feeling again.

One does not try to square the clubface. It just gets squared up in a good swing.

Players readily admit, "I'm a golf nut," or "I'm a golf addict."

They get addicted to the joy of hitting good shots.

When you begin to square your clubface, you will satisfy your addiction much more often.

Remember—a little bit is a little bit.

Harvey Penick's Little Red Book

Three things there are as unfathomable as they are fascinating to the masculine mind: metaphysics, golf, and the feminine heart. The Germans, I believe, pretend to have solved some of the riddles of the first, and the French to have unraveled some of the intricacies of the last; will someone tell us wherein lies the extraordinary fascination of golf?

ARNOLD HAULTAIN

The Golf Lie

WALTER SIMPSON

To some minds the great field which golf opens up for exaggeration is its chief attraction. Lying about the length of one's drives has this advantage over most forms of falsehood, that it can scarcely be detected. Your audience may doubt your veracity, but they cannot prove your falsity. Even when some rude person proves your shot to be impossibly long, you are not cornered. You admit to an exceptional loft, to a skid off a paling, or, as a last appeal to the father of lies, you may rather think that a dog lifted your ball. "Anyhow," you add conclusively, "that is where we found it when we came up to it."

The Art of Golf

If You Dare to Make the Ball Suck Back

GREG NORMAN

There's an old story about the budding golfer who asks the old pro how he can get more backspin on his 5-iron shots.

"How far do you hit your 5-iron?" asks the pro.

"About 110 yards," says the pupil, to which the pro replies, "Then why do you want to make it come *back?*"

The fact is, if you hit your 5-iron only 110 yards, you do not have the strength or ability to make your iron shots spin back. If, however, you can hit a 5-iron at least 160 yards, then that suck-back shot you've seen me and other pros hit on television or at tournaments is definitely within your capability.

It's a wonderful shot to have, particularly when

you're playing hard greens, or when you need to get close to a pin that's positioned just beyond the lip of a front bunker. And the way I see it, if I can spin the ball back and they can't, I have a big advantage on my opponents—they can only make the ball go in from the front of the hole while I can use either the front or the back!

The gallery loves to watch these shots, and I admit that I do too. One of my favorites came in the Italian Open a few years ago. They were offering a Lamborghini Countach that year for the first player who could make a hole in one on any of the par-threes. When I teed off for my second round, no one had done the deed.

At the second hole I hit an 8-iron that landed 15 feet past the pin, took one hop, and sucked back straight into the hole. Boy, was I excited. Fast cars are one of my greatest loves, and I had never driven a Lamborghini.

Well, when I got to the clubhouse, I was informed that a young Italian club pro had aced one of the other par-threes 10 minutes before I had made mine. That $100,000 car had pulled out of my pocket just as quickly as it had parked. And what did I get for making the *second* ace? A leather carry-all!

But I still have the memory of that hole in one, and of countless other shots that I've been able to hit into or near the hole because of an ability to apply extra backspin.

Shark Attack!

The average golfer does not improve stroke by stroke. Improvement comes in plateaus.
HARVEY PENNICK

Dr. Johnson on the Links

ANDREW LANG

On the morning after our arrival in St. Andrews Dr. Johnson expressed a desire to see the ruins of ecclesiastical antiquity for which this place is famous, or, I should say, infamous. Yielding to a roguish temptation of which I am ashamed, and which even now astonishes me, I determined to practice on the credulity of my venerated friend. I therefore, under pretense of leading Dr. Johnson to the ruins, carried him to that part of the vicinity which is called the Links. It is an undulating stretch of grassy land, varied by certain small elevations, which I assured Dr. Johnson covered all the ecclesiastical ruins that time and the license of the rabble had spared.

He was much moved, and refused to be covered, as on consecrated ground, while he walked along the Links, a course of some two miles. Often he would pause, and I heard him mutter *perierunt etiam ruinæ*. I ventured to ask him his opinion of John Knox, when he replied, in a sensible agitation, "Sir, he was worthy to be the opprobrious leader of your opprobrious people." I was hardly recovered from this blow at my nation, when Dr. Johnson's wig was suddenly and violently removed from his head, and carried to a certain distance.

We were unable to account for this circumstance, and Dr. Johnson was just about stooping to regain his property, when a rough fellow, armed with a few clubs, of which some had threatening heads of iron, came up hastily, saying, "Hoot awa'! ye maunna stir the hazard."

It appears that his golf ball, struck by him from a distance, had displaced Dr. Johnson's wig, and was still reposing in his folds. Before I could interfere the fellow had dealt a violent stroke at the perruque, whence the ball, soaring in an airy curve, alighted at a considerable distance. I have seldom seen my venerable friend more moved than by this unexpected assault upon his dignity.

"Sir," said he to the fellow, "you have taken an unwarranted liberty with one who neither provokes nor pardons insult." At the same moment he hastily disembarrassed himself of his coat, and appeared in his shirt-sleeves, which reminded me of his avowed lack of partiality for clean linen.

Assuming an attitude of self-defense, he planted one blow on his adversary's nose, and another in his abdomen, with such impetuosity and science that the rascal fell, and bellowed for mercy. This Dr. Johnston was pleased to grant, after breaking all his weapons.

He then resumed his coat, and with an air of good-humored triumph, he remarked, "It is long, sir, since I knocked a man down, and I feel myself the better for the exercise."

At this moment we came within view of the Cathedral towers, and I instantly felt considerable apprehension lest, on discovering my trick, he might bestow one on me the same correction as he had just administered to the golfer. I therefore hastily took the opportunity to call his attention to the towers, remarking that they were the remains of certain small chapels, which had suffered less from the frenzy of the rabble than the Cathedral, on whose site, as I told him, we were now walking. Thus I endeavored to give him a higher, and possibly an exaggerated, idea of the ancient resources and ecclesiastical magnificence of my country.

"Sir," he said, "we will examine later the contemptible relics which the idiotic fury of your ancestors has spared; meantime I must have a Roll. It is a long time, sir, since I had a Roll."

He then, to my alarm, ascended the highest of certain knolls or hummocks, laid himself down at full length, and permitted himself to revolve slowly over and over till he reached the level ground.

He was now determined to exercise himself at the game of Golf, which I explained to him as the Scotch form of cricket. Having purchased a ball and club, he threw himself into the correct attitude, as near as he could imitate it, and delivered a blow with prodigious force. Changing to strike at the same time both the ball and the ground, the head of his club flew off to an immense distance. He was pleased with this instance of his prowess, but declined, on the score of expense, to attempt another experiment.

"Sir," he said, "if Goldsmith were here, he would try to persuade us that he could urge a sphere to a greater distance and elevation than yonder gentleman who has just hit over that remote sand pit."

Knowing his desire for information, I told him that, in Scotch, a sand pit is called a Bunker. "Sir," said he, "I wonder out of what *colluvies* of barbarism your people selected the jargon which you are pleased to call a language. Sir, you have battened on the broken meats of human speech, and have carried away the bones. A sand pit, sir, is a sand pit."

I was somewhat deadened by this unlooked-for reception of an innocent remark. Meanwhile he had fallen into an abstract fit, from which I attempted to rouse him, by asking him what he would do if landed on a desert island, with no company but a Cannibal.

"Sir," he said, "I should consider myself more fortunately situated than when landed on an island, equally uncultivated, with no companion but an inquisitive Scotchman. From a Cannibal, sir, I could learn much. From you I can neither learn anything, nor have I any confidence in my power to communicate to you the elements of civilized behavior."

He burst on this into a heart fit of laughter, which was concluded by a golf ball, which suddenly flew, from an incredible distance, into his mouth, and produced an alarming fit of coughing. When he had recovered from this paroxysm he appeared somewhat disinclined for further conversation, and on arriving at our inn, he said, "Sir, do not let us meet again till dinner. Sir, you have brought me to a strange place of singular manners. I did not believe, sir, that in his Majesty's dominions there was any district so barbarous, and so perilous to travelers."

Finding him in this mood, and observing that he grasped his staff in a menacing manner, I withdrew to a neighboring tavern.

Dr. Johnson on the Links

To a Golf Ball

J. H. HAYES

Long ago, when first I bought you,
You were white and fairly round,
And a little gem I thought you,
Teed upon the teeing ground.

But, alas! the months have vanished,
And, if I must speak the truth,

They have altogether banished
The resemblance to your youth.

For I've "pulled" you and I've "sliced" you,
And you've lain in banks of gorse,
And I've temptingly enticed you
From the cart-ruts on the course.

So, though quite devoid of beauty,
I would claim you as a friend
Who has nobly done his duty
From beginning to the end.

And receive my thanks unsparing,
That you've heard with dumb assent,
The perhaps too-frequent swearing
Which I've used, though never meant.

Golf

"Let's let this guy play through, okay?"

Memory Losses

HORACE G. HUTCHINSON

Again, if you hear a man complaining of have "lost all interest" in a match which he has lately played, you will be pretty safe in inferring that he lost it. The winner very seldom experiences this feeling.

Hints on Golf

The Perfect Golfer

SIR OWEN SEAMAN

As a set off to that common character, the very human golfer, who ascribes his failures to his opponent's luck and his own liver, I am tempted to submit a slight sketch of the perfect match-losing temperament as I observed it —for the last time, I hope—in the person of that paragon of golfers, Gabriel Goodwin.

When we met on the first tee yesterday his face wore an extreme pallor, the result of a recent nasty attack of influenza.

'Going strong?' I asked, for I am not in the habit of making concessions to the health of my opponents.

'Never fitter in my life,' he answered cheerily.

'Been playing much lately?' I asked.

'No,' he said; 'but I'm always better after a rest. I ought to do pretty well to-day.'

He drove off and topped the ball badly. As it approached the cross-bunker a brave smile lit up his filmy eye.

'Serves me right,' he said genially. Then, as the ball

scrambled over and lay clear beyond, 'Tut! tut!' he said with a frown; 'just my luck!'

I responded with a hard low drive that should have traveled 250 yards at least, but it caught the bunker full in the face and fell in.

'Just your luck!' he said, and was obviously pained. And indeed I could see that he took little pleasure in winning the hole with three strokes to spare.

On the second tee he sliced hopelessly into the rough.

'Funny thing,' he said; 'it isn't as if I wasn't feeling fit.'

I followed suit in the same direction.

'A bit of colour—what?' he said sympathetically.

Both balls were lost. He left his caddie to search for his, and came over and found mine for me. His own was never retrieved.

'All square,' I said. I saw no occasion to refer to his bad luck, but he clearly felt that the thing might be weighing on my mind, so he just said,

'Mine was much the worse shot; and anyhow, if I'd found my ball I doubt if it would have been playable.'

At the seventh green (he was now three up, in face of the most execrable fortune) a marvelous recovery from a bunker laid his ball dead.

'Good,' I said, for I could afford to be lavish, having something in hand this time.

'Pure fluke,' he answered.

I had three putts for the hole and scratched the first two of them.

'I'm afraid you're not in the best of health,' he said.

'Oh, I'm all right.' I answered snappily.

I had still a four-foot putt to win the hole and missed it.

'Have it again!' said Goodwin; 'I put you off by telling my caddie to keep still.'

'The hole is halved,' I said coldly.

After the turn, where he was five up, he visibly tired, and once or twice he swayed as if he would fall. Indeed, at the thirteenth hole, where a gallant brassey shot just trickled him into the water-bunker (two strokes later I hopped it with a fluffed iron, without protest on his part or comment on minezzz) a touch of vertigo nearly toppled him in while he was fishing his ball out.

'Anyhow, it wanted washing,' was all he said.

At the sixteenth hole, after an unparalleled run of luck, I had him down to one. Every time I just fell short of a bunker he would say, 'Well judged!' and when I scraped through he would say, 'Hard luck! Took all the run off your ball!'

At the seventeenth he could hardly stand, and missed a 9-inch putt.

'All square!' I said, on a note of triumph.

'Anybody's game,' he replied brightly.

At the eighteenth he was within a foot-and-a-half with his third. I had to play the odd from fifteen yards away, and the match was as good as over. At the best I could only hope to halve it. I putted desperately and lipped the hole, laying him a dead stymie. He had two for half, and his plain business was to take no risks. But a gay smile broke over his wan cheek as he called aloud for his niblick.

'One seldom gets a chance of trying this stroke,' he said, 'and now's an excellent opportunity.'

I breathed a short sharp prayer that he might knock me in and remain outside himself.

He did.

'I've often wanted to see that done,' he said, with a rippling laugh.

'My game!' I said.

'And well deserved,' said he, as he offered me the price of a first-class ball.

'But we had not bet,' I said.

'Oh, but surely we had,' said he.

Being flushed with victory and in a generous mood, I hadn't the heart to deny him.

●   ●   ●   ●

'How did you get on with Goodwin?' said the Secretary after lunch.

'Oh, I won all right,' I said.

'Then you've made him a happy man. If there's one thing he enjoys more than winning, it is being beaten.'

'Well, next time,' I said, 'I think I'll play with some one who makes excuses on the score of health, and blames his luck and complains of mine and hates losing. You get more satisfaction that way. There's no fun in beating these inhuman angels. I'd as soon whack an india rubber bogie.'

Defense in Disbelieving

WALTER SIMPSON

The supposed necessity for pressing is born of too much respect for the enemy. Because they have got the best of you for the moment and played the hole perfectly up to a certain point, they are credited with being infallible, and you see no chance of their going into a bunker or taking four to hole off an iron. It is scarcely ever politic to

count the enemy's chickens before they are hatched. . . .
A secret disbelief in the enemy's play is very useful for
match play.

The Art of Golf

Withholding Praise

HORACE G. HUTCHINSON

Though the henchman who carries your clubs may be a
most able adviser, you will seldom, as a beginner, derive
much encouragement from his criticism. If he should
happen to remark, "Ye learnt your game from Mr. So-
and-so, I'm thing?—" naming the celebrated player from
whom as a matter of fact you did receive your first
instructions—you must not conclude too hastily, and in
misconception of the Scottish idiom, that this comment
is an inference from what he has observed of your play. If
you should unwarily reply with too great eagerness in the
affirmative, the remark which has been known to follow,
"Eh! ye've verra little ou' his style aboot ye," will quite suffice to show you your mistake.

Hints on Golf

---

*Babe [Zaharias] would attempt to psych her
opponents in every possible way.
She would hit a five-iron, quickly stuff it in
the bag and tell everyone it was a seven.
She would stride onto the putting green
before a tournament and shout,
'Are you girls practicin' to come in second?'*
WILLIAM OSCAR JOHNSON AND NANCY WILLIAMSON

A Traitorous Handicap

HARRY VARDON

Very many golfers handicap themselves far more than they imagine by using implements which come into their possession in a more or less promiscuous way. They walk into the stores; see a club which takes their fancy; and emerge five minutes later with what they fondly regard as a treasure, but which ultimately proves to be a traitor.

Pacific Golf and Motor

The Firm Putt

GENE SARAZEN

A lot is said about bold putters, but I'll never forget Bobby Jones' remark that a dying putt has three chances to go in the hole: by the front door, the left side door, and the right side door. But the bold putt has only one chance, and that is in the front door. And it must hit the back center of the cup at that. I don't believe in hitting the ball short of the hole, but try to get just past it; practice hitting a dying putt just to the hole, and you'll find that you will hole more putts. The bold putter who misses usually has a long one coming back. You know, nothing is more tiring than hitting a ball three feet past the hole and holding that putt back for a par when all the time you had a birdie in mind. The sudden struggle for a par unnerves you. So if I miss, I always like to miss it close to the hole. I think the time to be bold is on the three- or four-footers coming back. Not really bold, but firm. Remember, on those short putts, cut down on that backswing as much as you can, and keep the clubhead right along the ground all the way back. Don't raise it, as a lot of people who break their wrists do. You're bound to cut the putt and miss the hole.

Better Golf After Fifty

About Golf

E. V. KNOX

Golf is obviously the worst game in the world. I doubt indeed whether it is a game at all.

It is played with a ball, about which, though I could say much, I will say little. I will not decide whether it should have a heart of oak or a heart of gold, whether it should go through a 16-inch ring or a plate-glass window, whether it should sink like the German Navy or float like the British. Enough, if not too much, has been said about the standard ball.

Golf is played with a number of striking implements more intricate in shape than those used in any form of recreation except dentistry. Let so much be agreed.

Now, quite plainly, the essential idea underlying all games played with a ball, whether a club, stick, mallet, bat or cue be added or no, is that some interference should take place with the enemy's action, some thwarting of his purpose or intent. In Rugby football, to take a case, where no mallet is used, it is permissible to seize an opponent by the whiskers and sling him over your right shoulder, afterwards stamping a few times on his head or his stomach. This thwarts him badly. The same principle applies, though in a milder form, to the game of cricket, where you attempt to beat the adversary's bat with your ball, or, if you have the bat, to steer the ball between your adversaries, or at least to make them jolly well wish that you would.

Even with the baser and less heroic ball games, like croquet and billiards, where more than one ball is used at a time, action inimical to the interests of the good old days of yore, when croquet was not so strictly scientific, a shrewd sudden stroke—the ankle shot, we called it, for, after all, the fellow was probably not wearing boots—well, I dare say you remember it; and I have once succeeded in paralyzing the enemy's cue arm with the red; but this needs a lot of luck as well as strength, and is not a stroke to be practiced by the beginner, especially on public tables.

We come then again to golf, and see at once that, with the miserable and cowardly exception of laying a stymie, there is no stroke in this game that fulfills the proper conditions which should govern athletic contests involving the use of spherical objects with or without instruments of percussion.

And yet we read column after column about fierce encounters and desperate struggles between old antagonists, when as a matter of fact there is no struggle, no encounters at all. Against no other ball game but golf, unless perhaps it be roulette, can this accusation be laid. Ask a man what happened last Saturday. 'I went out,' he says, rather as if he was the British Expeditionary Force, 'in 41; but I came home'—he smiles triumphantly; you see the hospital ship, the cheering crowds—'in 39.' Whether he beat the other fellow or not he hardly remembers, because there was in fact no particular reason why the other fellow should have been there.

Golf matches ought to be arranged, and for my part I shall arrange them in the future, as follows:

He: Can you play on Saturday at Crump?

I: No, I'm not playing this week.

He: Next weekend then?

I: Yes, at Blimp.

He: I can't come to Blimp.

I: Well, let's play all the same. Your score this week at Crump against mine next week at Blimp, and we'll have five bob on it.

I'm not quite sure what his retort is, but you take my point. It is manifestly absurd to drag the psychological element into this cold-blooded mathematical pursuit. After all that England had done and come through in the last few years, is a man in baggy knickerbockers, with tufts on the ends of his garters, going to be daunted and foiled just because a man in slightly baggier knicker-bockers and with slightly larger tufts on his garters has hit a small white pellet a little further than he has? Hardly, I think.

That is why, when I read long letters in the principal daily papers about the expense of this so-called game, and calculations as to whether it can be played for less than twenty-five shillings a time, I am merely amused. In my opinion, if the relatives of members of golf-clubs cannot afford to support them, these institutions should either be closed or the inmates should be provided with some better game, like basketball. That is what I feel about golf.

All the same, if Enerby really thinks and believes that, because in a nasty cross-wind I happened to be slicing badly and didn't know the course and lost a ball at the twelfth, and he holed twice out of bunkers and certainly balked me by sniffing on the seventeenth, that I can't beat him three times out of five in normal conditions and not with that appalling caddy—well, I suppose one must do one's best to relieve a fellow-creature of his hallucinations, mustn't one?

Golf Nuts

DAN JENKINS

LET'S TALK about golf nuts.

I'll start with the runny little sixty-eight-year-old combatant who always insists on playing from the gold tees.

He says you can't really *see* a golf course unless you play it from the tips.

He finds something terribly intriguing, as opposed to insane, about a 7,200-yard golf course, particularly if it's infested with water, waste, sand, bulkheads, trees, moguls, deep rough, violent wind, severe pins, and slick greens.

He would never improve a lie. He is greatly offended at the mere suggestion of a mulligan.

He loves playing a par-5 hole with driver, 3-wood, 5-wood, 7-wood, sand blast; pitch, clip, and four putts.

He is enthralled by a long, brutal par-4 hole that he can attack with driver, lateral, spoon, unplayable, 5-iron, boundary, 9-iron, cart path, pitch, and three putts.

He is fascinated with a killer par-3 hole that he can bring to its knees with driver, water, 5-wood, bulkhead, wedge, chip, and three putts.

One day he hopes to break 126.

"How did you play today, dear?" his wife asks.

"Great. I had a putt for a par and three chips at birdies."

Next, I give you the tireless gentleman who calls me

every year or so to bring me up to date on the progress he's making in trying to play all of America's famous courses.

He has been at this for about twenty-five years, I guess.

In all of the phone calls over the past quarter of a century, he has asked me the same question.

Can I suggest anything that will help him get on Pine Valley, Augusta National, Merion, Seminole, Cypress Point, Oakmont, Los Angeles Country Club, Bel Air, Shinnecock Hills, Colonial, Winged Foot, Chicago Golf, Brook Hollow, or Olympic?

I used to say, "Crawl over the fence and don't play the first hole or the eighteenth."

Now I say, "Steal a hundred million dollars from your company and put a hyphen in your name."

I give you this retired fellow I've stumbled upon who plays six times a week and makes all of his own clubs. They are rather crude-looking things but he makes them in his workshop.

Although golf is obviously his life, he has been pleased to inform me that he has never attended a tournament, doesn't watch golf on TV, doesn't read golf books, doesn't read golf magazines, and doesn't even read the sports pages of the newspapers.

One day he asked what I did for a living. I said I was a writer.

"What do you mean?" he said, looking at me as if he had just heard of the most bizarre profession imaginable.

I said, "Well, among other things, I write articles for a golf magazine."

He looked at me for a long moment, and then he said, "Why?"

I excused myself hurriedly and went home and reported to my wife that I thought I had just met the mysterious sniper who fires at motorists from a freeway overpass.

Also in my neighborhood is this elderly man who only plays on weekends but spends the rest of the time hunting golf balls.

He's always out there during the week, creeping through the trees or poking around at the edge of lagoons.

It is rumored that he has over 10,000 golf balls in his garage, where he keeps them neatly arranged on shelves.

More than one person has told me I *must* visit this man's garage—his collection of golf balls is astounding.

"It's on my list," I say nicely.

As amazing as anyone I've heard about lately is the dentist. He is said to be a lifelong fan of Arnold Palmer. He is said to be such a fan of Arnold's, it borders on mental illness.

I don't know if it's true—I can only hope—but the dentist is purported to carry in his pocket a ball marker made from the gold that was extracted from Arnold's teeth.

This might not make him the biggest Arnold Palmer fan in the world, however.

There was a journalist in Great Britain whose unbounding hero worship of Palmer became a legend. He was never satisfied, one hears, with autographs, scrapbooks, photos, paintings, or articles about Arnold.

One day he got the inspired idea to begin collecting the divots Palmer would take out of fairways in England and Scotland. Eventually, the entire lawn of his home near London was made out of Arnold Palmer divots.

Actually, if I were to follow through on a thought I had the other day, I think I could be exempt on the Golf Nut Tour myself.

You see, I have this habit of knocking balls into the woods when they betray me. I might add that it doesn't take much for me to feel betrayed. A four-foot putt that curls out, a pulled 7-wood that winds up in a bunker, a chip shot that races across the green and into the frog hair, a tee shot that defies its stern warning and seeks out the forest.

I've been leaving these balls in the woods, but I've come up with a better idea. A small cemetery in my yard. It could be fenced in by a variety of broken shafts. Call me the Mortician.

In this cemetery I will bury all of the golf balls that betray me, because if they can betray me once, they will certainly betray me again. Planted into the earth, however, they will have nothing to do but rot in eternal hell forever.

Never again will they be able to bring unwarranted grief and anguish to some innocent golfer, like myself, who never meant them any harm whatsoever.

It's what they deserve, I say. All I've ever asked of them is a simple string of bogeys.

Fairways And Greens

If your adversary is badly bunkered, there is no rule against your standing over him and counting his strokes aloud, with increasing gusto as their number mounts up; but it will be wise precaution to arm yourself with a niblick before doing so, so as to meet him on even terms.

HORACE HUTCHINSON

Idiot's Game

SIR WALTER SIMPSON

Excessive golfing dwarfs the intellect. And is this to be wondered at when we consider that the more fatuously vacant the mind is, the better for play. It has long been observed that absolute idiots, ignorant whether they are playing two more or one off two, play steadiest. An uphill game does not make them press, nor victory within their grasp render them careless. Alas! We cannot all be idiots. Next to the idiotic, the dull, unimaginative mind is the best for golf. In a professional competition I would prefer to back the sallow, dull-eyed fellow with a 'quid' in his cheek, rather than any more eager-looking champion. The poetic temperament is the worst for golf. It dreams of brilliant drives, iron shots laid dead, and long putts held, whilst in real golf success waits for him who takes care of the foozle and leaves the fine shots to take care of themselves.

The Art of Golf

On the Links

GEORGE HIBBARD

It was a trying moment. In the clear sunlight the links lay trim and clipped before me. At varying intervals the little red flags dotted the course, while here and there the vermilion coats of the players shone brilliantly against the emerald grass. The scene was a pleasant and peaceful one, but I did not enjoy it. My heart sank, and my hands grew cold while my head grew hot, for Emily only in the last few days had I dared to think of her as Emily—stood looking on.

My visit to the Harrisses had at first been delightful. If Emily at times appeared indifferent, at other times she was gracious, and I was not hopeless. Then suddenly the blow had fallen.

But, in order to be understood, I must explain the state of mind of the Harrisse family. I saw, a short time ago, a book, "The Manias of the Middle Ages." I am sure that no medieval persons were ever more thoroughly "possessed" than the members of this very modern household. They were all golf enthusiasts, or fairly golf mad. Harrisse *père* never thought of anything else, and Emily of but few other things. I had tried to appear interested, and they had been politely indulgent. Then the fateful moment came. One evening, on entering the drawing-room dressed for dinner, I saw that Mr. Harrisse held a letter in his hand. I could not help noticing a singularly beaming smile on his jolly old face, and with some astonishment I detected a new light of interest gleaming in Emily's eyes.

"My dear boy," he cried, hastening forward in his impetuous way, and grasping me by the hand, "why have you been so modest? To have one of the best golfers in the country here in the house, and not know it! We can't forgive you."

In an instant I saw what had happened. Some person, knowing that I was staying in the house, had mistaken me, Launcelot Schaw, whose reputation as a minor poet, I will confess, extends beyond my own country, for my cousin "Sam" Schaw, whose collection of cups, won at everything from tennis to polo, is almost as great as my collections of first editions. The same thing had occurred before. I should have been equal to the occasion, but I was not. I saw Emily's admiring glances. These were something I had never hitherto encountered, and, in my delight, I yielded to temptation. Not actively. I did not assert anything; still, I did not deny anything. In a moment I wished earnestly that I had; but then it was too late. Almost at once I began to discover the difficulties and dangers into which I had plunged myself. Dinner was a torture. With an air of profound deference, I was asked questions by my host, and even by Emily, that I could not answer, and that, indeed, I could not in the least understand. It was delightful, but distressing. After-dinner was for me something like a session of the Inquisition. I do not know how I passed through it; but the worst was yet to come.

"There's one thing you must do," whispered Emily's father, pushing his chair toward mine; "you must beat Stewart Elyot for us."

Beat Stewart Elyot! Beat a man who did nothing but talk golf, who did not attempt to make any concealment of his victories, and who was clearly my rival with Emily!

"I tell you," said the father, "ever since he has been staying at the Blakeley's his boasting has been insufferable, and you must take him down a bit. You must do it for me."

Would you do? I was asked by Emily's father to "take down" my own rival, and to do it for him. No human being could have had the strength of mind or character to own up then and there. Better go on and be found out, since I had already committed myself, gaining at least a few days in which something might happen.

But nothing had happened, and there I stood. A caddie was beside me with my bag, holding a number of knobbly sticks, that reminded me, with my disturbed imagination, of the bunch of instruments from which my dentist made selections before he said, "A little wider, please." Emily's father was there, intently absorbed; Emily's friend Miss Allyn was there, coldly critical; Emily herself was there, charming in her loose golf cloak, and looking maddeningly enigmatical. Stewart Elyot, my opponent, was there, and, to my surprise, visibly anxious. I knew what they expected me to do. I had seen many do it. With one of those sticks I was to knock that miserable little pebble of ball some altogether absurd distance. What if I had only the night before written the lines beginning,

In ambient loveliness my goddess queen,

a poem I think not unworthy of Emily, and certainly one that will take its place among the sonnets of the early twentieth century!

"Watch the stance," I heard her father whisper.

The hour had come, if not the man. But I must act or stand confessed impostor—the unwilling one, to be sure, but still the impostor—that I really was. I did not know what the "stance" was. I did not care. I seized a club.

"Hush!" exclaimed Mr. Harrisse as Miss Allyn giggled in the way that always annoyed me.

A solemn silence fell on the party. A silence seemed to fall on the universe. There was a certain haziness before my eyes. The ball was there, for I had seen the caddie put it on a little heap of sand. I grasped the club despairingly. I also shut my eyes firmly. I drew back the stick, and seemed to swing it through illimitable space. Suddenly I heard a dull click. I opened my eyes.

"Where is it?" I demanded wildly, scanning the heaven.

"There," said Emily.

Looking down, I beheld the glittering little thing peacefully reposing on the grass, and as the sun shone on its brilliant surface, it would seem, almost winking at me in derision.

"I'll venture you don't 'top' it often like that," said the father, consolingly.

"Very strange," I stammered.

I glanced at Elyot. The anxious expression that I noticed on his face lifted a little. He came forward, placed his ball, and with an airy swing sent it rolling—at most fifty feet. I felt perceptibly encouraged. If a great performer like Elyot did no better, I might for the moment escape. I caught a surprised whisper as I advanced to take another stroke. I hit the ball this time. I actually hit the miserable little object, taking, to be sure, a good deal of ground with the stroke, but still sending it, with a rise, on and on down the side of the hill.

I had thought it something wonderful, and was distinctly disappointed. However, I remained silent. The walk was short to the place where my ball had fallen, and I blessed the occasion which gave me the chance.

"There is no other game in the world that would give me such an opportunity—such a blessed opportunity as this," I said tenderly.

"Oh," she exclaimed, "can you play and talk? So few great players can."

I found I was in the wrong, but I braved it out.

"Of course, under ordinary circumstances; but to speak to you—alone—I can do it so seldom."

She was silent, but did not seem displeased.

"Look!" she exclaimed suddenly. "Mr. Elyot is going to play."

I glanced in the direction of my opponent and my rival. I watched him as he drew back his club, watched him with growing anxiety, and saw him miss his ball altogether. I could not understand it at all. Was he so "rattled" because Emily was there?

There was a queer light in Emily's eyes that I did not comprehend. Elyot tried again. This time he did not miss. It was my turn. Once, twice, thrice, then hit the ball squarely, and away it spun. The mocking glance in Emily's eyes increased. I was decidedly troubled by it.

"You must see," I said with what I considered great presence of mind, "that there is an influence that makes accurate play for me difficult, and golf is a game requiring perfect poise."

"Have you a headache, or is it the day?" she asked in her direct way.

"It is you," I replied bluntly.

"Then I will remove the influence," she said haughtily, and joined the others.

I had made a fool of myself when I had thought to do so well. Viciously I hit the ball, and, to my amazement, it rose gracefully. It fell, rolling hardly six inches from where it struck the ground, and rested within a foot of the flag.

"Bravo!" cried her father. "A splendid approach!"

And I would have given worlds not to have made the shot exactly at the moment Emily left me, after I had said that I had. I thought I saw in her face an expression of displeasure, also of surprise. In the next I "holed out"; no one could have helped it. I had won. I did not understand how it could have happened.

At the next tee I started first. I say "started," for that was all. I may have gone ten feet. I doubt it. This time Elyot missed altogether. I was puzzled. So was Emily's father.

"Gentlemen, gentlemen," he exclaimed reproachfully, "you're both woefully off your game."

It really hurt his kind old heart to see such golf. I don't wonder.

This time Emily walked with Elyot, and I plodded on, cursing my blundering stupidity. Before, my desperation had enabled me to make a good shot; now the result was quite the opposite. I swung over the ball, I hit behind the ball, I went on both sides of the ball. My score on the putting green was something awful—fourteen, I think. And Emily and her father were looking on. However, Elyot, although he won easily, was eleven. I was certainly perplexed.

At the next hole Elyot led off, or, as I heard them express it, he had the "honor." He did well. His ball rose with a sudden up slant and shot off into the air. Her father applauded; so did Emily. And again I missed altogether. Miss Allyn giggled. I liked her less than ever. Clenching my teeth, I hit wildly, and missed again. It was getting serious. They must see the truth.

"Curious game—golf—*very*," commented her father. "There are days when *I* am almost as far off myself."

They would not find me out. There seemed some malevolent destiny in it, some diabolical play of Fate, to make me suffer to the uttermost for my deception.

At last I got away; not very far, in truth, but it was something. I glanced at Elyot. He did not seem to be having very much better luck. What was the matter with the fellow? Suddenly I found Emily again with me. She was distinctly smiling.

"Oh," she exclaimed, as I looked at her, "I am *so* amused!"

"It's serious enough for me," I said gloomily, and I have no doubt that my looks proved the sincerity of my words. "But you misunderstood me," I hurried on, "about the influence. You inspire me. I can do better. I want you by my side—always."

I had never ventured to say so much, and I was terrified by my own boldness.

"There!" she cried as I again missed the ball, "is that my inspiration? You pay me a poor compliment to play so badly. You must do better, or I will go."

What could I do? The ball was so painfully small, and the space about it where the club's head might go so absurdly great. I felt that I must concentrate. There were times when I had been mildly facetious about golf. I wished that I had not. I did not feel that way now.

"Stay, stay!" I besought wildly. But by some accident the next shot was a fairly good one, and as we talked I advanced little by little. At last I found myself on the green.

Elyot was a stroke or two "more," as they put it, but after going past the tin-lined orifice several times, and once or twice over it, I was even with him. At last, when in despair, I went in. He missed, and I had won.

We had played two more holes. Suddenly I found Emily again by my side.

"I have concluded to forgive you," she said sweetly.

"For what?" I gasped.

"I don't know exactly, but for something."

"You are so good!" I murmured.

"Besides, I want you to beat."

"You do!" I exclaimed ecstatically.

"I like Mr. Elyot so much, but if he beats *you*," she said seriously, "he would be made so vain that it would not be good for him."

The more I considered this sentence the more I was puzzled as to whether I should be pleased with it or not. There was certainly one for me in this accented "you," but weren't there two for Elyot? Emily was often maddening.

"See!" she exclaimed, "Mr. Elyot has lost his ball!"

I expected she should go look for it, as all were doing, but Emily was unexpected. She sat down on the grass near me. I sat down too. There was no reason why I should look for Elyot's ball; moreover, I had quite forgotten about him and it and almost everything else. With Emily's last glance all prudence fled.

"I have so few chances to speak to you," I murmured, "and I am going away."

"Not at once," she said quickly.

"In a day or two," I said, sighing hopelessly.

"I know."

There was something in her tone that encouraged me.

"Emily," I said tremulously.

As I spoke the name a perfect panic seized me. I was appalled at my own daring; it seemed as if something must happen, but nothing did. Emily remained motionless, with her head adverted.

"You know I never want to go away from you—that I want to be always with you—that I only live in the hope of winning your love—that—"

"Fore!" cried Stewart Elyot, and I jumped perceptibly.

I heard a humming sound; it seemed within a few inches of my ear. The next moment they were all down on us, and her father announced that it was my play.

I was too dazed to understand as I staggered to my feet. I had spoken,—not in the poetic words in which I had fancied myself speaking, but still I had spoken—and I was appalled by my temerity.

I appeared only to regain consciousness at the "quarry." I had seen it before, and viewed it merely as an ordinary excavation of some size, with water covering its rocky floor, and luxuriant vines trailing along its steep sides. Now it seemed endless in width, bottomless in depth. I was thankful Elyot had to go first. I was more thankful that his ball, when hit, rolled gently across the intervening grass, over the edge, and into the stagnant water below.

I stepped forward. As I did so, I passed Emily.

"He is two up," she whispered.

The fact that Emily had listened to me encouraged me. I felt that I could do anything. What I did was drive the ball into the water with a sounding splash. I saw Emily clasp her hands. Elyot's second attempt was no better than the first, but no more was mine. Elyot's third was even worse. I had given up all hope as I stood again over a new ball. I was astonished, therefore, as I opened my eyes, to hear a burst of applause.

"Neatly placed!" said her father.

Emily's eyes sparkled, and I tried to look as if I were not surprised.

"I might be starting on," I said airily.

As I spoke, Elyot cast a glance at me that, for utter downright loathing, I never saw equaled. I moved away.

As I did I heard the rattle of Elyot's fourth ball as it rolled down the stony bank.

I have had my rare moments, when the "Athenæum's" praise—but never mind that; when the third edition—but let that pass; still, I had never experienced such a period of perfect bliss as was mine when I stood on the opposite shore while Elyot sent ball after ball into the water. I had often derided my cousin Sam when he had described to me the delight of feeling an opponent's arm slip over one's own in a neat parry in boxing, the pleasure of taking a stiff jump in the lead of the field, the joy of gaining a well-contested yard of football, or a long drive between the flags at polo; but at that moment I felt that I had been wrong. The bays of the poet are good, but there are more exhilarating conquests.

At the eleventh hole a long stretch of over four hundred yards lay before us. Both Elyot and I drove miserably and wildly, he to the left, I to the right. I expected Emily to go with him. She did not. She came with me. I could feel my heart beat. I did not care about the game, for I was with her. But her first words troubled me.

"You *must* win," she said decidedly.

"But my mind—my heart is so full of so much else," I replied gloomily.

"Of course," she replied as we strolled along. "I have been thinking of what you said just now—and of course you didn't mean it—"

"But I did," I interrupted quickly; "and you know it," I added impatiently.

She seemed a bit taken aback by my tone, and went on more meekly.

"Why, if you did, I must think it over again—in a different way," she murmured.

"But don't you know?" I continued, emboldened by my success.

She looked at me for one short instant, as I thought, appealingly.

"I know that this is no time for me to speak," I continued desperately, "but there are so few times when I can."

"But if I—give you other times?"

What I felt was beyond utterance.

"You see, I didn't understand," she said slowly; "I didn't know what you thought—or," she concluded slowly, "what I did."

"And you do now?" I cried.

"Y-e-s," she answered.

I started with joy, and then it occurred to me that what she thought might easily be unfavorable to me. I was assuming too much. Instantly I was cast into the deepest gloom.

"But you must play *now*," she urged.

"How can I," I exclaimed, "with this awful suspense— if it is suspense," I concluded mournfully.

"Don't you know what I think?" she said again, glancing at me.

"No," I cried.

"But—but I can't tell you now," she continued, looking about.

"When, then?" I demanded.

"I had made up my mind to tell you—before you went," she continued.

"Then you knew what I was going to say!" I exclaimed joyfully and stupidly.

"How could I?" she replied, rather disconcerted, but haughtily. "Still," she went on, "if you will not let him beat you—"

"Yes," I said breathlessly.

"—I'll tell you—" she paused, "twenty-four hours sooner."

"Won't you—without?" I begged.

"That's my condition," she said, and quickly left me.

I looked, and found that, while I had been pounding the ball along, Elyot had already reached the green. I gathered myself together. One stroke hit the sod; the next, though, brought my ball beside his.

"What's against me?" I demanded.

"Ten," said her father, reproachfully.

"Dead!" he cried delightedly.

I did not understand, but I felt it were better so. Elyot was within six inches of the hole. His next shot would put him in it. With deliberate care he bent over, for he was afraid of hitting too hard. Miss Allyn again giggled, and this time I did not mind. His putter just stirred the ball. I went in. Elyot was again only one up.

Elyot won the twelfth hole. The thirteenth we halved. I saw that my state was desperate. Twenty-four hours— how could I?—twenty-four hours, when it lay with me to shorten that time!

"Two up and five to play," muttered her father.

Elyot, of course, had the honor, and marched proudly to the tee. After he had placed the ball, I saw him glance rather anxiously before him. The hazard in front was a peculiar one in this: the end of a narrow pond came half across the course, thus leaving any player a choice whether to drive over its hundred yards of water and its sandy shore, or go round the bend, where there was open land with smooth grass. I saw Elyot hesitate, then gently drive his ball off the tee in the safer direction. My blood boiled. In my heart I said it was a most unsportsman like thing to do. I had hoped that he would attempt the pool and go in. It was my turn. I felt that in boldness was my only hope. Anyway, I had noticed Mr. Harrisse's disapproving look as he had seen Elyot's action, and it was better to fail grandly, since fail I must. I made up my mind to try to drive directly across.

"Take the cleek, sir, take the cleek," my caddie whispered. I had feed him well before we started.

I took what the boy gave me, and hit. Again, as I opened my eyes, there was applause. I had gone over. I had gained a stroke, at least, on Elyot. All might not be lost. I was on the green.

Passing Elyot angrily pounding his ball, I waited at the hole until he came up. Then I went in on the fourth stroke. It was a glorious moment.

I was excited, I will confess. Never, even when I wrote "Roland at Roncesvalles," had I felt so thoroughly stirred by the white heat of intense emotion. I had the honor. I understood what that meant now. The cleek had saved me before, so I took it again, although I saw Mr. Harrisse's astonishment. I clung to it as my only hope. I hit, and I hit well; at least the ball rose and then rolled. In the semi-unconsciousness of many mingled emotions I walked forward.

"Fore!" cried Elyot, and I dodged.

His ball, I saw with consternation, had gone farther than mine; but I might gain on the next stroke. I did. He missed his ball altogether. I swung the club once, and once more I hit. Elyot was away behind. I was almost on the green. Suddenly I heard a buzzing in the air, a whir, and something passed me. It was Elyot's ball; he was beside me.

"Your mashie," suggested my caddie.

I took the proffered club, and brought it down with all my strength. I felt it strike the sod, and believed that all was lost; but no: almost straight up the ball rose, and going higher and higher in the air, fell finally, beyond the hole, to be sure, but still within putting distance of it.

"That's something like," commented her father.

I was too dazed for utterance, for the strain was telling on me. It was not golf; it was roulette. But I went in. I expected Fortune to take it out of me some day for that outrageous piece of luck; but I went in.

The hole was mine. We were even.

Even! Even! It seemed incredible to me, when I considered with whom I was playing. But I had to play. Golf, it seemed to me, was a constant repetition, with infinite variation. In this case the variation was not great. I abandoned my cleek, and my drive was as bad as ever. But, again, so was Elyot's, and there was no advantage for either of us. As I walked forward, I felt, rather than saw, that Emily was beside me.

"Don't you *want* to know sooner?" she whispered.

"*Don't* I want to know!" I exclaimed almost angrily. "What wouldn't I give to know—the best!"

"Then play!" she commanded, and left me.

I groaned inwardly. I may have groaned outwardly, for my caddie looked at me curiously; but it was only a moment. He was evidently accustomed to all possible expressions of human emotion on the links. But I felt perceptibly better. If it should be that she really—

"Fore!" cried Elyot, and again his ball whizzed past —hurrah! only to bury itself against the post of a fence far out of the course. I watched him with delight as he dug at it, beat at it, pounded at it. At length it rolled out. He had counted seven strokes. Made careless with delight, I hit jauntily, lodging under the very same fence. I had thought what a fool he was to get excited. AS I look back at it, I must have become quite fanatic. In a sort of automatic frenzy I used my club. At last I, too, was free, and together we played for the green. Why go into detail? We halved the hole.

Still eve, and still my honor. I felt as if I were staggering up for the last round. But the end was near. As I looked back it seemed almost pathetic to me that all my efforts should at last go for nothing. I found myself pitying myself in anticipation.

"An exciting game," said her father, rubbing his hands, "although I must say, gentlemen, it might have been better played."

Again the honor was mine. The stream that we had crossed in coming out again lay before me. It was at a distance nicely calculated to catch all balls not well driven. I could not drive at all. I was safe so far, for I fell short of the hazard by fifty yards. I saw that Elyot was preparing to follow my example. His idea, evidently, was not to hit hard, but he did what he had not done before. He hit cleanly and truly, and the small force accurately applied was enough to land him squarely in the ditch, for it was little more.

"Hard luck, old fellow, for a fairly good stroke!" I cried.

He glowered thunderously at me and passed on. A stroke more took me to the edge, another over. He tried three strokes, paused, and wiped his brow; then tried two more. My heart bounded. I am sure my eyes lighted up. But he was across, and we were pounding in for the green. I got in a rut. I got in a thistle. When we reached the verge of the green we were even.

"You're farther off," said Mr. Harrisse.

I obediently took the club my caddie gave me, and, stooping, played. Elyot's ball was within a foot of the hole, and our strokes were even. I saw I was lost, but I played. My ball stopped directly between Elyot's and the hole.

"You're stymie!" cried the father. It sounded like a deadly insult, but I knew that he could not mean it.

Still, I did not know what this was, and for a moment I thought all was over. But it was all right.

Elyot had to play round me. Mr. Harrisse said something about lofting a stymie, but it was after Elyot had played. This stroke left him as far from the hole as he was before, but one more. He played again and missed— missed by half an inch, but missed. He had played too hard, and his ball was still farther off than mine. I could see his hand tremble. He played. Again he missed! At the next putt I went in. The hole was mine.

I was dazed, but I played. Playing had become a second nature to me, and I believe that I could have played in my sleep. Indeed, there was something of a somnambulistic character in my action. At least, it seemed almost as if I awoke when I heard Emily speaking.

"I am *so* glad!" she said.

"Why?" I asked stupidly.

"Why," she replied impatiently, "you're dormy now, and he can't beat you."

She seemed to describe my condition, but I understood that she was speaking of the game.

"Why?" I gasped.

"Because you are one up, and there is only one hole to play."

"Oh!" I exclaimed, with a glance of intelligence. "But I haven't beat him yet—and I suppose I can't know."

"I—I," she murmured, "only said that you must not let him *beat you.*"

"Oh!" I cried, this time rapturously. "And I may—you say he can't beat me. Then tell me. I have waited so long. Tell me. You are not unwilling to have me love you."

"What a way to ask me!" she said impatiently.

"How should I ask?" I demanded anxiously.

"So that I could answer you properly," she said gently. "You should say, 'Do you love me?' "

"Do you?" I cried.

"Yes," she whispered.

It was exasperating. I could not take her in my arms then and there out on the broad expanse of the sunny links. I had dreamed of quite another scene when I learned my fortune. But I did not care. I had her. She was mine at last for good and all. I wanted to say something intense, poetic.

"This is a beast of a game," was all that I managed to answer.

She smiled.

"Do you think so?"

"No, no," I exclaimed hurriedly; "I'll always think of this with gratitude, with rapture. It has made me the happiest man in the world. But, thank Heaven! there's only one more hole, and we can walk to the house."

"Yes," she said shyly; "and now beat."

"I can't," I replied hopelessly. "I only wonder that I have done so well."

"*Do* you?" she said, with the same curious smile I had noticed at first.

"Yes," I replied, "against such a great player as Elyot." I could afford to be generous now.

"Why," she said, "didn't you know?" Then she laughed outright. "He never had a club in his hand before to-day. I found it out, and I have been so amused. He was only boasting, and that is why I wanted him beaten."

I was astonished. And I had been pluming myself on coming off so well against a "crack." Suddenly my conscience smote me.

"Do you know," I said contritely, "I think perhaps I ought to tell you something. No more have I ever played."

"I was *sure* of it," she said calmly, "and I thought it was so fine and strong and brave and noble of you to go in and try to do it—when papa made the mistake about the letter—for my sake."

I had been thinking all the time that it was rather a mean and sneaking performance, but of course if she looked at it that way! And it is curious how a woman will look at a thing when the man happens to be the right man.

"It has been an awful experience," I said boldly.

"Poor dear!" she whispered tenderly. "I am so sorry!"

Of course we told her father, when we told him the other news, that Emily had consented to marry me. He was so pleased with my having won the match that he did not seem to mind. Since then I have played the game with such diligence and enthusiasm that he is now entirely contented. Indeed, the day when I beat him four up and three to play, I could feel that he was perfectly satisfied with me as a son-in-law. I do not abuse golf anymore. I won too much in my first game ever to do that. Moreover, I am quite as mad about it now as all the rest of the family.

Luck and Sympathy

HORACE G. HUTCHINSON

However unlucky you may be, and however pleasant a fellow your adversary, it really is not fair to expect his grief for your undeserved misfortunes to be as poignant as your own. Remember, too, that it is not altogether impossible for him to have bad luck also, and that with such measure as you mete out sympathy to him, will he be likely in turn, to show sympathy for you. I do not remember to have met any golfer who did not consider himself on the whole a remarkably unlucky one.

Hints on Golf

---

*How fast is our golf ball traveling? We would of course
like to know, but even our most careful estimates
smack of the wayward melancholy of oafs
speculating in a pasture: Is there a face in the sun?*

JERRY BUMPUS
"OUR GOLF BALLS"

The Common Sense of Golf

H. J. Whigham

The real game of golf is the play by holes and not by score. It is in the play by holes that all the elements which make the game so human come in. A man may go around in eighty by himself, but when he comes across a player who is just a class better than himself and has to try to defeat him in match play he is more likely to take ninety. To the younger player the score card is particularly injurious because he is apt to try all sorts of tricks in order to get there somehow and so he loses all freedom of style. It is better to miss the shot a hundred times in the right way than to play it successfully in the wrong.

To most of us medal play is nothing more or less than a beastly nuisance, but we should not despise it altogether. In the first place, it is excellent discipline for the finished player; it teaches above all control of the nerves, for it is absolutely impossible to do a good score if you get either anxious or irritable. IN the second place, it is a capital test of steadiness and temper, and for that reason the American system of deciding the amateur championship, including as it does both medal play and match play, is distinctly better than the English system which excludes medal play.

But, after all, the most important thing for golfers of all ages and handicaps is not that they should play golf well, but that they should play it cheerfully. One often wonders why some people choose to play a game at all which apparently gives them about two hours of complete misery. The habit of being irritable at golf grows upon a man without his knowing it, until at length he is a burden to his partner, opponent, caddie, and most of all to himself. If he is not careful he will carry this irritability into everyday life and become a burden to his family as well.

For golf is like a patent medicine; it either kills or cures. If you realize at the beginning that to be a good golfer you must, before all things, control your temper, you will find after a while that it is just as easy to be cheerful as not and a great deal more pleasant. And the result of this schooling of the temper is that you are a better and more lovable person in all relations of life. But if you once begin getting angry and morose at golf, you will rapidly become worse until there is no playing with you or living with you. So be warned in time. When you top a drive into a bunker or miss a short putt at a critical point of the match, remember that you are playing a game for amusement, even if you are desperately keen to win, which you have every right to be. Tell yourself that your only chance of winning lies in forgetting past errors.

About Good Losers

When you have any bit of hard luck, don't keep talking about it for several holes afterwards. In the first place your opponent, though he may condole with you for form's sake, really does not think that you had such bad luck; if he were honest with you, he would tell you that he thinks you played the shot badly. The more you talk about such things the more he thinks that you are getting old and cranky and really rather a nuisance to play with. In the second place, talking about your bad luck only makes you dwell on your sorrows and tends to spoil your play. It is not true that you consistently get worse lies than the other people. When a man tells you that he always holds bad cards at bridge you never think of believing him; you take him to mean that he always plays them badly.

Perhaps the best way of curing yourself of the tendency to become irritable and morose when you are playing badly is to pull yourself up and think how objectionable and ridiculous other people look when they are in the same state. Nothing in the world is so unlovely as a bad temper; real loss of temper is deplorable.

It has often been said about bridge and other games that the only thing worse than a bad loser is a cheerful winner. Surely this is true of golf. The man who gloats is singularly detestable. Remember here again that you are playing a game and you want your opponent to have a good time as possible, even though he is losing. Nothing indeed is more necessary than courtesy to your opponent. If you find that it annoys him to get too near to him when he is playing, or to walk ahead of him, or to make remarks to him just as he is going to attempt a difficult putt, remember that to do any of these things is just unfair as it would be to tee your ball in a bunker when he is not looking. The best advice to all golfers is to play the game for the fun of the thing; take your defeats cheerfully and your victories with modesty.

Finally to make the game enjoyable and at the same time to improve the skill of players, your courses should be well laid out and properly bunkered. I lay stress on this point because the science of bunkering is so woefully misunderstood in this country. I do not at all insist on penalties. There must always be luck about the game; that is one of its charms. On the contrary, I object very strongly to the penalty of having to hunt for your ball in long grass every time you go off the course. But I do hold that the bunkers and penalties should be so arranged as to make the player try the fine shots. A course is hardly worth playing on which has not several really big carries off the tee and also for the second shot.

Why do all golfers like the Alps at Prestwick and the Sahara at Sandwich? Surely on account of the great carries. Secondly, the putting greens should vary in size and contour and the bunkers close to the hole should be deep, although you may easily go too far in this matter of depth. Of course, mud holes are bad. All bunkers should be filled with clean sand and then you will find it is not at all difficult to get out of them. But unless your greens are well bunkered you lose half the fun of the game. Jerome Travers found in Scotland that men like Hilton and Maxwell could play shots which he had never thought of.

Our players in this country do not learn to play golf in the best sense of the word because they never have to put back-spin or side-spin on the ball to hold it on the green; and they rarely have to play for slice or a pull.

It is all nonsense to argue that the majority of players being poor performers ought not to be punished by having to play over difficult courses. All the bad players in England flock to St. Andrews and Prestwick and Sandwich. And Americans do just the same thing. It is a noteworthy fact that most Americans praise Prestwick more than any other course abroad, and Prestwick is noted for the size of its bunkers. Bad players have a way of objecting to new bunkers before they are put in; but they very rarely object to them once they are made.

It is only those who do not play golf as a game, but take it as medicine, that really object to bunkers being properly placed, and we cannot make our courses to suit the physically and mentally weak. There is a lot of talk about driving away the poor players when the new bunkers were put in at Garden City; some bad players became quite fierce about it. I have yet to hear of a single player who has left Garden City now that the bunkers are there. In other words, no one has suffered and a large number get more pleasure out of the game.

No one really knows anything about golf until he has played over a course at least as good as Garden City. And so we get back to the original point of this article: if you want to become a golfer—and you are very foolish if you do not—go and play on the best courses available and watch the best players.

The Learned Skill

CHI CHI RODRIGUEZ

The irony of my learning to play this great game of golf —initially with a guava stick for a club and a crushed-up tin can for a ball, and later with a "real" ball, but only a five-iron, is that it was an *advantage*, not a disadvantage, as one might naturally perceive it to be. Both of these rather rustic types of apprenticeship sharpened my hand-eye coordination and heightened my sense of touch or "feel" for hitting a particular distance.

But playing one club golf was mostly responsible for my educating myself to work the club precisely on different paths and planes, and also at varying speeds, because this is the only way you can improve and hit a variety of shots with only a five-iron. For example, to play a 20-yard shot out of the rough to a pin tucked close behind a greenside bunker, I had to exaggeratedly open the clubface of the five-iron and swing very slowly on an upright out-to-in path so that I cut across the ball at impact, thereby imparting a small degree of cutspin on it, which is what enabled it to hold the green. Of course, once I was fortunate enough to own a complete set of "sticks," I chose a more lofted sand wedge to handle this lie and course situation, because this club features 56 degrees of loft (24 degrees more than a five-iron), which is a key ingredient for hitting a high, soft, quick-stopping greenside shot. What I found so amazing, once I had the luxury of holding a wedge in my hands, is that the basic principles I had adhered to while hitting the impoverished short shot with a five-iron essentially remained the same with a wedge, thus making the execution of the shot easier. Now I could stick the ball close to the hole, not just get it to stay somewhere on the green.

I think you probably have guessed where I'm headed: My shotmaking prowess is a learned skill, an art. It is not inborn.

101 Supershots

Pilgrimage to St. Andrews

J. A.

It has frequently bee observed that St. Andrews is to the golfer what Mecca is to the Mohammedan. The comparison is apt in many respects. The Mohammedan turns his face towards Mecca when he prays, and gives utterance to words expressive of his belief in the Prophet. The golfer turns his thoughts towards St. Andrews. Each of their kind holds his city to be sacred in the eyes of true disciples. Both places too are reached by a certain pilgrimage, and, when the desired haven attained, the happy pilgrim forgets all but the supreme delight of the moment.

St. Andrews having been reached, and the gauntlet of the younger fry of the caddie tribe having been run, the first thing to do was, of course, to visit the shrine of that deity of the place, Tom Morris, who received his visitors with the genial cordiality which has made him more than esteemed by all who have come into contact with him.

To play Golf well at St. Andrews requires an intimate knowledge of the course. Many hazards are quite unseen from the tee, and after playing what appears to be a beautiful shot the ball may be found trapped in one of the numerous bunkers with which the links is honeycombed. But the bunkers are by no means to be condemned. St. Andrews without its bunkers would be as a jewel without a setting. They greatly add to the zest of the game, yet, unless one knows beforehand exactly where the bunkers lie, the best and steadiest playing in the world may result in a tall score. This is probably true on all greens, but it is specially applicable to St. Andrews. Again, there is hardly a hole where a hazard requires to be carried from the tee, and where it is not better and safer to "dodge" it. It is, no doubt, a fact that long and straight driving may save a stroke at some holes; but is not this more than compensated by the risk of being caught in some bunker and losing more than the advantage gained?

St. Andrews men have always been more noted for long driving than for anything else, and the green encourages the cultivation of this part of the game.

There are good many holes where two long shots should lay the globe near the disc and where a weaker driver would require an iron shot in addition; but this is bound, to some extent to cramp iron play, and more than one golfer has remarked upon the absence of the necessity for good iron play at most of the holes. The hard putting-greens, too, are rather against approaches pitched up, rendering it difficult to make the ball fall dead.

St. Andrews has been justly described as a "heaven" of Golf. Every advantage has been taken of the great natural capabilities of the green. Its beautiful velvety turf has been carefully tended and fostered; and seldom indeed is a bad-lying ball to be got even at the end of the year.

Who has not heard of the bunkers? And who, after having visited the place, is not acquainted with their terrors? All sizes and shapes are there, and most of them are deep, necessitating strong and skillful play to extricate the unfortunate gutta entombed in their depths.

St. Andrews was a prominent place in Scottish history. It teems with objects of interest; but those who are interested in subjects of this kind should go and glean for themselves—not forgetting to take their clubs.

Golf

Golf is the cruelest of sports. Like life, it is unfair.
It's a harlot. A trollop. It leads you on.
It never lives up to its promises. It's not a sport.
It's an obsession. A boulevard of broken dreams. It plays with
men. And runs off with the butcher.

JIM MURRAY
LOS ANGELES TIMES

The Greatest Thing in the World

W.G. Sutphen

The president of the U.S.G.A. sat in his private office at
the Marion County Golf Club, a prey to painful perplex-
ity. In the anteroom a secretary waited as patiently as
might be for the important document over which the
president had been working all through the night. It was
getting on to nine o'clock, and in half an hour the players would begin to arrive. They would expect to see the
announcement displayed upon the bulletin board, and
they would make it unpleasant for the secretary if it
should not be there. The young gentleman puffed nervously at his cigarette, and began again on his self-
imposed task of committing to memory the club
handicap list that hung on the opposite wall. The clock
struck nine.

President Nicholas Longspoon groaned aloud, as he
looked at the broad sheet spread out on the table before
him with that dreadful blank still unfilled. But he, too,
had heard the clock striking nine.

"I shall have to chance it," he muttered. "It will give
me three weeks of grace, and in that time I shall surely be
able to think up something. So here goes for 'The Greatest Thing in the World.'"

The president took his pen and wrote quickly. The
secretary appeared in answer to the summons of the call-
bell, and the chief having committed the precious document to his subordinate's care, entered his automobile
carriage and was steered away to the nearest Turkish
bath. The secretary posted the notice upon the club bulletin board and went in with a light heart to his long-
delayed breakfast.

Ferdinand Baffy entered the clubhouse, and, tossing his bag of clubs on a settle, walked up eagerly to the bulletin board. The notice was there, and he read it over with a light frown contracting his high, bald forehead.

"So!" remarked Mr. Baffy, proceeding to check off on his fingers the several items of interest. "On October 2d, 3d, and 4th—annual match play competition for mixed foursomes—married couples barred—first prize, 'The Greatest Thing in the World.'"

" 'The Greatest Thing in the World,' " repeated Mr. Baffy, meditatively. "I sounds attractive, but a trifle indefinite. Wonder if Nick Longspoon knows what it is himself, or where to get it when he wants it? 'The Greatest Thing in the World!' Bah! It will be a sorry day for Nicholas Longspoon when that promissory note comes due." And Ferdinand Baffy threw back his head and emitted a gurgling chuckle from which both sound and mirth were conspicuously absent. And then, with renewed gravity: "If I could but win that prize it would be a sweet revenge for by-gone wrongs. I have not forgotten how Nicholas Longspoon once stymied me at the eighteenth hole when we were playing for a bag of sweet potatoes, and the match was all square. That night the children went supperless to bed, for I had been having poor luck in the club grocery handicaps. And that jade Cicely, his daughter! I can hear her laugh yet as I missed my putt for a half."

A frightful expression distorted for an instant the usually impassive and gutta-perchary-like features of Mr. Ferdinand Baffy. The newspaper files shivered in their racks, and a full-length portrait of old Tom Morris turned itself hastily to the wall.

"And I could win," he continued, "Were it not that

Jack Hazard is paired for the event with Cicely Long-spoon. They are just a shade better than Charlotte Brassey and me, and they will beat us out. I cannot deceive myself, and yet I would give anything to have the chance of humiliating Nicholas Longspoon!"

At such periods of spiritual crisis the devil is never far away from those who would invoke his aid. Even now he was standing behind Ferdinand Baffy and whispering softly.

"Speak up, won't you?" said Mr. Baffy, irritably, at the same time putting his hand to his ear.

The infernal communication evidently commended itself to Mr. Baffy's mind; for, after assuring himself by a hasty glance around that he was still alone in the room, he crossed over to the glazed cabinet in which was kept the club's collection of antiquities. By some oversight it had been left unlocked.

Prominent among the curiosities displayed was a golf ball of a make that had been very popular during the closing years of the nineteenth century. Now, in 1999, it had been advanced to the dignity of a relic, and was catalogued as an exceedingly rare specimen of its kind. Hastily appropriating the venerable object, Ferdinand Baffy stowed it away in an inside pocket and left the room on tiptoe. The wheels of destiny had begun to move.

In order to fully understand the situation, the intelligent ready must now be content to swallow a few historical crumbs from the loaf of universal knowledge. As every schoolboy knows, golf was carried to the Western World in the last decade of the preceding century. Its advent was almost unnoticed, save by the comic weeklies, and its existence was more than once seriously menaced by the rival sport of afternoon tea, as pursued upon the west piazzas of the leading clubs. But, in spite of all, golf continued to spread. Persons suffering with chronic golficitis were permitted to land upon our shores without the slightest let or hindrance from immigration commissioners, and they carried the infection into every nook and corner of this broad land. Golf-courses began to multiply by tens, by hundreds, by thousands, and by 1925 the official map of the United States resembled nothing so much as a gigantic spider's web. And in that web lay entangled the entire population of the country, without distinction of age, sex, or previous condition of servitude. The United States had become golficized.

In 1950 the offices of President of the United States and President of the U.S.G.A. were merged into one, under the second title, and the seat of government was removed from Washington to Lauriston, the latter being the home of the Marion County Club, and a convenient golfing centre. In 1952 Congress passed the Compulsory Golf Bill, which made the exercise of the game obligatory upon all citizens between the ages of eighteen and forty-five, the provision applying to women as well as to men. The agricultural, industrial, and commercial interests of the country continued to be of vast importance, but their active direction was committed to cripples, persons afflicted with defective vision, and the great army of idiots who persistently refuse to see any difference between golf and shinny.

From the economic standpoint, the new system was immediately successful. The hours of labor were short, being from half after nine in the morning to early putting light, and no player could be compelled to do over thirty-six holes a day. In order to avoid even the suspicion of professionalism, an ingenious system of prize coupons was devised, under which a hard working golfer could easily obtain anything that he might desire in the way of provisions, clothing, furniture, while fancy groceries, tickets to the opera and other luxuries were a regular feature of the Saturday afternoon handicaps. A player had only to do his daily rounds, honestly holing out all his putts, and he was sure of a comfortable livelihood during his working years and a pension upon retirement.

It was indeed a new order of things, and, of course, it could not please everybody. Human nature remains the same, and there was a rapidly growing class of the disaffected, who were opposed to the practical blessings of compulsory golf. Some of these malcontents had gone so far as to disable their driving arms, with the deliberate intention of unfitting themselves for the exercise of the noble sport. The idea was, of course, that they would then be assigned to some department of manual labor, or, perhaps, to the aristocratic retirement of shopkeeping. But the government quickly put a stopper on that game by decreeing that these malingerers should, upon conviction, be punished by being assigned to duty as golf reporters. Now, if compulsory golf be an irksome task, what can the compulsory reporting of compulsory golf be called? The remedy proved immediately successful.

Along with the universal diffusion of the game had gone its improvement at the hands of the American inventor. Self-centering play clubs, range-finders, anti-foozling mashies, wind gauges, automatic cleeks, hypnotic putters—these are but a few of the wonderful improvements upon the old fashioned tools. Fossils, like old Hugh Dormie, used to insist that this sort of thing was not golf. How poor human nature repeats itself! There were old Hugh Dormies in the consulship of Horace Hutchinson, and they talked in exactly the same way about bulgers and *Colonel Bogey*. But in truth, golf had come to be an exact science, and the personal equation had been wee nigh eliminated. Theoretically, every match should have turned out a tie, but in practice there was diversity of gifts, as of yore. It required brains to use the range finders, and one might easily make a mistake in the calculations. There were other players, too, who would insist upon falsifying their scores. The weakness was in their blood, inherited from famous handicap winners of the nineteenth century, and it could not be eradicated.

But perhaps the most radical of changes was that which had been made in the golf ball. The ball of 1899 was an irresponsible piece of gutta-percha, and chockfull of that total depravity which is characteristic of all inanimate things. By a special process, the ball of 1999 had been deprived of all its unamiable propensities and rendered completely subservient to its owner's will. Such a ball could neither be sliced, pulled, nor topped, and under no circumstance did it ever find its way into a bunker. The worst novice could drive it three or four hundred yards at will, and, as the advertisements say, it was a perfect ball for putting. Does all this read as though it must be too good to be true? Alas! There is another and a darker side to the picture, and this must now be presented.

The "innocuous" golf ball had indeed been achieved, but it is dangerous work experimenting in nature's laboratory. The indestructibility of matter is a truism of science, and the same law applies in the spiritual world. Evil is not necessarily destroyed by being driven out of its accustomed habitation. The golf ball had been freed of its concentrated fund of total depravity, but the devil that had been cast out had to go somewhere, and he promptly entered the system of the golfer himself. The golf player of 1899 was a cheerfully plumaged biped, overflowing with love and charity for all mankind (handicappers alone excepted). The golfer of 1999 was a sad-colored creature, breathing forth envy and the east wind, an object of detestation to his fellows and a torment to himself. Remember, too, that he had become but a mere cog in a vast machine. The State controlled and regulated his every action, from the cradle to the tomb, even marriages being arranged on the basis of the official handicaps. The very conception of what we call love had passed out of men's minds and died within their hearts. And so with faith and courage and patience, and a dozen other of the graces and virtues. Indeed, the words themselves had dropped out of common speech, and had been replaced by such outlandish expressions as "Play two more!" "Hoot, mon!" "Keep your e'e on the ba'!" and the like. Men groaned under the iron tyranny of the "gowff," but there was none to deliver them. They had made their bunker, and they must lie in it. Such was the situation on the day that Ferdinand Baffy walked away from the Marion County Golf Club with an 1899 ball in his pocket. There is a limit to everything, and it had now been reached.

Jack Hazard was to be married shortly to Cicely Longspoon, daughter of the president of the U.S.G.A. That is, the young man was officially betrothed to Miss

Longspoon, and he really disliked her less than any other girl he knew. They both belonged to the Brahmin caste (players who give odds to *Bogey*), were of a congenial age, and played admirably together in a mixed foursome. Everybody agreed that it would be a most excellent match.

Strange as it may seem in an age so utilitarian, the golfer still had his little weaknesses. One of them was for winning prizes. And so when Hazard read the announcement of the autumn competition for mixed foursomes he was mightily taken by the glittering generality of President Longspoon's offer of "The Greatest Thing in the World" to the winners. That ought to be something worth having, and he strolled over to the home putting green to consult Cicely Longspoon.

"You know, Cicely, that everything helps when you're starting in at housekeeping. Perhaps it's some new dodge for splitting kindling wood by hypnotic suggestion, or biscuit making without a master. Hasn't your father said anything more definite?"

"No, and he doesn't intend to do so. All I can get out of him is that we shall know when the time comes. And to tell you the truth, Jack, the poor old pater looks a bit worried."

"Don't wonder at it," returned Hazard, with energy. "Every year the prizes in this particular event have been growing more and more extravagant and out of all proportion to its real importance. But custom is custom, and every new president, under penalty of impeachment is obliged to over-top, by at least a hair's breadth, all that his predecessors have done before him. In 1899 the prize was a pair of butter coolers; in 1998 President Bulger presented the State of Illinois to the successful competitors. What was there left for your poor father except to offer 'The Greatest Thing in the World'? And the thing for us to do is to win it."

Cicely Longspoon gave her hand in frank amity to John Hazard.

"As you say, it should come in useful for housekeeping," she murmured, softly.

"And I bide my time," hissed Ferdinand Baffy, as he crawled out of the bunker, which men call "Tophet," and gazed malevolently after the retreating couple.

The 2d and the 3d of October had come and gone, and today was Saturday, the 4th. The great competition for mixed foursomes had narrowed down to the finals, Miss Charlotte Brassey and Mr. Ferdinand Baffy being pitted against Miss Cicely Longspoon and Mr. John Cheviot Hills Hazard, and the match had just been called. The men were to drive from the first tee, and Jack Hazard had the honor. The range finder was already in position, and Hazard had only to read off the indicated angles.

"Twenty-one degrees, four minutes, and nineteen seconds, and one degree, six minutes, and eight seconds," repeated Cicely, as she took down the figures upon her scratch pad. "Dividing π by the cosine of the asymptote, we get two pounds eight and fourpence ha'–penny." She turned to the table of logarithms, and the pencil fairly raced over the paper. "Sight for eight hundred and sixty-one yards," she said, turning to the caddie.

The boy turned the indicators on the play club and handed it to his master. Hazard shut his eyes and whacked away. The ball fell to earth, and finally, after a tremendous roll, came to rest.

"Eight hundred and sixty-one yards two inches and a quarter," came back in megaphonic tones from the fore caddie. It was the most brilliant piece of calculation that had ever been seen upon the Marion County grounds, and Cicely had to bow again and again to the plaudits that greeted her success. Even the miserable chain gang in the "gallery" shuffled their feet and raised a feeble shout of "Fore!" It was great mathematics, as everybody agreed delightedly.

Ferdinand Baffy, with a sneer, sighted his play club by pure guess work, and drove exactly eight hundred and sixty-two yards. And so honors were easy, although no one gave *him* any applause; anybody could do *that.*

The whole assemblage—players, scorers, referee, and "gallery"—piled themselves solemnly into automobiles and were trundled away to the scene of action.

Whatever else may be said about the golf of 1999, it was at least up-to-date, and even old Hugh Dormie was glad enough to get a lift for the weary half mile.

It was Cicely's turn to play, and Hazard accordingly took charge of the wind gauges.

"East nor'east by one half nor' nor'east!" shouted Jack. The distance was less than two hundred yards, but the course just given out was a difficult one, and Cicely's friends looked a trifle anxious. could she do it?

Miss Longspoon selected her favorite "lay-'em-dead" mashie (as club endowed with an intelligence almost human), and after consulting the tiny jewelled compass inlaid in the grip, she pitched the ball within six inches of the cup. More applause. Miss Brassey did equally well, and the hole was halved in three.

Both women drove well from the second tee, but Hazard misplaced a decimal point in calculating his elevations for the second shot, and overplayed the hole by a quarter of a mile. This made Baffy and his partner one up, but the score was squared again at the fourth, Miss Brassey failing to bring off a forty-yard steal on account of defective insulation in her new electric putter.

With varying fortunes the match went on, and now the contestants were at the eighteenth tee with the score all square. Through the hushed ranks of the "gallery" Cicely Longspoon made her way to the teeing ground, and smilingly indicated to the caddie where to build his little mound of moist sand. But who had the ball? The caddie looked at Miss Longspoon, and Cicely in turn appealed to Hazard. It was very strange, but no one knew where it was.

You and I, dear reader, being behind the scenes, are entitled to know that the missing ball was at this very moment quietly reposing in the right hand pocket of Mr. Ferdinand Baffy's red coat. He had managed to appropriate it a moment before, when nobody was looking, and his heart beat high as he realized that his hour of triumph was at hand.

"Where is the ball?" said Miss Longspoon, for the third time, and with a slightly acid accent.

"I beg your pardon," spoke up Ferdinand Baffy, "but I must have picked yours up by mistake; here it is;" and putting his hand into his pocket he took out a golf ball and gave it to the caddie. Had, then, Ferdinand Baffy repented him at this last moment of the evil that he purposed: One would gladly think so—but alas! it was from his *left hand pocket* that he had taken the ball which Miss Longspoon was now about to drive. It was a new ball, white and clean—but then the "innocuous" golf ball never showed any marks of usage. To all appearances it *was* the missing ball.

The curve of the parabola was generally used in playing this, the home hole; and Miss Longspoon accordingly selected a driver, whose striking surface was a frustrated cone, and confidently banged away. Great Scotland! the ball, instead of describing the beautiful curve of the parabola, was trundling disgracefully along the ground; another instant and it had disappeared into the depths of the bunker, "Tophet."

Cicely Longspoon had topped her ball!

For a full minute the vast throng stood motionless, stupefied. Such a thing as a topped ball had not happened for three generations; with the exception of old Hugh Dormie, not a soul among them all had the slightest conception what a top really was. And now the miracle had happened before their very eyes.

Four newspaper reporters started off on a run for the nearest telegraph office, and the crowd drew its breath again with a long, shuddery sigh. What was to happen now?

It was with profound feeling of awe that Jack Hazard took his niblick and descended into the gloomy depths of "Tophet," untrodden by human foot for more than half a century. And yet, strange to say, there was the ball lying in the exact middle of an old heel print. How inscrutable indeed are the ways of golfing Providence!

It had been many years since anybody had occasion to use a niblick, and in consequence the club had not enjoyed the attention of the inventors and paten makers. It was still the plain old niblick, and treacherous as of yore. Hazard played at the ball, but only succeeded in digging a large hole in the sand. Cicely followed suit, and buried the ball in the hole.

In playing the sixty-seven more Jack just managed to get the ball over the edge of the bunker cliff, and then fell back exhausted into the arms of his ever faithful caddie. This is the moment that the artist has chosen to immortalize in the famous oil painting of the match that now hangs in the rotunda of the national capitol. Observe the expression on the face of the niblick, and not that Ferdinand Baffy is smiling behind his hand. He never smiled again.

"Perhaps we had better pick up," said Hazard to Cicely, and there was just the hint of discouragement in his tone. "You have to play sixty-eight more, you know."

"Never!" returned Miss Longspoon, firmly, as she waggled her driving iron over the ball. "A hole is never lost until it's won, and we are playing for 'The Greatest Thing in the World.' Sixty-eight more."

Miss Longspoon's iron ploughed up the ground in an astonishing manner, and the ball, instead of flying on towards the green, shot almost vertically into the air. Everybody stared at it open-mouthed—a dangerous procedure, as Ferdinand Baffy found out a moment later. The ball, descending with frightful speed, struck him squarely on the upper lip, incidentally destroying a large amount of expensive artificial work, and giving him full two minutes of exquisite agony.

Mad with pain, Ferdinand Baffy fell writhing to the ground, and the curious crowd closed in around him. But Mr. John Cheviot Hills Hazard stood apart from the hurrying throng, and his face was as one who had looked upon a new heaven and a new earth. And truly, had he not just seen, with his own eyes, the most wonderful, the most fascinating sight in all the world—*a pretty girl in the act of foozling an iron shot!*

Jack came up close to the pretty girl, and gently imprisoned that little fluttering hand. "Cicely," he said, softly; and for a little while these two were quite content to let the world go by.

Mr. Ferdinand Baffy had been assisted to his feet, and some one had tied a handkerchief about his wounded jaw. But his appearance was still far from prepossessing. "Looks like fifteen cents, marked down from thirty," remarked young Swiper, in a loud whisper.

"All right," growled Mr. Baffy. "You wait till you see Nick Longspoon's face when I request him to hand over 'The greatest Thing in the World.' Come along, Charlotte. Hazard has picked up his ball, and we win by one up."

The hum of many voices floated in through the windows of President Longspoon's private office, and he knew that the great match must be over. They would be looking for him to appear, and he must go out to meet his doom. He had not been able to think of anything that could beat ex-President Bulger's State of Illinois, and now he must acknowledge his defeat and accept its humiliating consequences. He had offered as a prize "The Greatest Thing in the World," and he had not got it to give—more than that, he did not even know what it was or where it could be found. The mind of man could not conceive of anything bigger than the State of Illinois in the way of a golf prize, and yet he had promised "The Greatest Thing in the World." Pulling himself together by a heroic effort, President Longspoon stepped out upon the club piazza and looked upon the purple face of his old enemy, Ferdinand Baffy, standing in the fore-front of the vast crowd. With an evil smile, Ferdinand Baffy ascended the steps and stood before the president of the U.S.G.A.

"How about those sweet potatoes, Nick Longspoon?" sneered the scoundrel, in an undertone of concentrated malice, and then, aloud, with an accent of mocking cour-tesy: "Having won the match, Mr. President, I shall be happy to receive at your hands 'The greatest Thing in the World.'"

"One moment, Mr. President." It was old Hugh Dormie who spoke, and the crowd made way for him, breathless, and yet triumphantly waving aloft an old and tattered volume.

"Well, what is it?" said the president.

"'If a player's ball hits his opponent, . . . the oppo-nent loses the hole,'" quoted old Hugh Dormie, solemn-ly. "Mr. Baffy having me with that unhappy accident, the hole and match go to Mr. Hazard and partner."

"What is your authority for such a statement?" inter-rupted Ferdinand Baffy. His face was white and his eyes glassy.

"The RULES OF GOLF," thundered old Hugh Dormie, in a terrible voice, and involuntarily every head was bared.

Incredible! and yet the reader must remember that for over half a century patent clubs and the "innocuous" golf ball had held undisputed sway, and the very memo-ry of fines and penalties had faded from the minds of men. But old Hugh Dormie had remembered—he used to win his matches by those dear old rules, and he knew what they could do.

Ferdinand Baffy jumped into the nearest automobile and motioned to the chauffeur to go on.

"Where to?" inquired that gentleman.

"Gehenna!" yelled Mr. Baffy, as he sank back on the cushions.

And so Jack and Cicely had won their match, after all. Friendly hands were drawing them forward, and now they stood, still hand in hand, before the president. But even though Ferdinand Baffy had been discomfited, Nicholas Longspoon must still drink his bitter cup. He drew a long breath.

" 'The Greatest Thing in the World,' " he began, firmly. And then his voice wavered. "Perhaps I ought to say— er—" he went on, lamely, "that—er—'The Greatest Thing in the World,' you know—" He stopped short, in pitiable confusion.

"Got it right here, sir," said Jack, cheerfully.

"Eh, what's that?" stammered the president.

"'The Greatest Thing in the World,' " returned the young man, unabashed, as he drew the blushing Cicely to his side. "And if you have no objection, sir, we would like to have the cards go out by Wednesday of next week."

And men's hearts softened and their eyes grew dim as they realized that this was, indeed, "The Greatest Thing in the World." Alas! and for how many weary years had they turned aside upon the unprofitable worship of strange golf.

"By St. Swithin!" swore Haggis Glenlivat, as he stepped forward and confronted the throng. "I for one have holed my last putt. Monday morning I open a stock-broking office, and Mary Glenlivat shall have her sealskins for Christmas."

And with that he deliberately smashed his favorite play club across his knee and hurled the fragments far out on the home putting green. Now, Haggis Glenlivat was as good a golfer as ever swung a caddie, to use the old familiar phrase.

In an instant the crowd had taken his meaning and had broken for the locker rooms. The crash of iron and the splintering of wood resounded on every side, and the pile of wreckage on the home putting green was quickly as high as the clubhouse. Old Hugh Dormie applied the match, and, as the flames shop up into the evening sky, the people raised a great shout. The revolution had begun, the tyranny of compulsory golf was at an end.

Five years later. A more highly blessed and prosperous country than the United States it would be difficult to find, even among the Utopias of the Bellamys and their tribe. The golf-stricken hordes of Europe gaze longingly at our happy shores, but we have at last learned the necessity of self-protection. The immigration laws are now so strictly drawn that no one whose Christian name is Willie is ever allowed to get inside Sandy Hook.

Jack Hazard is the happiest young quarryman in all the State of New Jersey, and he handles a maul with all the grace and energy that was once expended upon the useless occupation of swinging a brassey. Golf is never mentioned at his pleasant dinner table, and yet, curiously enough the chiefest treasure that he and Mrs. Hazard possess is an old scarred and battered golf ball, a relic of the nineteenth century. I dined with him yesterday, and over the cognac and cigarettes the name of Ferdinand

Baffy suddenly cropped up. A shadow passed over Jack's handsome face.

"Don't you know?" he said, in answer to my query. "Poor of Baffy! Judge William Williams gave him ninety-nine years in State prison at hard labor. The trial came off last month."

"And the crime?"

"He had tried to patent an improvement upon the niblick," said Jack, in a low tone.

The Nineteenth Hole

GOLFBALLS THE SIZE OF HAILSTONES

Oops!

H.S.C. EVERARD

Perhaps nothing gives rise to such a feeling of idiotic impotence, or rather of misapplied power, than a succession of 'tops:' one can sympathize with the historic gentleman, provoked with himself beyond measure, in whose breast the fire burnt, so that at the end he spake with his tongue, and right forcibly, to the effect that he wished his ball had no top.

Golf in Theory and Practice

The Stymie

REX COLVILE

I was, I admit, pleased with myself. I had beaten the Colonel by no less than four up and three to play, and the club secretary had said to me, when we returned to the club-house, that, if I went on like that, I'd pretty soon have my handicap reduced to twenty-four. All this—and perhaps a little more—I had told Mollie during tea; but her interest had been languid until I chanced to mention that the Colonel had stymied me at the fourteenth hole.

'What's "stymied"?' asked Mollie, arresting a yawn.

Now I was so charmed by Mollie's intelligent question—for hitherto between us twain (otherwise in perfect accord) there had been a great golf fixed—that I determined to spare no trouble in elucidating the matter to her. Therefore I threw back the north end of the table-cover beneath. Women are like children, they must be shown things; besides I *wanted* to show her.

'I'll explain,' I said, 'by ocular demonstration. Let's suppose that this'—and I tapped the table-cover—'is the fourteenth green, and you and I are playing a match. Here'—and stretching back my hand to the writing-table, I took the ink-well out of its stand and placed it on the green—'is the hole; this'—and I selected a lump of sugar out of the basin and put it within six inches of the hole—'is my ball. And this'—putting another lump of sugar on the edge of the green—'is yours. Do you follow?'

Mollie nodded eagerly. All her languor had gone. She actually clapped her hands. I glowed responsively.

'Now then,' I began.

'But,' she interrupted, 'it's a match, isn't it? Oh, *do* say it's the final of an awfully important match!'

'All right,' I agreed indulgently; 'it's the final match. Now—'

'But if it's a final there would surely be a crowd of spectators,' she urged.

'Oh, I think we can imagine them,' I suggested a trifle testily.

'*I* can't,' said Mollie firmly. 'I must see them or else they won't be there. Look! Here they come!'

I leaned back in my chair with a gusty sigh. The whole thing seemed to be degenerating into child's play; instead of a scientific demonstration of one of the most ticklish golfing problems, the lesson was fast assuming all the characteristics of a nursery burlesque.

'Come, come,' I snapped, for my patience was on the ebb.

But Mollie, unperturbed, continued marshaling the spectators at the edge of the green. Innumerable little blobs of bread (so she assured me) represented the rank and file; a bit of shortbread was the Scots professional, MacGrouch; chocolates were flapper enthusiasts (who all wanted *me* to win); a minute portion of the last crumpet was the Vicar, and a bit of crust Colonel Cursit.

'And these,' she declared finally, putting a morsel of gingerbread near the hole and another morsel near her ball, 'are our caddies. Yours is a bit crumbly, because, of course, he's nervous. Now, then, I'm ready. What do I do?'

I was struggling to regain my original attitude of indulgent instructor when Mollie threw me back again into one of incipient irritation.

'Oh,' she cried in dismay, 'wait a minute. We haven't got Colonel Cursit's spaniel. It always goes with him to the links, doesn't it? To find other people's lost balls, you know, and bring them back to the Colonel, so he can sell them back to the people who lost them. There'—and she bit a chocolate flapper in half, exposing its pink interior —'that's the spaniel; the pink part's its tongue, all lolling eagerly for a lost ball. Now go on; I'm waiting.'

Her smile was so disarming that I could not help smiling with her.

'Well, then,' I conceded, 'your object is to place your ball between mine and the hole, so that it prevents my holing-out next hole. That's what laying a stymie is.'

Mollie, laughing excitedly, seized a teaspoon.

'This is my stick,' she announced.

Of course I had not intended that she should use a club at all in this miniature demonstration. I thought she would just flick the ball with her finger and that I would guide it to the desired spot. But somehow I couldn't find it in my heart to disappoint her.

'Very well,' I said; 'aim for this.' And I indicated the

stymie position. Mollie addressed the ball by tapping it repeatedly on the summit with her stick. And each time she tapped she chuckled.

'Right!' she cried at last. 'Look out!'

She measured the distance carefully. I leaned forward over the table. In spite of my kindly disdain for the affair I was conscious of a slight degree of excitement. Suppose, by some chance, she really *did* lay me a stymie. It might prove to be the nucleus of a lasting and intelligent interest in golf. My excitement increased. Mollie flourished the teaspoon.

'Go!' she cried. (I suppose, dear ignorant child, she meant 'Fore!'). The teaspoon fell.

Her lump of sugar, I mean her ball, rose, described a graceful arc and flopped fair and square into the ink-pot —I mean the fourteenth hole. And some of the ink spurted into my face, and some of it on to my collar, and a little up my nose and the remainder into my mouth.

'Hurrah!' cried Mollie. 'Goal I've won!'

And she popped Colonel Cursit's spaniel and Mac-Grouch, the professional, into her mouth.

Golf tales at the nineteenth hole rival golf shots on the other eighteen. The sport's best medium is not television, radio, or the eye. Even more than baseball, it's a sport of words.
THOMAS BOSWELL

Golf is the only game in which the fields of play are as highly valued as the greatest players. The golfers come and go while the courses last forever. . . . Great golf courses are of the earth.
MIKE BYRAN

Advice: To Ask or Not to Ask

HORACE G. HUTCHINSON

In partnership with a stronger player, it will not be needful for you to make this careful study of the times to advise and at times refrain from advising. Ask for advice if you want it, but not otherwise. Do not think it necessary, out of deference to your partner, to be continually soliciting his opinion. It is quite sufficient to apologize once for a topped shot. Do not be constantly referring to it, as if such a mistake was a rarity. Nor when you have made what is, for you, a fair shot, apologize to your partner for "having made such a bad one." He will soon form an estimate of your game, quite apart from the effect produced by these remarks—an estimate probably more correct, and possibly lower, than your own.

Hints on Golf

The Long Ball

HARRY VARDON

I don't believe in the long ball coming from the wrists. In defiance of principles which are accepted in any quarters, I will go so far as to say that, except in putting, there is no pure wrist shot in golf. Some players attempt to play their short approaches with their wrists, as they have been told to do. These men are likely to remain at long handicaps for a long time. Similarly there is an idea that the longest drivers get in some peculiar king of 'snap'— a momentary forward pushing movement—with their wrists at the time of impact, and that it is this wrist work

·at the critical period which gives the grand length to their drives, those extra twenty or thirty years which make the stoke look so splendid, so uncommon, and which make the next shot so much easier. Generally speaking, the wrists when held firmly will take very good care of themselves.

The Complete Golfer

Golf

HENRY E. HOWLAND

The original of the royal and ancient game of Golf is lost in obscurity. Whether it was an evolution from the kindred games of Kolf, Hockey, or Jeu de Mail, whether developed in Scotland or carried thither from Holland, may never be definitely ascertained.

Its record is woven into Scottish history, legislation, and literature from the beginning of recorded time. More than four hundred years ago it was a popular game in Scotland, and archery, the necessary training for the soldier, so languished in competition with it that, by the stern ordinance of Parliament and royal decree, it was proclaimed "that the fut ball and golf be utterly cryit doun and nocht usit." But although forbidden to the people, it was a favorite royal pastime. King James played it with Bothwell in 1553, and the royal accounts show that he had money on the game; Queen Mary played it after the death of Darnley, perhaps as a solace in her widowhood; James VI, an early protectionist, laid a heavy tariff on golf balls from Holland, and gave a monopoly of ball-making at four shillings each ball to a favorite. The great

Marquis of Montrose played at St. Andrews and Leith Links, and was lavish in his expenditure for golf-balls, clubs, and caddies.

The news of the Irish Rebellion came to Charles I while playing a match at Leith. James II, when Duke of York, won a foursome, with an Edinburgh shoemaker as a partner, against two Englishmen; the shoemaker built a house in the Canongate with his share of the stakes, and, in order to commemorate the origin of his fortunes, placed on its walls as escutcheon a hand dexter grasping a club, with the motto, "Far and Sure." John Porteous, of the "Heart of Midlothian," Duncan Forbes, of Culloden, who turned the tide of Prince Charlie's fortunes in 1745, were adepts at the game, and Covenanter in their sermons, poets, philosophers, and novelists have paid their tribute to the royal sport.

With lingering feet it crossed the Grampian Hills in the wake of his somewhat sportive Majesty James VI of Scotland, and made its home at Blackheath, where it maintained a precarious existence under the scare of Scottish Londoners, until the establishment of the famous clubs of Bandbury, Westward Ho, Wimbledon, and Hoylake, when, with a suddenness unexplainable, and unparalleled popular favor, it extended all over England; since then it has spread to the uttermost parts of the earth.

The nurseries for golf in the United States are many and varied, and are increasing so fast that the tale outruns the telling. The first one, established at Yonkers on the Hudson, some five years ago, by Mr. John Reid (of course a Scotchman), bears the name of St. Andrews, in honor of the Royal and Ancient Golf Club of the East

Neuk of Fife, in the shadow of "Auld Reekie," the clustering point for the great mass of golfing history and tradition. It is an inkland course of stone-wall hazards, rocky pastures bordered by ploughed fields and woods, and is prolific in those little hollows known as cuppy lies; the Saw Mill River meanders in its front, and a fine view of the Palisades from its highest teeing ground makes it an attractive spot for tired city men to whom it is accessible for an afternoon's sport.

The links of the Shinnecock Hills Golf Club, established three years since by Mr. Edward S. Mead, with Willie Dunn as its keeper, is a golfing Eden. The great rolling sand-hills, covered with short stiff grass, lying between Peconic Bay on the north and Shinnecock Bay on the south, with the ocean beyond, are picturesque in their beauty, and since the resolution of matter from chaos have been waiting for the spiked shoe of the golfer. The hazards are mainly artificial; there are some stretches of sand, railroad embarkment, and deep roads, that are tests of skill and temper; the breezy freshness of the air, the glory of the boundless expanse of downs and water, and the splendor of the sunsets, make a perfect setting for the beauty of good golfing.

Newport is a well-to-do club with a large investment in land and a tasteful club-house now in course of construction. From its site the whole course is visible, and the panorama of Narragansett Bay, with the fleet of yachts lying in anchor on one side, and of the ocean on the other, is most pleasing. It is a course of nine holes, with turf of the true golfing quality, stone wall, and artificial hazards—and a tricky quality to its putting greens which require careful approaches to save many extra strokes. Its members are enthusiastic sportsmen, who are not diverted by the giddy attractions of that favorite resort from the serious work required of a good golfer.

The Tuxedo Club has its links partly in Tuxedo Park and partly outside of it, about ten minutes' walk from the club-house. The Ramapo Hills rise abruptly a few hundred yards on either side of the course, the curve of the valley at either end making a beautiful nest, which is traversed by the Ramapo River and its tributary, the Tuxedo Brook.

There are nine holes in the course, which crosses Tuxedo Brook four times and furnishes great variety in its hazards of hills, stone walls, railroad embankments lined with a blast furnace slag, apple-trees, and a combination of terrors in front of what is known as Devil's Hole, consisting of brook, bowlders, and road, which has spoiled many a score. The course is known as a "sporting links," where straight, long drives are the only hope for preserving the temper, and the hazards are such that they make glad the heart of man when surmounted, but to the beginner, are outer darkness where is weeping and gnashing teeth.

The game was first introduced into New England by the Messrs. Hunnewell, who laid out a course on their estate at Wellesley. Since then golf clubs have sprung up as if by magic in the neighborhood of the modern Athens, a full list of which, with their characteristics, would exceed the limits of this article.

A player who has done a round at the Country Club of Brookline will have passed over various points of avenue, steeple-chase course, race-track, polo-fields, and pigeon-shooting grounds; he will have come triumphantly through a purgatorial stone wall jump, a sand-bunker and bastion, a water-jump, and finally a vast gravel-pit or crater, which has made many a golfing heart quail, and whose depths the great Campbell himself (the Scotch professional keeper) has not disdained to explore. As in the case of the embarkments at Shinnecock, it requires but a true drive or a fair cleek shot to negotiate it; but the moral effect of these hazards is such that the true drive or the fair cleek is problematical. Stone walls, trees, ploughed fields, fences, and chasms, however, present excellent sporting requirements on a course, for variety is the spice of golf. It is difficult to picture a prettier sight on a fine golfing morning, than this course with its red-coated players, the shepherd, his dog, and his flock, in a lovely setting of undulating land, fine trees, old-fashioned colonial club-house, race-track and polo-field.

The course at the Essex County Club of Manchester-by-the-Sea, consists of eleven holes, all visible from the piazza of its pretty club-house. The hazards are nearly all natural, consisting of fences, barns, roadways, a broad valley of cleared land filled in with sand and traversed by a winding brook, which is also met and crossed at other points. The teeing-grounds and putting greens have been made with great care, and the course will always be a popular one.

At Pride's Crossing is a private course of nine holes, laid out over the estates of several of its members. The green is mostly lawn and pleasure grounds, extending along the front of handsome summer-houses, the whole by the gifts of nature exceedingly attractive, with nothing formidable save the impossibility of driving a ball accurately through parlors and kitchens—some amateurs, however, have essayed it to the discomfiture of the ladies and servants—and a trying bit of corn-field, which yielded a far more valuable crop of lost golf balls in the harvest-time of 1894, than of corn.

The Myopia Hunt Club of Wenham, famous in polo and hunting annals, is an admirable golfing land, with good distances, natural hazards, commanding extensive views of the adjoining country, which is dotted with fine residences and covers, where the whistle of the quail tickles the sportsman's ear, and the music of the kenneled hounds testifies to the varied sports of its members. At the last hole is a pond in whose depths lies a hidden treasure of golf-balls, and over whose surface has been wafted many a smothered and unsmothered curse. The story is told of one enthusiastic tyro who drove two or three balls into the water, and sent his caddie to the club-house for a fresh supply; then, opening the box, he drove the whole dozen into the placid pond. Such exhibitions are common to the game, and a great relief to the surcharged heart.

The Weston Golf Club has among its officers General C. J. Paine, who, when not holding the tiller of an unconquered yacht, does not disdain the cleek and the mashie, and ex-Governor William E. Russell, an enthusiastic golfer, who has laid aside the cares of state to compete in tournaments.

The Rockaway Hunting Club, of Cedarhurst, Long Island, is a prominent club, and has fine seaside links of nine holes. The members are enthusiastic golfers and the play is constant through the year. The hazards are sunken roads, high cedar-tree hedges and ravines. The tasteful club-house, recently completed, is well patronized both in winter and summer.

In addition to these may be mentioned the Nahant Club, which has received less than all others of the gifts of nature and art, but is frequented by players who make up for its defects by their enthusiasm; the Dedham Polo Club, the Cambridge Golf Club, and the Kebo Valley Club at Bar Harbor, the Warren Farm Golf Club, the Westchester Country Club, the Staten Island, Meadowbrook, Philadelphia Country Club, Morristown, Morris County, Tacoma Golf Club, Tacoma, Wash., and Chicago Clubs, all of which have fostered the interest of the game.

It has been played for twenty years in Canada, the Royal Montreal Golf Club being the pioneer. The course commands a fine view of the city and the St. Lawrence with the Belœil Mountain and the Vermont hills in the distance.

The course of the Quebec Golf Club is over the Plains of Abraham, and is full of historic interest. The scenery is unequaled in its grandeur, the St. Lawrence lying far below and the beautiful Isle of Orleans not far distant.

There are important and well-established clubs also at Toronto, Kingston, and Ottawa, and the number is rapidly increasing throughout the Dominion.

To prevent the friction and the uncertain results which necessarily follow from having a number of clubs each offer prizes for so-called championships, a National Association has been formed to give authority to certain meetings where, each year, the amateur and professional championships shall be played for, as in England and Scotland, the amateur championship being well guarded from professional play, while the "open" events will admit amateurs and professionals alike.

There is no Anglomania about this game in America —it has its own inherent charm. To the novice it seems the simplest of all sports, but to the expert the most complicated; to him it is "a thing of beauty and a joy forever." The scoffer who speaks with contempt not born of familiarity, or views it with assumed indifference, may assert that the game, with its system of strokes and score, will restore the unhealthy atmosphere of the croquet ground; that it will try the souls of the clergy and become the undoing of the parishioners. "It is simply driving a Quinine pill over a cow pasture." He may watch with a pitying and ill-disguised contempt the frantic effort of stout elderly gentlemen to extricate a ball from a hazard, and say, as an old farmer did, who leaned over the fence and smiled placidly at a perspiring banker, "Don't you think you are pretty big for that little marble?"—yet he cannot stay its triumphant progress.

Jeers at the paraphernalia of the game have some justification. Red coats are not becoming to the American landscape, and on a warm July day are fairly distressing; the various wrappings with which some men adorn their legs, as for defense against whin gorse and "fog," which we have not, are suggestive of adornment rather than utility, and excite laughter in the cynical observer; but such criticism is the veriest dalliance. From the moment one of the Philistines essays a stroke, and by accident makes a fair drive from a tee, his conversion is assured, he has gone through all the phases, and learned "to endure, then pity, then embrace"; the game then becomes dangerously near being interesting; henceforth he will strive persistently, in season and out of season, to show "the golf that is in him"; he will regret the neglected opportunities of his youth, and the disease which has no microbe and no cure is chronic and seated on him in life. Henceforward he will adopt the motto of the Hittormissit Club, "Drive it if you can, club it if you will, kick it if you must."

The game illustrates the analytical and philosophical character of the Scotch mind. In it muscle and mind, hand, ball and eye, each play a part, and all must be in perfect accord. Some of its fascinations lie in its difficulties—there are twenty-two different rules to remember in making a drive; some golfers write them on their wristbands, others have them repeated by their caddie at the beginning of their stroke; one enthusiast, after painfully obtaining the proper position, had himself built into a frame, which thereafter was carried about each teeing ground, that he might be sure of his form. The loose, slashing style known as the St. Andrew's swing, in which the player seems to twist his body into an imitation of the Laocoön, and then suddenly to uncoil, is the perfection of art. It is a swing and not a hit; the ball is met at a certain point and swept away with apparent abandon, the driver following the ball, and finishing with a swing over the shoulder in what is almost a complete circle.

A jerk is an abomination; the true motion requires a gradual acceleration of speed, with muscles flexible, save that the lower hand should have a tight grip on the stick —a swing like "an auld wife cutting hay;" if this does not convey the idea, "Eh, man, just take and throw your club at the ba'." Oh! the careless ease of that swing and the beautiful far-reaching results that follow! But be not deceived, over-confident beginner, wise in your own conceit; a topped ball that rolls harmlessly a few yards, or some practical agriculture with perhaps a broken driver, or a wrench that follows a fruitless blow, will be your reward, if you venture to imitate that dashing, insolent, fearless stroke, which seems so easy because it is the very perfection of art and crown of skill. It is but the fruit of a life spent club in hand, for the best golfer, like the oyster, is caught young.

The recognized styles of the drive are as varied as the players, a fact attributed by golfers to the errors of greatness, easy to imitate, but dangerous without the genius to turn them to good account. An admirer of a famous Scotch champion declared, as a result of patient and anxious observation at the end of a round, that the great player had every fault at golf that he himself had been taught to avoid; genius, however, is not trammelled by rules, and the greatest players have always adapted their game to their anatomical configuration.

In addition to the recognized styles of famous golfers there are swings of diverse and wonderful grotesqueness —the "Pig-tail" style, the "Headsman," the "Pendulum," the "Recoil," the "Hammerhurling," the "Double-jointed," the "Surprise," and the "Disappointment"— whose respective names are in a measure their explanation, the last-named not being applicable to the state of mind of the player, as one might suppose, but to that of the spectator, who finds that a faulty style in the beginning of a swing may often result in as clean a stroke as one could wish. These styles have been characteristic of famous golfers, and with all of them the ball starts low-flying from the club, skims like a swallow's rise as the initial velocity begins to diminish, continues in its career for two hundred yards, and drops to the ground as gently as a bird alights.

But who shall tell of the unrecognized styles, the hooking, slicing, heeling, toeing, foozling of the would-be golfer in his game of eternal hope and everlasting despair, of bright anticipation tempered by experience, playing as if he owned the green instead of using it, cutting out divots of turf, ploughing the waste places, larding the lean earth as he walks along, plunging down the escarpments of a hazard, and keeping the recording angel busy during his sojourn there, driving into those in front, and passed on the green by succeeding players—

"While those behind cry forward
And those before cry back."

Let kindly forgetfulness draw a veil over this stage of his career.

The drive, however, as many insist, is but the prelude, and, therefore, the least important of the shots. It passes many a pitfall, reduces the dangers that lurk in cuppy lies, bastion bunkers, pit bunkers, and hazards, but the approach shots in playing "through the green" are a test of skill, nerve, and temper, and cut a greater figure in the score than the drive from the teeing-ground. The term "approach shot," in its common acceptation, conveys the idea of a stroke played with the iron with something less than the full swing, and involves differences in distance, elevation, and style. Then comes in the nice judgment as to three-quarter shots, half-shots, and wrist shots to cover the distance, the straight forward stroke, or the cut in making any of these; then must you choose whether to run the ball up along the ground and risk the irregularities of turf and soil, or loft with accurate judgment, and pitch the ball dead on to the elevation, so reaching the putting-green where you would be.

To see a finished artist at his work is a sight that

lingers long in the memory—his glance to measure the distance and assure himself of the direction, the momentary rest of the club behind the ball, the knuckling over of the body toward the hole, the cross-cutting downward stroke with its clean blow, and then triumph as the ball pitches with its reverse "English" on to the ground far short of the distance the unpracticed eye would have measured, and grips into the earth as if with inanimate intent to save the player any unnecessary trouble in holing out. Even though one may know nothing of its difficulties by experience, he grasps intuitively an enlarged idea of the merits of the game; but to a player the success of such a shot, made with a clear purpose, gives the same exquisite thrill of ecstasy as a two-lengths lead in a boat-race or the strike of a three-pound trout.

On the putting-green the work seems easier—indeed, a scoffing onlooker once said he could hole the ball with his umbrella, and did; but there is as much nicety of judgment, accuracy of eye, and delicacy of execution in this stage as in any other part of the game. The approach putt brings you near the hole; then should come a careful survey of the ground with objects to guide the eye on the line, which will be facilitated by diligent practice on the drawing-room carpet; a rest of the putter for a moment behind the ball, near the right foot, the forearm resting against the leg, a following pendulum-like swing of the club, without a jerk, and the ball will roll as if in a groove to its appointed resting-place.

It would be wise for a tyro not to watch a professional match until he has made a trial himself. "Can you play the violin?" a boy was asked. "I don't know," he replied, "I never tried;" and the novice at golf, to whom it all looks so easy, would probably make the same answer. When from actual experience he has learned its difficulties, when modesty and humility have entered into his soul, when he has tired his brain with diagrams and rules in books of instruction, with their nice distinction between an upward swing and a lift, and a downward swing and a hit, and a complicated formulæ for every kind of club or iron in every kind of lie on the course, when he has had burned into his memory, as with a red-hot cleek, the five injunctions of the golfer's Koran, "Slow back"; "Keep your eye on the ball"; "Don't aim too long"; "Aim to pitch to the left of the hole," and "Be up"—then let him with meek heart and due reverence follow Willie Dunn and Willie Campbell in a match-play over a round of eighteen holes, and take an object-lesson in the art which he has labored so painfully and fruitlessly to acquire; then will his respect for skill, patience in play, judgment in the selection of the proper club, and nerve in critical moments, rise proportionately to the descent of his own self-conceit; and his vaulting ambition for a record as a golfer will receive a spur that may help him to acquire it.

The game is too young in America to have developed players of remarkable note, though creditable records have been made; but coming years may cast the halo of championships on heads now young that shall link their names with Allan Robertson, old Tom Morris, Anderson, the Parks, Dunns, Piries, Straths, and Kirks of a previous generation who made history in the golfing world, and with that of "poor young Tommy," as he is always affectionately called, the son of the famous old keeper at St. Andrews, whose play was so incomparable that, although he died at the early age of twenty-four, he was the most formidable golfer of his time. At twenty he had three times won in succession the championship belt, and to his golfing career the motto "Capite et supereminet omnes" was universally accorded.

It is one of the traditions of these great players at St. Andrews, that it was their guiding principle never to make a bad shot, an easy theory to enunciate, but the great army of amateurs who with heart-breaking efforts have striven to rise to that standard, and the record of their toppled balls, broken clubs, misses and foozles at critical stages in a match, can bear witness to the difficulty of reducing it satisfactorily to practice. The merit of these fine golfers was that their play was sure—as they played to-day so they would play to-morrow; there was nothing unequal in them, no wavering, no unexpected breaking down at a moment when the championship might depend on a single stroke. They have been known to play ninety consecutive holes without one bad shot or one stroke made otherwise than as it was intended; and it was this dead level of steadiness under all chances of hazards and bad lies, and all conditions of cold, wet, wind, or snow, as in young Tom Morris's last famous match before his death, that placed them in the front rank of golfers.

The true golfer is critical of lucky strokes or flukes; in his estimation they are as discreditable as bad ones; certainty and precision is his standard, and his comment in broad Scotch, the real golf language, after a bad shot by a good player, calculated to draw applause from ignorant bystanders, would probably be "My, but yon was a lucky yin, bad play—didna desaire it." George Glennie, a famous player whose purism was proverbial, once in a "four-some" drove his ball into a burn; his partner wad-ing in with boots and stockings, took the ball on the wing with his niblick, as it floated down, and laid it dead at the hole. "Well, what about that stroke?" said his partner to the sage, who had preserved unyielding silence. "Not golf at a'"—then, in a soliloquy, as he advanced to the teeing-ground, "just monkey's tricks."

The game can be played in company or alone. Robinson Crusoe on his island, with his man Friday as a caddie, could have realized the golfer's dream of perfect happiness—a fine day, a good course, and a clear green; if Henry VIII had cultivated the more delicate emotions by taking to the links of the Knuckle Club, he might have saved his body from the gout and his name from the contempt of posterity; he might have dismissed the sittings of the Divorce Court and gone to play a four-some with Cromwell, Wolsey, and the papal legate; and all the abbey lands which fell to the nobles would have been converted into golfing greens by the flat of the royal golfer. He might with Francis have established a record on the Field of the Cloth of Gold. Such a game would have cemented their friendship, for the man with a keen love of golfing in his heart is more than the devo-tee of an idle sport, he is a man of spiritual perceptions and keen sympathies. As a teacher of selfdiscipline the game is invaluable. The player is always trying to get bet-ter of the game, and, as Allan Robertson said, "The game is aye fechtin' against ye."

The fascinations of golf can only be learned by expe-rience. It is difficult to explain them. It has its humorous and its serious side. It can be begun as soon as you can walk, and once begun it is continued as long as you can see. The very nature of the exercise gives length of days. Freedom of movement, swing of shoulder, and that suppleness of which the glory had departed, all return to the enthusiast. He has a confidence in his own ability which is sublime, because it is justified by performance, and that self-control which chafes the ordinary adversary.

His sense of the ultimate purpose and the true proportions of his existence is unruffled, whether he views life from the exaltation of a two-hundred yard drive on to the hill, or the lowest heel mark in the deepest sand-pit on the course; while the feelings of momentary success or depression which so possess the souls of weaker men, pass over him with no more influence than the flight of birds. His soul is so wrapped in the harmony of earth and sky and the glory of the game, that no buffets of fortune can come at him.

This is what makes it a tonic to the nerves, while the temper goes through a personally conducted tour, beginning with the impatience and ending with complete equanimity. Egotism is powerless to excuse a fault, for that can lie only with the player himself. He cannot vent his fury upon his opponent, even though a tree opportunely situated may land a ball on the green, while his own flies hopelessly into the woods; for the game is born in the purple of equable temper and courtesy, and the golfer's expletives must be directed against his own lack of skill, or lies, or hazards, and the luck and vengeance must light, and often do, on the unoffending clubs, even to their utter extermination. To the language with which every golf course is strewn, differing more in form than in substance, from the "Tut, tut, tut" of the ecclesiastic to the more sulphurous exclamation of the layman, the divine quality of forgiveness must be extended; but as it is a compliment to call a man a "dour" player, it seems to be recognized that the characteristic of all language in golf should be its brevity. The difficulty of contending with an uncertain temper in others is nothing as compared with ruling our own, and the dust and bad language that rise from the depths of a bunker emphasize the truth of the words of Holy Writ, "He that ruleth his own spirit is greater than he that taketh a city"; but yet it is certain that he who hath not lost his temper can never play golf.

Golfers as a rule are an exceptionally honest race of men, but uncertain arithmetic is occasionally encountered on the green. "I aim to tell the truth," said one; "Well, you are a very bad shot," was the reply, and there is often an area of low veracity about a bunker. Accuracy is a cardinal virtue in the game, and a kindly judgment may attribute such errors to forgetfulness; but as the chief pleasure is to beat your own record for your own satisfaction, and as this form of deception makes real progress continually more difficult, for the discount is always in your path, the man of trecherous memory gets small comfort out of his duplicity.

With the development of the game comes the development of the caddie, who is one of its principal adjuncts. In America he is still the small boy with no special peculiarities to distinguish him from others. In Scotland he is as much of an institution as the player himself. He has grown up on the links, and is the guide, counsellor, and friend of the player, whose clubs he carries. One of his principal qualifications there is that he should be able to conceal his contempt for your game. He is ready with advice, reproof, criticism, and sympathy, always interested, ready at critical times with the appropriate club, and, if need be, with the appropriate comment. He is anxious for the success of his side as if he were one of the players. His caustic remarks are borne with equanimity, and his contemptuous criticisms with the submission they deserve.

The relation of the fairer part of creation to golf varies between that of a "golfer's widow" and that of a champion. Singleness of thought, concentration of purpose, quietude of manner, are essential in the game, and the expert golfer, whose tender mercies are ever cruel, will unhesitantly cry "Fore" to the flutter of a golf cape of the tinkle of light feminine conversation, so distracting by reason of the natural gallantry of man. In the words of a promising young golfer, who found it hard to decide between flirtation and playing the game, "It's all very pleasant, but it isn't business." But the sincerity of their enthusiasm is so apparent, and their adaptability to the nicer points of the game so great that there are few clubs now where they are not firmly established, and where a man who has finished a hard day's play cannot take pleasure in an aftermath of tea and blandishments.

Health, happiness, and "a spirit with a' the world content," lie on the golfing ground. The game is a leveller of rank and station. King and commoner, noble and peasant, played on equal terms in days gone by, and rich and poor, clever and dull, are "like as they lie" when matched in skill.

"There's naething like a ticht-gude-gowing mautch to soop yer brain clear o'troubles and trials." It is so fostered by companionship and wrapped about with the joys of friendship, that he who has his soul's friend for his golfing mate is on fortune's cap the very button. With such company, when the November wind streams down the course, whipping out our little clouds of breath into streamers, we can stride over our eighteen holes with the keen joy of living that comes at intervals to the tired worker. And then, oh! weary soul, what joys await the faithful! The putting off of mud-caked shoes, the brisk plunge or shower-bath, and the warm glow thereafter; the immaculate shirt-front that crackles at your touch, the glad joy of dinner and the utter relaxation of content, "with just wee drappie of guid Scotch to follow."

The poet, scorning the material things of life and the pursuit of wealth, sings thus:

"But thou, O silent mother, wise, immortal,
To whom our toil is laughter, take, Divine One,
This vanity away, and to thy lover
Give what is needful,
A stanch heart, nobly calm, averse to evil,
The purer sky to breathe, the sea, the mountain,
A well-born gentle friend, his spirit's brother,
Ever beside him."

Mr. Santayana should go a-golfing.

---

*Too much technical knowledge can be harmful in golf,
I believe. You don't have to know why a particular shot
is working well for you just so it does work and
you can do it over and over again.*
SANDRA HAYNIE

---

*I've had a hell of a great life. For some of the pros,
after a while, it all gets like a job. It is a lot of work,
I don't deny that, but I've never found a kick to beat just
whopping that old ball onto the green.*
SAM SNEAD

A New Golf Alphabet

CARRIE FOOTE WEEKS

A stands for Aptitude, Accurate Aim,
Which will make an Adept at this popular game.

B is a Bunker; it takes Brawn and Brain
To land your golf Ball in the fair green again.

C is the Caddie who carries your Clubs;
He calls you a "Corker," in spite of your "flubs."

D is the Driver you use at the tee;
The dirt which you Dig, and that other "big D—"

E is the Energy ever displayed
When Engaged in a round with a pretty young
    maid.

F is a Foursome, a Foozle, and "Fore"—
If you Form in the first F is bad, you're a bore.

G stands for Grip; the professional's Grasp;
And the Green which you reach, if you conquer
    this clasp.

H is the Hole, not as deep as a well:
And sometimes it's Heaven, and oftener H—?

I can be Iron, or mashie, or cleek,
You know best yourself which Iron you seek.

J is a Jerk. If your ball finds a cup,
To play with a Jerk often sweeps it right up.

K is to "Keep your eye on the ball";
If we follow this rule, there is hope for us all.

L stands for Links, and for "Like as we Lie,"
Which is different from "Lie as we Like,"
    by-the-bye.

M stands for Medal play, also for Match,
At both you are beaten if you play at scratch.

N is a Niblick, respected by all;
For it is good friend in Need, to a ball.

O stands for Oxygen, Ozone, and Odds,
Which golfers accept as a gift of the Gods.

P is "to Press"; "Don't" makes a good rule,
One can Play pretty well, and yet Putt like a fool.

Q is the Question beginners must ask:
"Is my club the right length?" "What's wrong with
    my grasp?"

R stands for Reply made by old golfers keen:
"A good stance; have patience. Watch me Reach
    the green."

S is the Swing that we practice in dreams.
A Stymie looks simple. 'Tis not what it seems.

T is to Top. Sometimes sign of Terror;
If hazards or bunkers win balls by this error.

U means Unpopular people who play,
Who borrow your clubs, and stand in your way.

V is the Virtue of one Scotch high-ball,
To lengthen your golf yarns, and drives, in the Fall.

W is a Wrist shot, Whippy and free;
Those who do it well, good golfers must be.

X might stand now for "great eXpectations,"
Day dreams of golfers, in all ranks and stations.

Y is Yesterday; a word hardly known.
It's this Year, and new heroes sit on the throne.

Z stands for Zenith. The golfer whose fame
Touches this point can die, saying, "I've played
the game."

---

*Now, I take it that there is no other game in which these
three fundamental factors—the physiological,
the psychological, and the social or moral—
are so extraordinarily combined or so constantly
called into play. Some sports, such as football, polo,
rowing, call chiefly for muscular activity, judgment,
and nerve; others, such as chess, draughts,
backgammon, call upon the intellect only.
In no other game that I know of is, first,
the whole anatomical frame brought into such strenuous
yet delicate action at every stroke;
or, second, does the mind play so important
a part in governing the actions of the muscles;
or, third, do the character and temperament of your
opponent so powerfully affect you as they do in golf.
To play well, these three factors in the game must be most
accurately adjusted, and their accurate adjustment is
as difficult as it is fascinating.*
ARNOLD HAULTAIN

A Gossip on Golf

Horace G. Hutchinson

Ten or twelve years ago a lighthearted lady following a very great golf match round the St. Andrew's links in Scotland dared to observe to her grave male companion:

"How funny it seems, being so solemn over the *game.*"

"It's not a game," came the reply in the shocked tone in which it seemed to him natural to rebuke such irreverence. "It's not a game; it's a study."

The remark of this light-hearted lady was but the expression of that spirit of slight veneration for that "grand old manner" in which our forefathers pursued the Royal and Ancient Game in the dignified habiliments of high hats, knee-breeches and swallow-tailed coats.

When a nation borrows from another an art, a sport, a pastime—anything of which the nature is progressive —the borrower generally takes up the novelty at the point to which the lender has brought it, and modifies it according to its national characteristics. Thus England, a jovial, cricketing nation, in assimilating the game in Scotland, a serious, golfing nation, did not fail to modify it by the influence of English cricketing joviality.

A second borrower has come on the scene. America, taking her golf from England rather than from Scotland, at a stage of its development at which the traditions of the old kind were already modified, has grafted upon it her own characteristics.

Comparing infinitely little things with infinitely big ones, I see a strong analogy between my personal position at the time I took up golf, and that of the States, in respect to golf, at the present date. For I had not the chance of learning the game at any of the great Scottish centers (there were no great centers, in those days, that were not Scottish), and they were immensely far, by the British measurement of distance, from the Westward Ho, the nursery of my golf. There were at Westward Ho, none of the classic models, available to me, on which youth should form its style; for learning golf it is particularly true that the example is better then precept, and it is likely to puzzle the American beginner, as in days past it often puzzled the English beginner, to find how wide the difference is apt to be between the teaching of example and the teachings of precept.

When, now and again, it happened to us to see one of the classic models, we found him violating all those maxims of "Slow back," "Don't press," and the rest, that had been impressed upon us from the date of our eariest studies in golf. It was only a later wisdom that showed us that the violation and the contradiction were apparent rather than real; that the "slowness"—relative to the pace of the downward swing; that "Don't press" did not mean "don't hit hard," but "don't try to hit harder than you can."

When one is a boy it appears inevitable that one's style of learning should be imitative, and to be a boy and to have good golfing models before one's eyes is the ideal condition of the tyro.

In the absence of all teachers, you must condescend to learn from a book. It is not impossible, if you will only apply your mind to it. One of the best and freest and strongest styles known to the writer is that of a man who began golf after he was grown up, with no "coach," but with a book to teach him. He studied this book—it was not a big one—and worked with it at his swing for a week *before he began to try to hit the ball at all.* This was a very wise and very self-controlled young man, and the secret of his singular success is beyond doubt to be read in the italics. No doubt he had a dull week, but he had much better times ever after than the beginner who persists in caving in the ball's head.

I played a good many years ago in the United States, when probably I was the only man that did. The game was over an improvised course at the Meadowbrook Club on Long Island—not an ideal links, but quite as good as many of the "best inland links" in England. Far better, in all likelihood, nowadays are those links of the Shinnecock Hills, St. Andrew's, Morristown, Newport and others. But it is only on soil where the turf is of the right royal sandy nature, with crisp, short grass, that the game can be played in its perfection. All the good links-ground of the old country is made by alluvial deposit, aided by the sand blown up off the beach and washed up by the waves.

The Meadowbrookites of that day were kind enough to say that they thought golf seemed "a very good Sunday game." Nowadays it appears that some Americans think it quite good enough for some of the week-days. Considering all the clubs that are springing up all over the country it is impossible that there should be a sufficient supply of good professional teachers. One fears that it is inevitable that the golfer should have to resort to the book.* The membership of those clubs we may perhaps

---

*Mr. Hutchinson, no doubt from motives of modesty, does not mention two books which should be in the hands of every serious golfer, viz, the volume entitled "Golf," in the Badminton Library, and "Hints on Golf."—ED.

roughly estimate, on a very moderate average, at some two hundred or three hundred each, say two hundred thousand in all; and to this figure must be added a large number, an immensely large number, of players not attached to any club.

The American tyro who takes up golf after reaching years of discretion does not start from quite the same point as his British compeer. The latter almost inevitably grafts his building golf on a stock of cricketing experience. He will begin with a relatively open mind. There is much in his favor in this attitude. The cricketer is handicapped by the past use of a bat—a slogging weapon (whereby let us not be thought to speak disdainfully of the great game of cricket)—a weapon which he clutches with the right hand while his eye is kept hopefully forward, not bent on the ball, but projected whither he proposes to smite that ball. The youth of America is not brought up so universally on one game. A great deal of base-ball, a little polo, a little tennis and lawn-tennis are his occasional lessons; all aiding no doubt in the harmonious movement of hand and eye, but none of them, except perhaps the first, directly teaching that right-hand grip of a weapon wielded by the two hands which is a stumbling block in the path of the English cricketer commencing golf.

Polo is of all games the one which most resembles golf in style of stroke. The club must be swung back with comparative slowness, and the forward stroke must be carried well through. As illustrative of the affinity between the strokes of gold and polo it may be noticed that the Peat brothers, noted polo players, quickly acquired considerable skill with the driver as soon as they took up golf. We generally find that the Englishman who comes to golf with his original cricketing vices strongly possessing him, strikes the golf-ball better with an iron than a wooden club, because the former is more like a bat. For that very reason it is not the best kind of club to begin with, if the learner desires to acquire the proper golfing swing; and the American tyro will not have this special temptation of the Englishman to begin with the iron club.

Equally fatal both English and American is the tendency to look forward, whither the ball should go. The British and the Columbian eye, equally, must be kept fast on the ball until the latter is struck—this is imperative. Neither must the right hand of either nation be allowed to become the "predominant partner" in the golfing stroke. The functions of the right hand should be analogous to those of the House of Lords—to correct the too erratic vigor of the stroke whose main energy is wielded by the left. All beginners have a tendency to sway the body away from the ball as they raise the club. This, however, is all wrong. The body should not sway; it may, and should, turn from the hips, the shoulders swinging round as if the backbone were their pivot (this, of course, is not an anatomical correct description), but the whole body must not be allowed to sway away.

Smoothness is the quality to aim at in the swing. Remember to let the arms go out to their full length at once as you withdraw the club-head from the ball, and, similarly, follow on after the ball, when struck, with arms well outstretched (or outflung rather, by the energy of the stroke), for in this way you will make your club-head travel longest on the ball's line of flight. This is important both for length of drive and accuracy. If you are slicing or pulling the ball, so that it describes a curve, out of the vertical plane, in its flight, you may be sure that your club-head at the moment of meeting the ball is not traveling in the line of flight which you wish the ball take. Recognition of the cause of the evil will help you to cure it.

Stand with your knees slightly bent and your legs moderately wide apart, so as to give you a firm hold of the ground, with the ball nearer the left foot than the right and about at such distance from you that when you lay the heels of the club to the ball its shaft reaches to your left knee as you stand upright. Grip the club firmly in the palm of the left hand, lightly in the fingers of the right hand, and then swing up quietly, remembering the instructions as to the direction of the swing and the mode of turning the body, keeping your eye on the part of the ball which you want to hit, the while, and increasing the rate of the swing so that the club-head shall be traveling with its greatest velocity at the moment that it meets the ball.

Just now there is so great a demand for golf-clubs in England that the trade is hard put to it to supply them in sufficient numbers and good quality; and the sapient club-maker is apt to reflect that the beginner has not the knowledge to discriminate between a good club and a bad one, and, moreover, that his performances will be very little affected by the character of the instrument he uses. It is very likely that America, in the initial stages of her golf, will be deemed by the club-makers a fair field for the planting out of crooked shafts and green heads. When the States have got their golf into something like organized order, Americans will probably reflect that the importation of clubs from England is rather analogous to the importation of Welsh coal by a Newcastle man, for the great bulk of the hickory used in the making of shafts comes originally from America.

America already has its National Golf Association, and thereby, has already solved a problem in golfing matters which has vexed the soul of very many English golfers for a long while, has been the occasion of much public correspondence, of a good deal of heartburning, and is now no nearer its solution than the day of its first being propounded. Scotland naturally looks with some jealously on the rather intemperate zeal with which England has "taken up" her national game. She resents the slight alterations and modifications of rules which England wishes to introduce. If England chooses to play golf on places to which the rules of Scottish golf are not quite applicable, that is not Scotland's fault, but England's misfortune. Thus Scotland is apt to argue. And between the desire of another set of rules which shall be applicable universally, nothing is done; there is no headquarters to which moot questions can be referred, no central authority. It is a felt want, though it is very possible that no central authority is better than an injudicious central authority whose decisions might not carry weight. The States are fortunate to have settled this matter satisfactorily and without friction.

Under the authority of the association the question of the superiority of tournament or competition by score as the best test of golf in such a contest will be ultimately settled. Other things being equal, all that remains to be said is in favor of the tournament plan, in which men play matches by holes—the original way of playing the game. But other things are so often unequal—such as the hazard of the draw, which often lets one man in easily, while two others of the strongest fall to Kilkenny-cat work on each other in the first round. The method which we in England call "the American tournament" suggests itself as most obviously appropiate—that the method by which each competitor plays all the rest, and that the winner of most matches wins the palm. Unfortunately, its propriety is only apparent, for a round of golf takes half a day, virtually, and in a year of three hundred and sixty-five days too many of them would be occupied, on this plan, in finding out the champion. Moreover, a round of eighteen holes is short enough for an adequate comparison of men's mettle. So what is to be done? We in Great Britain have no decided answer to send over, for we play our amateur championship by tournament. You ought to explain, when you say "by tournament" that you do not mean every man against every other, but, by drawing your opponent, playing by holes—our open championship by score. By tournament, in English sense, we mean a competition by holes in which the players are drawn against each other at the start. The winners of the first round engage in mutual contest in the second, and so on until all have been beaten save one, who survives as victor of the tournament. In order to modify the inequalities of fortune often felt by those who enter for the tournament, it has been proposed that, for one day or two days, competitors shall play scoring rounds, and that those whose scores fall beneath a certain figure shall then play off, tournament fashion, for the ultimate glory.

Then there is the "bogey" plan, wherein a certain bogey or imaginary score is fixed, for each hole, by the committee which regulates the competition; and the competitors fight this bogey score, hole by hole. The victor is he who is fewest holes "down" or most holes "up" to the bogey. The worst feature of the bogey method is its name. Scottish golfers cannot get over that: it is so shocking to the grand old traditions; it smacks almost of levity, and, remotely, of profanity. But the bogey plan, nevertheless, has much to recommend it; it obviates all unfairness and many of the objections urged against the decision by score, which, after all, is not the game of golf but a mere means for comparing the play of a number of golfers in a single round.

One can but refer to these various modes of competition: it is wiser to decline the invidious task of deciding their rival merits. Bogey, though he has a bad name, has much to recommend him. In Great Britain we are too conservative to embrace him heartily; it may be that a democracy may see its way to his reception with due honor.

It is not one of the least merits of this Royal and Ancient Game that two players of very unequal caliber can make a mutually interesting match together. It is not here as with those games, like tennis and racquets, in which one player's stroke depends on that of the opponent. Where players are so unequal at those other games that immensely long odds have to be given, there is little fun for either side. But at golf, each pursues the slightly uneven tenor of his way unaffected—in any direct manner—by the other's doings. By strokes given at certain holes, or by certain holes of vantage given before starting, an equality of result can be produced from the most unequal play.

Still a match in which the players are well paired, without odds, is the most enjoyable, and the learner should always try to play with those who are more advanced than he, for thus he will himself advance quicker. Pleasant matches are those foursomes in which a first-class player on either side is in partnership with a player of inferior class. The latter has then the satisfaction of feeling that he is aiding and abetting the great performances of his partner, and at the same time inevitably learning the lessons which will enable him, in days to come, to rival them.

But he must not expect those days too soon. The learning of golf is a slow and tedious process at the best; though illumined by many bright flashes of hope, the clouds of despair darken it at least in equal number. The exasperating thing is that the secret seems always to be escaping you; for a day, perhaps for a week, you may surprise and delight yourself by playing your iron to the general admiration. You think you have acquired the stroke of beauty as a joy forever: the next day it may have utterly gone from you. The consolation is that it will return. At a certain, tolerably advanced, stage of your education you are likely to find yourself playing your iron well one day, your driver well the next, and your putter well the third. "Oh," you keep explaining, "if only I could catch a day on which I could play all three!" But that glad day does not hasten to arrive: you will know the sickness of hope deferred again and again, before it comes to you; and when at length it comes, it passes. You have to catch that day again and again before you can make certain of repeating its success, and even then the best success is so merely relative—so infinitely less than the success with which you can achieve as you consider the strokes over in your armchair; the ideal is so very far removed from the actual. And it is the glory of golf that this great gulf between hope and achievement exists in the game of the finished player no less than in the game of the merest tyro. Nay more, the gulf only grows the wider as knowledge of the game increases.

The neophyte of this cult has no notion of the subtleties and secrets that it contains. To him it is a matter of hitting the ball—and it will go. He knows nothing of playing the drive with a "pull," when the wind is from the right front, with a slight "slice" when the wind is from the left, in order that in either case the ball at the end of its flight may find the wind assisting it. He does not even know the thrill of sensuous delight that quivers through the fingers from the lofting shot nicely cut to fall dead on its alighting. Even such a simple secret as cutting the ball with a brassey to make it rise quickly over a steep bank straight in front is utterly beyond his ken. It is fully as much as can be hoped for him if he have some remote comprehension of the methods of hitting the ball with a soaring flight when the wind is behind him, and of sending it low-skimming, like swallows when rain is coming, in the face of the adverse breeze.

For him most of these subtle delights do not exist; he has not yet come to his inheritance of them. And no golfer yet has ever entered so fully into such an inheritance as to exhaust it. After a quarter of a century of assiduous golf in many lands, the Sphinx still startles one by showing herself in a new aspect, with new subtleties, unsuspected before, which one lights on wholly by accident. It seems that she will never yield up all her secrets. "Age cannot wither nor custom stale her infinite variety."

And from this panegyric of the great game, which to some—but not to those who know it—perhaps will seem too unmeasured, may be inferred the writer's diagnosis of the terrible mania for golf which is besetting all our intelligent classes. We borrowed golf from Scotland, as we borrowed whisky, not because it is Scottish, but because it is good. The sole form of flattery that America bestows on England is that sincerest form of flattery, the imitative. It may be that she has borrowed golf from us, because it is "quite English, you know"; but she will continue to use the loan, not because it is quite English, but because it is quite good. The most irreconcilable cricket, baseball, polo, or tennis player must admit that it is a fine thing to have discovered a game of great and varied excellence, which is played in the midst of the most delightful surroundings, and which will provide you with an inexhaustible interest from the time that you are becoming too old for the more violent games until the long-deferred day of your death.

For long-deferred it cannot fail to be, and of the many sections that have reason to bless the game of golf, surely the life assurance companies should bless it with the most grateful fervor. One cannot altogether ignore this aspect, though one may sympathize with the sourest scorn of the Scotsman for the Englishman who "plays golf for exercise." That the game provides charming and healthful exercise is a detail the more in its favor, but that any man should name this as the essential reason for which he follows a pastime so glorious in itself must be an idea forever loathsome to the mind of the rightly constituted golfer. Such a notion can only be the possession of the man who has never approached the shrine with sufficient piety to win from the Sibyl a single word of response.

Golf is a good walk spoiled.
MARK TWAIN

What Golf Means to a Big City

ARTHUR RUHL

One of the cartoons which Du Maurier drew for *Punch* years ago represented a very esthetic young man seated at a table in a restaurant gazing at a tumbler of water in which were a couple of lilies. The glass was the only thing on the table, and the young man regarded it with certain air of ecstacy, as was evident from his nether limbs twined one about the other. Opposite the young man, with his fingers resting deferentially on the edge of the table, bent the honest, round-faced British waiter.

"Can't I get you something more sir?" he asked. The young man replied, devouring the lilies with his eyes; "soon I will have done."

Although the purpose of the cartoon was to satirize the cult of esthetes, just then beginning to appear, it was doubtless suggested by the anecdote, since become almost classic, of the prophet of the new order, who, as I recall it, being late at a dinner party of which he was a guest, seized a bouquet of violets from the vase on the table, pressed them to his face, and with great apparent satisfaction sighed: "A-a-ah! I have dined!" The mental attitude therein implied is one which, in these days of athleticism, is rather distinctly deprecated. If one poses now, it is on the other side of the fence. One is rather embarrassed than otherwise to disclose the fact that he possesses sensibilities. The development of the more virile and Spartan virtues is generally reckoned to be the essence of the sport of the out-of-doors.

It is with a somewhat whimscical interest, therefore, that I recall a certain spring day on a golf course tucked away in the hills to the north of town. It was one of those days when the spring seems to come all at once, when the stir of growing things and the warmth and richness overpower and conquer us. All the things of winter seem suddenly old and dusty and frayed about the edges. We shuffle off our winter ideas and our hearthstone point of view as serpents shed their skins. Before we can quite adjust ourselves to the new world we drink to intoxication of the air and the colors and odors become for the moment overwhelmingly vital.

The St. Andrews course, than which none of the neighborhood of New York is prettier, was that day covered with violets. The fair green in the lower levels near the brook was purple with them. The air above them, hemmed in by the hills around, seemed to have an almost tangible velvetiness. One strode softly and played with a sort of exaggerated leisure and dignity as if afraid of breaking the charm. As a pair met in the greens they greeted each other with deference and conversed in lower voices as though they were in church. The moving figures, specking the green here and there in the distance, seemed less actual persons with whom one had come up in the train an hour or so before than parts of a painted picture or the fabric of a dream. Now and again a man would stop and raise his head and look all about him as though he wished to *feel* the day and the spring even more. And yet those playing were almost as far as possible removed from the type of person who would plunge his face into a bunch of violets and murmur, "I have dined!" They were lawyers and bankers and brokers and busy men generally, who, twenty-four hours before, had been hard at it in downtown New York, at downtown New York's cruel pace—fighting hard-headed battles in the realm of stock tickers and roaring exchanges and skyscrapers and trucks and trolley cars.

It is this esthetic value of golf, its appeal to the sensibilities, the rest and stimulus which it gives to the fagged-out and the world-weary which makes it more, probably, than any other sport to those who live in town. It is a game which we take up at any age and which we can play comfortably without any previous training or preparation. Almost any one may ride, but park riding is at best a somewhat artificial sport—an urban rather than a country recreation. Rowing is too violent an exercise for any but the young and very fit, and, as done in this country, one who goes in for it is likely to be lonesome. Walking without any object but exercise is a bore, and to all but the insatiable muscle-maker gymnasium exercise is likely to be more so.

Tennis and squash, although they answer the requirements of exercise, have little of that restful appeal to the sensibilities which one finds in the more leisurely, open, and freer sports. To a man nervously tired, as most tired city men are, the mere keying-up one's self to the strenuous pitch of violent exercise has somewhat the same grating effect that harsh sounds have to ears already wearied with noise. In short, from the point of view of pleasure, of practicability, and of results there is no sport which seems to be more adapted to the needs of the city man than golf. While it is putting air in his lungs and blood in his veins, it is smoothing out his puckered brain and attuning it to the eternal harmonies. The sum of the effect of a perfect day on a good course is similar to that of a cross-country run, a visit to an art gallery, and a symphony concert rolled into one.

Remembering St. Andrews

JAMES BALFOUR

The course is marvellously adapted to the game. It used to be flanked by high whins for the greater part of its extent, and these formed an interesting hazard. The turf is smooth and fine; the subsoil is sandy; the surface sometimes undulating and sometimes flat. There are beautiful level putting greens, while the Course is studded with sandpits or bunkers as golfers call them. These, with the ever-recurring hazards of whin, heather and bent, all combine to give endless variety, and to adapt the Links at St. Andrews to the game of golf in a way quite unsurpassed anywhere else. If there be added to its golfing charms the charms of all its surrounds—the grand history of St. Andrews and its sacred memories—its delightful air—the song of its numberless larks, which nestle among the whins—the scream of the sea-birds flying overhead—the blue sea dotted with a few fishing boats—the noise of the waves and the bay of the Eden as seen from the high hole when the tide is full—the venerable towers and the broken outline of the ancient city; and in the distance the Forfarshire' coast, with the range of the Sidlaws, and, further off, the Grampian hills, it may be truly said that probably no portion of ground of the same size on the whole surface of the globe has afforded so much innocent enjoyment to so many people of all ages from two to eighty-nine, and during so many generations.

Reminiscences of Golf on St. Andrews Links

Acknowledgments

"Golf Dreams" from *Hugging the Shore* by John Updike. Copyright © 1983 by John Updike. Reprinted by permission of Alfred A. Knopf, Inc.

"My Own Swing" from *Education of a Golfer* by Sam Snead with Al Stump. Copyright © 1962 Sam Snead. Published by Simon & Schuster. Reprinted by permission of Ann D. Snead, President, Sam Snead Enterprises, Inc.

Thanks to Little, Brown and Company for use of "To Play and Play and Play" from *Golfer's Gold* by Tony Lema with Gwilym S. Brown. Published by Little, Brown and Company.

"Hope on Ford" from *Bob Hope's Confessions of a Happy Hooker* by Bob Hope. Copyright © 1987 by Bob Hope. Used by permission of Doubleday, a division of Bantam Doubleday Dell Publishing Group, Inc.

"Winter Dreams" excerpted with permission of Scribner, a Division of Simon & Schuster, from *The Short Stories of F. Scott Fitzgerald,* edited by Matthew J. Bruccoli. Copyright © 1922 by Metropolitan Publications, Inc. Copyright renewed 1950 by Frances Scott Fitzgerald Lanahan.

"The Heart of a Goof" from *Wodehouse on Golf* by P. G. Wodehouse. Copyright © 1940 P. G. Wodehouse.

Author Index